Pluralism in Practice

T0244296

PLURALISM IN PRACTICE

*Case Studies of Leadership
in a Religiously Diverse America*

Edited and written by

ELINOR J. PIERCE

Afterword by

Diana L. Eck

ORBIS BOOKS
Maryknoll, New York 10545

Founded in 1970, Orbis Books endeavors to publish works that enlighten the mind, nourish the spirit, and challenge the conscience. The publishing arm of the Maryknoll Fathers and Brothers, Orbis seeks to explore the global dimensions of the Christian faith and mission, to invite dialogue with diverse cultures and religious traditions, and to serve the cause of reconciliation and peace. The books published reflect the views of their authors and do not represent the official position of the Maryknoll Society. To learn more about Maryknoll and Orbis Books, please visit our website at www.orbisbooks.com.

Library of Congress Cataloging-in-Publication Data

Names: Pierce, Elinor J., author.
Title: Pluralism in practice : case studies of leadership in a religiously
     diverse America / edited and written by Elinor J. Pierce ; afterword by
     Diana L. Eck.
Description: Maryknoll, New York : Orbis Books, [2023] | Includes
     bibliographical references and index. | Summary: "Twelve case studies based on
     Harvard's Pluralism Project method"— Provided by publisher.
Identifiers: LCCN 2023007217 (print) | LCCN 2023007218 (ebook) |
     ISBN 9781626985483 (trade paperback) | ISBN 9798888660065 (epub)
Subjects: LCSH: Religious pluralism—United States. | United States—Religion.
Classification: LCC BL2525 .P53 2023 (print) | LCC BL2525 (ebook) |
     DDC 201/.50973—dc23/eng/20230612
LC record available at https://lccn.loc.gov/2023007217
LC ebook record available at https://lccn.loc.gov/2023007218

Contents

Defining Pluralism

Pluralism is not diversity alone, but the energetic engagement with diversity.

Diversity can and has meant the creation of religious ghettoes with little traffic between or among them. Today, religious diversity is a given, but pluralism is not a given; it is an achievement. Mere diversity without real encounter and relationship will yield increasing tensions in our societies.

Pluralism is not just tolerance, but the active seeking of understanding across lines of difference. Tolerance is a necessary public virtue, but it does not require Christians and Muslims, Hindus, Jews, and ardent secularists to know anything about one another. Tolerance is too thin a foundation for a world of religious difference and proximity. It does nothing to remove our ignorance of one another, and leaves in place the stereotypes, the half-truths, the fears that underlie old patterns of division and violence. In the world in which we live today, our ignorance of one another will be increasingly costly.

Pluralism is not relativism, but the encounter of commitments. The new paradigm of pluralism does not require us to leave our identities and our commitments behind, for pluralism is the encounter of commitments. It means holding our deepest differences, even our religious differences, not in isolation, but in relationship to one another.

Pluralism is based on dialogue. The language of pluralism is that of dialogue and encounter, give and take, criticism and self-criticism. Dialogue means both speaking and listening, and that process reveals both common understandings and real differences. Dialogue does not mean everyone at the "table" will agree with one another. Pluralism involves the commitment to being at the table—with one's commitments.

—Diana L. Eck

Acknowledgments

Many years ago the Pluralism Project hosted a series of interfaith meetings with women leaders. In the small group of one gathering, participant Venerable Mushim Ikeda praised the diversity of the group assembled, but also asked us to consider another question: "Who is *not* at the table?" While the group was intentionally religiously diverse, it couldn't come close to being fully inclusive of the range of religions in America, to the internal diversity of each tradition, and to the intersectional identities within each community. That day, Ven. Ikeda underscored the critical importance of acknowledging who is not present, and whose voices are *not* being heard. More than twenty years later, I would like to carry forth her wisdom into this collection of cases. This is also a good question to ask during case discussions when coming up with collaborative solutions: "Who is not at the table?"

This portrait of pluralism in practice does not represent the full range of internal and external diversities of religious America. It is necessarily a selective portrait, which does not include Afro-Caribbean, Indigenous, Jain, nonreligious, and many other voices; it is limited to the American experience. It also does not intend—nor pretend—to represent the whole of one faith community through one person's experience. It is focused on progressive voices. In the future, my cases will feature more voices of young people, many of whom are reading and discussing these cases; while they may not be empowered as decision-makers now, they are actively creating our multireligious future and are vital to this conversation.

This volume would not be possible without the graciousness and generosity of those who have invited me into their religious centers, their homes and offices, and—for some—their lives. Sincere thanks are especially due to those whose stories are included within the pages of this book: Rabbi Anson Laytner, together with Dr. Marilyn Gist and Imam Jamal Rahman from "A Christmas Tree Crisis"; Dr. Brad Braxton and Michelle Banks from "A Festival of Faiths"; Dr. Karen Majewski, together with Rev. Sharon Buttry, Abdul Motlib, and Robert Zwolak from "A Call to Prayer"; Padma Kuppa from "Trouble in Troy"; Janet Penn from "A

Sign of Division"; Pastor Kent Brandenburg and Rucha Kaur from "Fliers at the Peace Parade"; Dr. Daisy Khan from "Center of Dispute"; Mayor Dean Koldenhoven, the late Sandy Broadbent, Father Alexander Cronin, Omar Najib, Rev. Peter Semeyn, Rouhy Shalabi, Dr. Michael Vander Weele, and, more recently, Edward Hassan, from "A Mosque in Palos Heights"; Rabbi Joel Sisenwine and Rabbi Charlie Cytron-Walker from "Showing Up for Shabbat"; Shinge Roko Sherry Chayat Roshi and Rabbi Sheldon Ezring from "A Question of Membership"; Aminta Kilawan-Narine from "A Quandary in Queens"; and Chenxing Han, Dr. Funie Hsu, and Dr. Duncan Ryūken Williams from "Forty-Nine Days." I would also like to thank those who spoke anonymously, including "Sam Smith" and others.

Other case protagonists gave generously of their time and insights but are not included in this collection: Dr. Jeff Young; Dr. Danielle Moretti-Langholtz; Imam Hassan Selim, and members of the Muslim community in Cedar Rapids, Iowa; Dr. Karen Spaulding; Cyndi Simpson; Dr. Parvez Ahmed and other leaders in Jacksonville, Florida; Jessica Bizub; Miriam Amer, Rev. Clint Twedt-Ball, and Michelle Stafford; Tom Spencer; and Steve Wareham and the taxi drivers who wished to remain anonymous. These and other cases can be found online: https://pluralism.org/case-studies.

Collaboration was key to the creation of many of these cases. Dr. Jennifer (Jenny) Peace, who exemplifies collegiality, has been a true thought partner for the case initiative. Most recently, Jenny did so together with her colleagues at Tufts University's Jonathan M. Tisch College of Civic Life—Dr. Brian Hatcher, Dr. Peter Levine, and Rev. Elyse Nelson Winger. "A Quandary in Queens" was developed with support from their interfaith civic studies program. Thanks to Dr. Emily Sigalow and Dr. Wendy Cadge for their roles in the co-development of "A Question of Membership" as part of the JewBu Project at Brandeis University. Thanks to the team at Global Spiritual Life at NYU for their support in the development of "The Christmas Tree Crisis," to Emily Chaudhari for her site visit to Sea-Tac, and to Mary (Polly) Hamlen for her initial idea for this case. Thanks to Wendy Goldberg for her interview of Rabbi Cytron-Walker in the postscript of "Showing Up for Shabbat," and to Rabbi Aryeh Azriel and the gardeners at Tri-Faith Initiative for their inspiring work.

Thank you to Jon Sweeney at Orbis, who shepherded both *Pluralism in Practice* and *With the Best of Intentions*. I appreciate my coeditors on *Intentions*, Dr. Lucinda Allen Mosher and Rabbi Or Rose, for their support of this sister volume. Lucinda generously provided additional editing expertise to, and enthusiasm for, this case volume. It would not be possible to mention every colleague who has informed this work: it includes those who teach with these cases—including those who participated in our case workshops. Willis Emmons at Harvard Business School's Christensen Center for Teaching & Learning provided critical guidance and expertise; Rev. Dr. Marcia Sietstra, the late Brendan Randall, and Kathryn Lohre were vital to the early years of this initiative. Through the years, advisers at the Pluralism Project, including Dr. Nancy Khalil and Dr. Neelima Shukla-Bhatt, provided key insights and encouragement.

I would like to express my considerable appreciation to my colleagues at the Pluralism Project—past and present. At the very beginning, the Project was energized by the creativity of Susan Shumaker and Rachel Antell; later, Whittney Barth and Alexis Gewertz provided critical thinking, enthusiasm, and support for the case initiative—including this volume; and, for nearly three decades, student researchers bring new ideas and energy. Finally, I want to express my deep and sincere gratitude to Diana Eck for her incomparable grace and unfailing optimism, both of which have been evident over these many years—especially as we experimented with the case method together.

Love and thanks to my family and friends, especially to my mother Paula O'Connor. Thanks to the Kurta sisters, Mariko Sakurai, and Shannon Floyd. I am grateful to my beloved trio of Asheesh, Skye, and Josh, who remind me, every day, "This must be the place."

Introduction

A decision-based case study is an invitation to engage. The cases in this volume are adaptations of a particular form of case study from professional education contexts. While many may understand a "case study" as an example or narrative, decision-based cases are also a method of teaching and learning. As Boehrer and Linsky helpfully suggest, "The relationship between the artifact of a case and its functional purpose is a crucial aspect of the case method. To grasp this, it is useful to think of a case in several ways: as a document or text, as a story, as a vehicle for discussion, and as an event."[1]

As documents or texts, the cases in this volume may provide microhistories of a dispute; as stories, they are told by a protagonist from their own perspective and location; as a vehicle for discussion (and reflection), they are structured around an actionable problem; as an event, each case discussion brings out unique observations, drawn from the participants. The participant-centered aspect of the case method cannot be overstated: the reader, or discussion participant, is challenged to read closely and empathetically, to reflect, to ask questions, and to come up with constructive answers to the dilemmas on the page.

Most of the cases in this volume are field cases, based on extensive research and interviews; only one, "Fliers at the Peace Parade," is a "library case," drawn from secondary research. As decision-based cases, they all have competing values, tension, and complexity; the case decisions are actionable, rather than abstract. The brief (A) case introduces the *problem*, the *place,* and a *person* (or people) confronted with a decision. We pause at the end of the (A) case—the point of decision—to ask additional questions and to reflect. Any analysis included in the case is that of the protagonist: in format and structure, the decision-based case creates space for analysis and critical thinking.

---

[1] John Boehrer and Marty Linsky, "Teaching with Cases: Learning to Question," *New Directions for Teaching and Learning* 42 (1990): 44.

Cases are incomplete both by necessity and by design. Yet in a case of any length, the discussion questions are similar. Based on the case narrative: What does the protagonist know? What does the protagonist need to know in order to solve the problem? As you consider how the protagonist might gather additional information, resources, or perspectives, consider how *you* would do so—whether as the protagonist or from your own location. What solutions might you suggest, based on the information in the case?

Protagonists and the Practice of Pluralism

Case studies focus on one primary point of view, a "protagonist," reminding us that there are real stakes and real people at the heart of any of these dilemmas or discussions of diversity. Each expresses a specific, situated point of view, grounded in their experience. While these stories are necessarily mediated by me as an interviewer and case writer, field cases are closely reviewed by the protagonist for accuracy—and to be sure they resonate closely with their personal experience.

As each protagonist determines a path forward, the reader is invited to join them, briefly inhabit their perspective, consider how they might respond, and then articulate their own point of view. The reader is encouraged to think critically about the problem, how it was handled, and what the protagonist may have missed. I would encourage you to bring empathy as you read these stories, recognizing that many of these decisions are made with the constraints of time, the confounding factor of limited information, and the complication of human frailty. Unlike you, who are reading these cases from relative comfort and distance, they didn't have the chance to practice with these dilemmas in advance.

For those who argue that these protagonists are sometimes treated as "heroes" in these case studies, I would agree. Please consider this: it is my intention to tell these stories from the protagonist's point of view, as it was happening for them at the time—and we are all the heroes of our own stories. Each case, in its own way, also suggests some of the blind spots and unanticipated elements: if they are heroes, they are certainly humble ones. As readers and discussants of these cases, we might bring the same sense of humility to the people—and the problem(s)—on the page.

Inhabiting these cases from the perspective of the protagonist enables us to move beyond simplistic criticism to complex problem-solving. It also helps each of us to practice pluralism: to understand that we, too, may be confronted by difficult decisions and complex dilemmas; we may experience—in relationship with ourselves or others—conflicting values and divergent truth claims. Cases help us to practice solving problems and confronting dilemmas. As we engage with cases, we practice forming and articulating our point of view; we also practice listening carefully, respecting other people's stories, and recognizing when we need to pause or seek additional information. I hope, as we practice pluralism through the case method, we might build some of the skills and capacities needed for living in our diverse society.

The Structure of This Volume

Pluralism in Practice includes the full text of twelve case studies, paired thematically as companion cases. It includes three more recent cases: "A Festival of Faiths," "A Quandary in Queens," and "Forty-Nine Days."

Each case opens with a brief scenario—a streamlined version of the problem—which serves as an introduction to the case text. These opening scenarios may also be utilized for discussion contexts with more limited time. Most of the cases in this collection are told in two parts: the (A) case brings thick description and detail to each dilemma and ends at the point of decision. This decision point structures the narrative, generates reflection, and energizes discussion as the reader pauses to consider an additional set of questions. Next, the (B) case describes how the decision or dilemma was resolved.

After each case appears a postscript or update on the dilemmas and controversies that served as the basis of these cases—both to under-score the changing nature and unseen aspects of these controversies, and to encourage readers to continue to follow these ongoing issues and unfolding stories.

The first part of the book, "Constructing Religious Diversity," approaches the display of religion in the public square: "The Christmas Tree Crisis at Sea-Tac Airport," about a contested holiday display at the airport, suggests the challenges of constructing a religiously diverse society. In "A Festival of Faiths," curators plan a large-scale festival of religion on the National Mall. Like its companion case, a working group is asked to consult on how to curate the complex, contested multireligious reality of religions in America—and how to think about lived religion.

The second part, "Religion in the American City," continues our exploration of religious diversity through two dilemmas in Michigan cities. "Trouble in Troy" follows one city's path toward inclusion of Hindu voices, and challenges to the presumptive Judeo-Christian identity, with the National Day of Prayer observance; "A Call to Prayer" looks at the controversy over the broadcast of the Muslim call to prayer in a town transforming from majority Polish to majority Muslim.

From the broader context of the American city, we move to thematic sections. In Part 3, "Fault Lines in Interfaith Relations," we explore some of the intractable divides in grassroots interfaith efforts: the issue of Israel/ Palestine, in "A Sign of Division," and the question of proselytization, as documented in "Fliers at the Peace Parade."

A thirteen-story Muslim community center in Manhattan may have little in common with the adaptive reuse of a church in a bedroom community of Chicago, yet both mosques face fierce opposition. In Part 4, "Mosques in the American Landscape," a Christian mayor and a Muslim community leader must each draw upon their respective faiths, and their inner resolve, as they navigate complex, charged disputes in "A Mosque in Palos Heights" and "Center of Dispute."

Part 5 explores interfaith and multifaith challenges through a Jewish lens. A rabbi called to host an interfaith event in the wake of the massacre at the Tree of Life Synagogue in "Showing Up for Shabbat" considers what "safety" means for the Jewish community and whether interfaith events are always appropriate. "A Question of Membership" explores multifaith identity through a request from a Buddhist leader to join her local synagogue.

The final part, "Navigating Crisis and Change," looks at two young leaders who must contend with community challenges: a first-generation Hindu American and community organizer faces issues, in "A Quandary in Queens," and Asian American Buddhists respond to anti-Asian violence in "Forty-Nine Days."

At the end of the book, Diana Eck offers some suggestions for reading and discussing cases in her afterword, "A Pedagogy of Pluralism."

A Postscript on Pluralism

The cases in this collection were developed over a period of more than fifteen years, with incidents taking place from the late 1990s to 2022. The postscripts, brief updates to each case, are drawn from more recent research and follow-up interviews. Here we ask questions including, How has the issue played out since the case was written? Has the protagonist's view changed over time? Would they offer any new reflections on leadership, or a new perspective on the existing case? Were there any unanticipated consequences? Or, in a few cases, might a postscript fill in what was missing from the original case?

Readers might do their own research on what happened after the case was resolved or read more about the city, the organization, or the individuals in the case; however, much might be overlooked or misunderstood doing a cursory Google search. Rarely in media coverage of a zoning battle, a difficult public decision, or a community dispute do we learn what happens in the aftermath. Much that unfolds does not become a matter of public record, and some of the assumptions we might make based on public sources—including my own, before speaking with people on the ground—may prove to be incorrect.

In most cases, these postscripts continue to center the voice and perspective of the protagonist; however, some include new voices. The postscript for "A Mosque in Palos Heights" integrates the voice of a minor character from the first case, Edward Hassan; "Fliers at the Peace Parade" expands the perspective to include a more prominent Sikh voice.

While this volume takes a longitudinal view on conflicts related to religious diversity and interfaith relations, these stories are ongoing, with impacts—and our interpretations—changing over time. Each case study and its postscripts are, in themselves, snapshots of a specific moment in time. This volume, accordingly, captures something of the current moment: it is not the same hopeful moment Diana Eck documented in *A New Religious America*. She wrote of a changing landscape, with emerging institutions and relationships, as well as some emerging challenges—but charged with a sense of possibility.

The mood here, as expressed by the protagonists in the postscripts, is decidedly darker: with follow-up interviews conducted in the midst of COVID-19, they describe a polarized political (and media) landscape, express concerns about the future of democracy, detail rising hate crimes against communities minoritized by race and religion, and chronicle the ongoing, seemingly intractable challenges of working across difference. In some cases, it becomes clear that their efforts—to build, repair, and reimagine—have not borne fruit. Yet the work continues.

Despite these stark realities, there are signs of hope in these post-scripts: an interfaith organization, formed out of crisis, still active twenty years later; a protagonist who didn't see her dream community center realized, yet has begun planning a new center; the leader refused membership to a religious community because of her dual religious identity who, years later, is welcomed. There is persistence to the practice of pluralism and, with it, a progressive vision for the future. There are also lessons here, common to these stories and evident to me as an observer and researcher of interfaith civic life: that having relationships in place before a crisis is critical; that effective leadership requires an ability to listen to other points of view—and to clearly articulate not only a vision but a plan; that we often can't avoid or anticipate crises, but we can learn from how others respond; and that constructive efforts require regular maintenance and constant cultivation.

One of our early cases, written by Marcia Sietstra, tells the story of the founding of the Tri-Faith Initiative in Omaha, Nebraska: here, a synagogue, mosque, and church chose to build side by side. In more recent years, they established an orchard called "Hope" on the thirty-eight-acre campus. Right now, Hope isn't thriving. Fruit trees take many years after planting before they can be harvested; the volunteers who tend to the trees recognize that the particular siting and soil conditions may not be ideal for the orchard to thrive, but they continue to search for solutions. Other aspects of the larger, aspirational Tri-Faith project are flourishing: the three communities constructed landmark religious centers—and an interfaith center—and have built programs for education, intentional relationship, and ongoing collaboration.

From the initial vision in the early 2000s to the vital thirty-eight-acre campus today, Tri-Faith understands itself as a new model of relationship, but also as a work in progress. It is a place of daily effort and ongoing cultivation, made visible in Tri-Faith's struggling orchard, but also in their vast, productive organic donation garden. Recently, Tri-Faith volunteers donated more than five thousand 5,000 pounds of produce to people in need across Omaha. The garden and orchard weren't part of the original plan for Tri-Faith, nor was the beautiful circular wooden bridge that connects the buildings: these ideas, like some of the new challenges facing Tri-Faith, have emerged over time. Will Tri-Faith become a model for other communities? How will they contend with increasing division—and rising hate crimes? Will they expand to invite other faiths? Will

Tri-Faith have relevance for an increasingly unaffiliated next generation? Will "Hope" survive—the orchard or the aspiration? Tri-Faith's visionary, Rabbi Aryeh Azriel, has something to say about this:

> Sometimes we need to stop using the word hope and actually try to effectuate, and change, and create the hope ourselves. There will be moments of rough coexistence. So what? We are responsible to continue this for the next generation, even if it is hard—even if there are obstacles. And there will be obstacles.[2]

This book documents some of the obstacles and difficulties of our multifaith reality in the United States, making clear the very real challenges that decision-makers face, as well as the deepening divides. This volume provides cautionary tales but also offers powerful examples of response and repair. Each case highlights one or more critical, constructive, and creative responses—of pluralism in practice—as tools for education, and perhaps, as a source of inspiration.

---

[2] Rabbi Aryeh Azriel, interview with the author, October 10, 2021.

Part 1

Constructing Religious Diversity

The Christmas Tree Crisis
at Sea-Tac Airport

The Christmas trees that appeared each year in the Seattle-Tacoma Airport, some said, were a "tradition." The fake but festive trees, decorated in red ribbons, were brought out of storage and put on display during one of the busiest times of the travel season. When the airport authorities received a complaint about the display's lack of inclusiveness, with a request to add a menorah, it went unanswered. When this was followed with a threat of legal action, the trees were swiftly returned to storage in the middle of the night. The removal of the Christmas trees, covered in the news with rhetoric about "the Grinch," was followed by a flood of hateful emails to the local Jewish community. The original request, which was not to remove the trees but to add a menorah, was swiftly withdrawn. Soon the trees returned, along with a newly appointed Holiday Decorations Advisory Committee to consider future displays. The committee was now charged with making a decision: Should they display all, some, or none of the local religious traditions? What should the holiday display look like? What are the implications of making a change to this "tradition"?

(A) Case

"What a mess."[1] Rabbi Anson Laytner shook his head as he read the media coverage of Christmas trees at Seattle-Tacoma International Airport (Sea-Tac). Laytner didn't agree with the request for a menorah to be added to the holiday display, the threatened lawsuit, or the airport's decision to remove the trees. He thought, *This is all such silliness.*

---

[1] All quotes from Rabbi Anson Laytner are from a phone interview with the author, January 15, 2016.

An article in the *Seattle Times* explained the airport's removal of nine trees by maintenance crews working the graveyard shift: "As odd as it might seem, Sea-Tac Airport officials were hoping to avoid controversy."[2] The article continued,

> The airport managers ordered the plastic trees removed and boxed up after a rabbi asked to have an 8-foot-tall menorah displayed next to the largest tree in the international arrival hall.
>
> Port of Seattle staff felt adding the menorah would have required adding symbols for other religions and cultures in the Northwest, said Terri-Ann Betancourt, the airport's spokeswoman. The holidays are the busiest season at the airport, she said, and staff didn't have time to play cultural anthropologists.
>
> "We decided to take the trees down because we didn't want to be exclusive," she said. "We're trying to be thoughtful and respectful, and will review policies after the first of the year."
>
> The decision, made in consultation with the Port's elected board of commissioners, interrupts a decades-long tradition at the airport. No sooner had the trees come down than their removal spread something less than holiday cheer across religious groups.[3]

The request for a menorah at the airport was initiated by another local rabbi, Elazar Bogomilsky. The *Seattle Times* article quoted Bogomilsky, who was "appalled" by the Port's reaction. "There are public menorah lightings at the White House and cities across the Northwest, he said.... Why not the airport?"[4]

Laytner hadn't made the request, but he knew he would have to respond. "As a liberal Jew who lived in Seattle for twenty years, I wasn't offended by seeing Christmas trees in public places. It didn't bother me," Laytner explained. "What bothered me was the Port's reaction, because I knew it was going to create backlash in the community, and sure enough, that's what happened."

---

[2] Jonathan Martin, "Airport Puts Away Holiday Trees Rather Than Risk Being 'Exclusive,'" *Seattle Times*, December 10, 2006, A1.

[3] Ibid.

[4] Ibid.

Backlash

Laytner soon began receiving emails and phone calls: "'Are you people the ones responsible for pulling down our Christmas trees at the airport? You people shouldn't do things like this—it will make people hate you more.'" Laytner, the executive director of Seattle's American Jewish Committee (AJC), was concerned. Earlier that year, a shooting at a local Jewish organization left one person dead and several wounded. "The Jewish community was still very much traumatized by that, and so we would take even mild threats more seriously than we would have otherwise. That included me."

The issue of the Christmas trees quickly became a matter of public debate in Seattle and beyond. Some questioned the request for a menorah; others criticized the airport's response. One online *Seattle Times* article about the removal of "holiday trees" received more than eight hundred reader responses, most of them opposed, some of them angry. Laytner recalled, "I think when the Christmas tree crisis hit, many people were talking like, 'Why should we change? We don't need to change.... This is our community, and we are going to do things the way we've always done it.' By the Port yanking the Christmas trees, that really yanked their chain."

Within the Jewish community, Laytner described conflicting concerns. "As with any other issue, I heard it in stereo. From one side, I was getting, 'This is terrible, we need to protect the separation of church and state'; 'This is putting our community at risk...', but on the other was: 'We Jews need to stand together' and 'What's wrong with having a menorah at the airport? Are you ashamed of who you are?'"

Laytner stated, "I wanted to see a separation of church and state. And for me, a menorah is a religious symbol, not a secondary religious symbol; it's *the* symbol of the holiday of Hanukkah." A dreidel, he thought, was more "comparable to the Christmas tree"; however, he added, "my preference was ideally always no Christmas tree and certainly no menorah."

The Port Responds

Within a few days, with Port officials under public pressure, and with the threat of a lawsuit withdrawn, the trees returned to the airport. That year, no other symbols would be added. Laytner noted, "I think that soothed the most vociferous complainers. That kind of diffused the crisis in the short term, and then the Port decided, 'Okay, let's look at this in a noncrisis mode.'"

Shortly after, Laytner received an invitation to join the Port's Holiday Decorations Advisory Committee, together with other faith leaders and representatives from the Port, business, law, and academia. The twelve-member committee included Dr. Marilyn Gist, a professor of management at Seattle University, and Imam Jamal Rahman, a local Sufi Muslim leader active in interfaith work.

Gist brought expertise in diversity and leadership; she also understood the perspective of the Port's managing director: "I could feel the pain from all of the criticism in the newspapers. [The managing director] was a leader embroiled in a controversy he didn't intend to start."[5] She added, "They took [Rabbi Bogomilsky's] concern to heart and removed the trees with the right intent. The public backlash had been surprising." Months later, she observed, "tension and woundedness" still surrounded the issue. Gist recognized that the airport was technically a municipal and private space but was thought of by most as a public space. Accordingly, for Gist, the question was simple: "As leaders, we need to ask: do we want to be welcoming to all, or welcoming to some?"

Rahman observed, "The Christmas trees at the airport brought up the issue of authentic inclusivity."[6] He emphasized the reverence for Jesus and Mary in the Islamic tradition, and explained, "We have respect for what Christmas symbolizes. We honor Jesus, but how can we also honor founders of other traditions? Inclusiveness is essential in a multireligious society." At the same time, he recalled, "I was particularly sensitive to the demonization and dehumanization of the Jews that was happening. . . . It was important not to generalize over particular incidents." Rahman wondered, "How do we live our interfaith ideals?"

Laytner reflected, "I wanted to see a community in which all of the different religions, different ethnic groups were treated with respect." Although initially he had no problem with the airport's holiday display, he noted, "Once the Christmas tree issue was raised, it kind of became an issue of respect." He wondered, "Are we going to remain the way we've

<hr>

[5] All quotes from Dr. Marilyn Gist are from phone interview with the author, January 8, 2016.

[6] All quotes from Imam Jamal Rahman are from phone interview with the author, January, January 8, 2016.

been since Seattle's founding, or are we going to move and take signifi-cant steps towards a different kind of vision for our community? And as a member of the Jewish community and an individual, I was invested in seeing change happen."

But another question remained for Laytner and the rest of the committee tasked with making a recommendation to the Port: what form should the holiday display take?

Questions for Reflection

- Did the airport make the right decision to remove the trees? Do you agree with their decision to reinstall the same display in response to public pressure?
- Imagine yourself as a member of the Holiday Decorations Advisory Committee, alongside Laytner, Gist, and Rahman. Consider the range of interests to balance and options avail-able, then the need to establish criteria for a successful outcome. What would you suggest?
- Is there a holiday display at your local airport? If you were creating a committee to evaluate that display, who might be a part of that committee? Would you have the same suggestion for displays at your local airport as you would Sea-Tac?

(B) Case

The newly appointed Holiday Decorations Advisory Committee met over a period of months at a downtown Seattle law office. Rabbi Anson Laytner appreciated having the time to discuss the question of holiday decorations at Sea-Tac without the pressure of the controversy and its backlash. Laytner explained, "Working in a noncrisis environment is definitely preferable. It was inspiring to have a committee that brought together people of many different faiths to try to work on this issue."

At the final meeting on June 6, 2007, the committee affirmed the purpose of decorations during the holiday season: "To make the airport a festive and welcoming facility during the holidays, which is a very busy and often stressful travel time."[7] Their formal recommendations read, in part,

---

[7] Holiday Decorations Advisory Committee Recommendation to Port of

The Committee recommends that decorations should reflect the Pacific Northwest environment and our diverse community, and convey universal values, such as peace and harmony. These values have roots in many religious faiths and cultures. Our goal is to create an inclusive and warm environment at the airport.

Committee members noted that the use of light and color is especially appropriate in Seattle due to our dark winter travel season. The use of fabric, garlands, color and light in decorations or celebrations is common to cultures worldwide. The committee recommends that no specific religious symbols should be used.[8]

The new holiday display previewed in October 2007; while newsworthy, it did not generate significant controversy. The *Seattle Post-Intelligencer* described the outcome starkly with the headline "Airport Will Celebrate Winter, but Not Christmas."[9] With only a brief reference to the "holiday hubbub,"[10] the article described the new decorations as "a grove of luminous birches up to 30 feet high and hung with crystals and mirrors to reflect colored, low-energy lights emanating from within piles of Dacron snow."[11] The article included a response to the display from Port Commissioner Pat Davis:

> What I was hoping for was something that was cheerful and evocative of the holiday spirit, and as much to do with nature and evergreens and trees as they could.... We wanted to move forward without something that would get us back into controversy, and I think it is very creative. I hope the public likes it—it will take a while to get used to.[12]

Laytner recalled, "Even though the result was kind of bland, I think it was still a very good effort. I think it was one of the first in our community." After the divisiveness over the Christmas trees, Laytner

---

Seattle, memorandum regarding Sea-Tac holiday decorations, June 6, 2007. From Perry Cooper, manager, aviation public affairs, to the author, December 11, 2015.

    [8] Ibid.
    [9] Kristen Millares Young, "Airport Will Celebrate Winter, but Not Christmas," *Seattle Post-Intelligencer*, October 19, 2007, A1.
    [10] Ibid.
    [11] Ibid.
    [12] Ibid.

explained, the committee focused on how the decorations might express "common values." Yet, he added, "How exactly do you display a value? It's very hard."

Committee member Imam Jamal Rahman reflected, "What stands out was that all of us were so eager. There were Christians and Buddhists, and besides religious leaders, academics, people from business." They generated a range of ideas, from decorating the trees with symbols of other traditions to developing an educational display on religious or spiritual literacy. But questions soon emerged: "Who do you leave out? Who do you include?"

Laytner noted, "Ultimately, the point of view that won the day was one that said we're going to have to do something that is really devoid of value and void of any kind of religious meaning." They were guided, in part, by the policy for decorations at Pacific Place, a downtown mall with decorations Laytner that characterized as "'Holiday Season,' but nothing specific." He observed,

> I think one of the ongoing issues for people doing interfaith work is how to manifest that respect of all different religions without falling into that swamp of who is a real, legitimate religion and who isn't? Or how do you do a program or an event that honors all the different religions and doesn't go on for five hours? So that's an issue.... So that's how we ended up with the values-neutral, holiday-neutral kind of decorations that they have now at Sea-Tac.

Dr. Marilyn Gist, the committee member from Seattle University with a background in diversity, equity, and inclusion (DEI), noted that the diverse group was able to quickly "pivot from the perspective of group rights, where parties are aggrieved, to 'What sort of a public space do we want to have?'" They recognized that the display would need to be "welcoming to all—either representing every group or none." She recognized that some would certainly miss the old Christmas decorations: "That is one of the losses." Yet she explained, "There are two ways of thinking about it: One, I am losing the right to being honored exclusively, or being able to have privilege; two, I am part of the pluralism of this society. My uniqueness has its place, but not necessarily in a public space."

Another New Display

Within a few years, the new holiday display was replaced. According to a Port spokesperson, the design with birches, birds, and snow "proved more fragile than expected."[13] Further, the Port received many comments over the years "that the birch trees in the new design were not representative of the Pacific Northwest."[14] Without fanfare or press coverage, smaller evergreen trees with white lights, fake snow, and poinsettia plants appeared in the Arrivals Hall. In an email to Laytner, the Port spokesperson explained, "The goal is to continue the direction given by the advisory committee to reflect the Pacific NW environment, create an inclusive and warm environment at the airport, and use light and color to help brighten the dark winter travel season of Seattle."[15] Laytner acknowledged, "It's gotten ... a little more back towards Christmas. But I guess, poinsettias are red and green. How far do you go with what's a real Christmas symbol? To me, you can get crazy about that." Overall, he expressed appreciation for the display, which conveys "a natural scene."

Beyond the Christmas tree crisis, Laytner observed, "What strikes me is the persistence of the issue of how profoundly entitled people from the majority culture feel. And that is still with us." Whether his own experience of hate mail or the rise of Islamophobia and political rhetoric against minority groups, Laytner explained, "People feel somehow threatened by diversity, that they are somehow on the losing end of things and are fearful. And how we can address that is a very significant issue, because it can lead to lots of different kinds of hateful manifestations if it is not addressed. Years later, we are still dealing with that pushback."

Postscript

When the Christmas tree crisis began at Seattle-Tacoma International Airport, Rabbi Anson Laytner dismissed it as "silliness." He didn't think a menorah should be added to the display, nor did he want the Christmas trees removed. At the time, Laytner noted that he wasn't bothered by the display of Christmas trees; he was upset by their sudden removal and the

---

[13] Perry Cooper, "RE: Sea-Tac Holiday Decorations Advisory Committee," email to Rabbi Anson Laytner, January 14, 2016.

[14] Ibid.

[15] Ibid.

backlash it triggered against the Jewish community. Yet today, Laytner explains, "I think I was being too accommodating.... In retrospect, it bothered me, but I just wasn't really in touch with that fact."[16]

He explains, "Growing up, what we were taught was this is basically a Christian country. Don't make waves and they won't bother you.... Accept what it is." At that time, he recalls, there was little sensitivity to diversity: at school assemblies, everyone sang Christmas carols. "So my initial reaction to the Christmas tree was, 'It's a Christian country, they're putting up a Christmas tree. I can live with the Christmas tree; at least it's not a creche.'" The consultative process of the holiday decorations committee began to shift his thinking. "'Wait a second. This is really not *their* country.... This is *our* country, and I am an equal member. And so why should this group have its values or its symbols prioritized over every other group's symbols?' So it was an awakening awareness for me."

Laytner's view on the display of religious symbols in public spaces remains unchanged. "I'm not in favor of putting in additional religious symbols because there's no way to be totally inclusive of every religious group, and even then, if you include every religious group in a place—in our area there's lots and lots of nonreligious people, so what do we do about them? Then they'll be offended by having this big display of religious symbols."

Less than an hour away from the Sea-Tac Airport, at the state capitol in Olympia, officials permitted the display of various religious symbols— for a brief time. In addition to the large "holiday tree" displayed in the capitol rotunda, a menorah and creche were added. There was also a large sign from the Freedom from Religion Foundation, framed in gold and placed near the creche. It read,

> At this season of the Winter Solstice may reason prevail. There are no gods, no devils, no angels, no heaven or hell. There is only our natural world. Religion is but myth and superstition that hardens hearts and enslaves minds.[17]

---

[16] All quotes from Rabbi Anson Laytner in postscript are from Zoom interview with the author, June 17, 2022.

[17] Richard Roesler, "Officials Draw Line on Holiday Displays; Moratorium Follows Uproar in Capitol," *Spokesman Review* (Spokane, WA), December 13, 2008, A6.

"That's the kind of thing that I would expect," Laytner reflects, noting that is one of the risks of displaying religious symbols in a public place. Once religious symbols are added to a display, he notes, "You can't, and shouldn't, say no [to some groups]." The sign from the Freedom from Religion Foundation, which generated some controversy, was stolen from the rotunda and later recovered by state troopers. When it was reinstalled, a small paper sign was affixed: "Thou Shalt Not Steal. Exodus 20:15."[18]

Laytner is grateful to the Port for convening the committee. "Symbolically it's quite important, and had it not been handled well, it could have easily escalated into religious tensions in the community." He notes, "And as we've seen in subsequent years, the flash points of religion and ethnicity are still hot buttons in our community, whether it's anti-immigrant or anti-Islam or anti-Jewish. They're still around." This sort of bias, he reflects, "is always there. And then a crisis exacerbates it and brings it to the fore."

Laytner sees the Christmas tree crisis as symbolic of "the state of our culture." With rising religious and ethnic diversity, groups want greater representation. "And that inevitably will cause pushback from the dominant group because they're used to having things their way and that's the way it's always been, right? So change is hard."

More recently, the holiday display at the Sea-Tac airport has undergone yet another change.[19] The new display features white, modern, evergreen-shaped forms. Small clusters of trees, no taller than six feet, may be found in the main terminal and each of the concourses. With their simplified design and infrequent appearance, they are easy to miss. They are accompanied by wood-paneled banners of multicolored snowflakes, some of which include LED lights. Airlines and staff are welcome to decorate individual ticket counters as they choose: recent displays included small wreaths, trees, gift boxes, and snowflakes.

If Laytner were appointed to the Holiday Decorations Advisory Committee today, he would suggest a winter scene, perhaps not unlike what they have now. "Just something to jazz up the public spaces. Bring some color ... and leave it at that. It doesn't have to be a loaded symbol. It can be neutral and simple and still spark joy, wonder, and delight."

---

[18] Ibid.

[19] All references to updated holiday displays: Port of Seattle, "Holiday Package 2021," email to Emily Chaudhari, and "Sea-Tac Holiday Display," email from Emily Chaudhari to author, December 31, 2021.

As Rabbi Laytner reflects upon his work in interfaith and community relations, he notes, "I think there are many stories that go into the making of the American story. And the challenge for every group is to make room for these other stories to coexist with its story." He continues:

The predominant American Jewish story is we came from lands where we were oppressed, we came to America as poor immigrants and we pulled ourselves up by our bootstraps, and now we are a strong, vibrant, prosperous community. Great for us to fulfill the American dream. My wife is African American, and that's not her story. They came from Africa, were brought here, impoverished and enslaved and persecuted, and they couldn't pull themselves up by their bootstraps because every time they tried to stand up the rug would get pulled out from under their feet. That's her American story. Somehow, my people's story and her people's story have to coexist, and there has to be room for her to embrace my story, and for me to embrace her story and all those other stories of other groups—including the dominant white Christian one.

A Festival of Faiths

Each year on the National Mall in Washington, DC, one million people gather for the Smithsonian Folklife Festival. For two weeks, visitors congregate to engage with the festival theme through crafts, food, story circles, and performances. The programming is intended for a broad audience—including children and young people—and is an immersive sensory experience. The Rev. Dr. Brad Braxton, who brought prior experience at the Smithsonian National Museum of African American History and Culture, was thrilled to help curate and advise the 2023 festival, with the theme of "Living Religion in America." Braxton and his colleagues at the Smithsonian hoped to honor the complexity, depth, and diversity of religious and ethical traditions in the large public festival. Yet as Braxton considered how to "tangibilitate" living religion—how to make religion visible and audible—he also had some concerns. How would they engage the next generation, many of whom did not identify as religious? How might the festival push the boundaries of the term "religion" in order to make the festival more inclusive? How, he wondered, could the festival address the "two poles of religion," of healing and hurt? And how might they cultivate conversations across lines of difference between and within faith traditions? The Festival of Living Religion might be a place for creative encounters, but it also had the possibility for conflict: indeed, the same grounds on which they would gather was also the site of the January 6 insurrection.

(A) Case

In the predawn hours, the Rev. Dr. Brad Braxton's neighborhood is quiet. As the sun rises along his tree-lined street in Brooklyn, Braxton has already completed four hours of work. Each day, he wakes between midnight and 2 a.m. Braxton finds that some of his best intellectual work happens before dawn. His busy, eclectic professional life demands the extra focus—and the extra hours—of the early morning. Braxton is the founding pastor of the Open Church in Baltimore and also leads diversity, equity, and inclusion (DEI) efforts at St. Luke's School in New York City; in 2020 he was appointed as a curator and adviser for the Smithsonian's Folklife Festival of Living Religion in America.

Shortly after his appointment to the Folklife Festival, Braxton sat before a blank computer screen: charged with planning a large-scale festival about religion on the National Mall in DC, he was undaunted, yet acutely aware of the magnitude of the task before him. Optimistic by nature and by faith, Braxton would need not merely to curate, but—in his words—to "tangibilitate" the complex, contested, diverse nature of religion in America today. It would need to be visible and audible, with arts and music, dance and theatre, storytelling and conversation. The audience for the large public festival would include varied perspectives within and among diverse faiths, and also those who did not identify as religious. The festival would also include many who understood their religious commitments in opposition to, rather than in dialogue with, others. Here, in the shadow of the US Capitol, this festival of religion in America was a matter of "moral significance" for Braxton. Simply put, he observed, "We need to create different conversations."[1]

Brad Braxton

Braxton's formal education includes a PhD in New Testament studies from Emory University and a master's degree in theology from Oxford, where he was a Rhodes Scholar; however, his most formative education, and the inspiration for his career, came from his parents. Braxton's father was a Baptist preacher; his mother was a teacher and gifted musician. Faith and family, for Braxton, are best described as Sunday mornings in Salem, Virginia: as a young boy, he would wake to the smell of French toast, pancakes, and sausage and the sound of his mother playing the piano. Most Sundays she'd be working out what she was going to play for the Gospel choir at his father's First Baptist Church; sometimes she'd play James Cleveland records, learning the music by ear. Braxton smiled

---

[1] All quotes by Brad Braxton are from Zoom interview with the author, July 16, 2020, and via email, May 3, 2021.

as he recalled climbing into his family's big white Pontiac with his father, heading to Sunday school: "I can feel it like it was today. My daddy was a Virginia farm boy: about six feet, had shoulders as broad as the Pacific Ocean. And he would put that big brown hand of his on my knee." It was a loving, "profoundly intimate" moment—an indelible part of his sense memory.

Even as he reflected on these warm Sunday mornings, Braxton paused to note that not everyone shares this experience of family and faith: like family, religion can be a source of healing, but it can also be a source of harm. He acknowledged the "two poles of religion ... in foisting upon us grotesque inhumanity and in fostering indomitable hope." Braxton emphasized, "There is a long arc of traditions in sponsoring social change: I want to move the needle for a richer appreciation of the role of religion. Black Lives Matter is rooted in the rich ethical—and pathological— aspects of religion." He explained further,

> At their best, religious communities are frontline "doctors of the soul" that foster healing in hurting communities. Whether regis- tering voters, supporting climate-change initiatives, or mobilizing congregations against police brutality, religious communities are compassionate and courageous creators of positive social change. At their worst, however, religious communities motivate bigotry and hatred, thereby engaging in social and moral malpractice.

He also acknowledged that, for some, "religion" was an inadequate term to describe their spiritual or ethical commitments. He reflected, "How we talk about religion is important: will it open up thought worlds or shut them down? Terminology can invite and exclude people."

Braxton joyfully pushes the boundaries of his Christian tradition toward inclusion, embracing his role as an ally of LGBTQ folk and as a DEI leader. He describes the Open Church of Maryland as an "experi- ment in radical religious openness," with a diverse congregation that is—in Braxton's words—"hat-wearing church mamas" coming together with skeptical social activists, young professionals, and others. Roughly half identify as LGBTQ. Braxton described the church as "a culturally inclusive congregation in Baltimore committed to courageous social justice activism and compassionate interfaith collaboration." Nearly one decade since its founding, he now challenges his congregation to consider whether "church" is the best description for the community, which includes members and visitors of diverse faiths.

His own identity as a Black Christian, he explained, is "deeply anchored in other ways of being that come from the African continent and African diaspora." While his spiritual autobiography began in Salem, Virginia, it also includes the insights gleaned from study trips to villages in the Gambia and Ghana when he was in his twenties and thirties. Writing about these experiences, Braxton later observed, "I began to imagine religion as a kind of African music—a complex, polyphonic performance of intertwining voices giving witness to all that is sacred. Christianity, for me, was an important voice, but it was no longer the only voice. The solo had become a chorus."[2] Today his embrace of pluralism includes an emphasis on dialogue across faith lines, and the "heat and light" that such conversations bring. Yet he also recognizes that such conversations across lines of difference can be far more difficult within a faith community than between them.

The Folklife Festival

Braxton was enthusiastic about the unique opportunities of the museum environment. With prior experience at the Smithsonian National Museum of African American History and Culture, he regularly recited the Smithsonian's six-word statement of purpose: "The increase and diffusion of knowledge." Braxton didn't have an opportunity to attend the Folklife Festival in person before he took on the role of curator and adviser; due to the pandemic, the 2020 and 2021 festivals would be hosted online. Yet conversations with colleagues and extensive multimedia coverage clearly conveyed to Braxton the many ways in which the festival is an immersive sensory experience.

The Smithsonian's introductory video states, "Every year, the festival presents a cultural dialogue in music, craftsmanship, work, and words. A peoples' museum, without walls."[3] Its website explains, "The Festival is

---

[2] Brad R. Braxton, "The Grace of the Lord Jesus Be with All: A Minister's Conversion to Religious Pluralism," *Harvard Divinity Bulletin* (Summer/Autumn 2016), https://bulletin.hds.harvard.edu/.

[3] Smithsonian Folklife, "Smithsonian Folklife Festival Introduction," YouTube, April 1, 2013.

an exercise in cultural democracy, in which cultural practitioners speak for themselves, with each other, and to the public. The Festival encourages visitors to participate—to learn, sing, dance, eat traditional foods, and converse with people presented in the Festival program."[4] Established in 1967 the Folklife Festival is DC's largest annual cultural event, drawing one million participants to the Mall over two weeks and ten million through online and print sources. Many of those who participate in the programming at the Mall are children and young people, eagerly engaging in crafts, eating new foods, and encountering new worlds through story circles. Braxton was drawn especially to the storytelling element, which—like contextual theologies (Black, womanist, postmodern, postcolonial, queer)—"insist that responsible theological discourse must be grounded in our personal stories and cultural histories and context."

When Braxton was appointed as a curator and adviser, he inherited the festival title of "Living Religion in America": it affirmed that faith and ethical commitments were not static, historical artifacts, but "breathing in the here and now." While the larger curation process leading up to the festival would include input from folklorists at the Smithsonian and integrate advice from a council of scholars and religious leaders, Braxton needed to create a foundation of core themes and messages upon which they could build. Unsure of how to honor the complexity, depth, and diversity of religious and ethical traditions in a large public festival, Braxton turned to "the elders." There, in his vast Brooklyn library, were the insights of "a council of elders"—authors, scholars, and activists. One of the first volumes off the shelf, *The Creative Encounter* by Howard Thurman, asked key questions: "What about religion takes us deep inside? And what about religion propels us to some form of external engagement?"

Braxton decided to call the festival "Creative Encounters," and after many hours of reading, writing, and reflecting with his esteemed council of elders, he shaped the festival around four themes: "1) Religion remains a vital force for creating meaning and motivating action; 2) Religion exhibits its creative energy in multidimensional ways; 3) The relationship between religion and politics is complex and creative; 4) Religion is a vital

---

[4] Smithsonian Folklife Festival, "About Us: Mission and History," accessed February 28, 2023, https://festival.si.edu/.

force for social change." He looked forward to exploring these themes with input from an audience as broad and diverse as those who would come to the National Mall: young and old, people of varied faiths, and those who don't identify as religious.

An Insurrection and an Invitation

By early 2021, Braxton and his colleagues at the Smithsonian began shifting into the practical matters of festival-making. He explained, "The 2023 Festival will be a living laboratory of diversity, as Buddhists, Christians, Hindus, Jews, Muslims, Sikhs, followers of Native American and African-inspired religions, and devotees of Humanism and other ethical traditions share, and learn from, their stories and practices." A few key issues remained: How might the festival express diversity within each tradition? Can the festival give space and credence to both exclusive and pluralist understandings of religion in America—and should it? And how might their programs reflect the two poles of religion?

As Braxton and his colleagues continued to translate complex themes into accessible programs, the home of the festival—the National Mall— became the site of a major insurrection. On January 6, 2021, much of the nation watched as angry crowds stormed the Capitol. Many rioters carried Confederate flags alongside flags with Christian images; others displayed nooses and carried crosses. While many observers were shocked, Braxton was hardly surprised by the intermingling of Christian and racist symbols in the riots. Braxton later explained,

> Intertwined within the founding narrative of America is the horrific story of how Christian discourse and practices were misused to perpetrate crimes against humanity. Christianity— or distorted versions of it—provided the religious justification for many nations to exploit and murder millions of Indigenous peoples through genocide, colonialism, and slavery. While courageously examining religion's harmful effects throughout US history—up to and including the January 2021 insurrection— I understand the festival as a creative opportunity to destabilize certain claims about religion and invite new conversations that foster healing and restorative justice.

As the festival drew closer, Braxton and his colleagues began to seek input from a wide range of religious groups, practitioners, and scholars. Together with the Smithsonian Folklife Festival team, they began convening working groups. For Braxton, this was an invitation to think creatively and constructively: "What creative encounters would *you* imagine at a Festival of Living Religion in America?"

Questions for Reflection

- Imagining yourself as part of the advisory council, what advice would you give to Braxton? What boundaries should Braxton push or respect? Are there any special concerns or risks he might consider given the topic of religion?
- How might Braxton balance the internal diversity of each community? Are there specific concerns you might identify from your own religious community—or from your own nonreligious identity?
- What practical ideas might you offer for what people see, do, and hear on the National Mall? How might you make religion tangible, tasteable, visual, audible?
- Braxton describes healing and harm as the "two poles of religion." How, if at all, would you reflect this in the Festival?

Postscript

When Michelle Banks was twelve years old, she took the Metro from her home in southeastern Washington, DC, to the National Mall and "stumbled across the festival."[5] She wasn't sure what was happening along the grid of green spaces and pathways, but was drawn in by an unfamiliar sound: live Reggae music. Decades later—after being a stage manager, assisting with volunteers, and even serving as a presenter and a participant—Banks would be appointed as lead curator for the Smithsonian Festival of Living Religion. The Rev. Dr. Brad Braxton, who shaped the vision for the festival, would continue to serve in an advisory capacity as he took on a new role: the fourteenth president of Chicago Theological Seminary.

---

    [5] All quotes by Michelle Banks are from Zoom interviews with the author, November 10 and November 28, 2022.

Banks identifies as a "cultural worker." With twenty-five years of experience working with children and youth across economic, racial, and ethnic lines, Banks brings a perspective grounded in practice and elevated through the arts: as a teenager, she cofounded the LatiNegro Theatre Collective in her hometown of DC. Banks is also a "reluctant academic" with cultural research experience: she has a master's degree in cultural sustainability from Goucher College and is currently completing her Ph.D. in Sustainability Education at Prescott College. Banks described Braxton's thinking—and contributions from a range of academic advisers—as "an incredible piece of work." She explained, "The words on the page were beautiful, but the sensory experience of the festival—the tastes and the sounds and the smells—that wasn't there." Banks thought, *How do I translate this into festival?*

As she read the notes from the consultations with academics, Banks appreciated the depth of the thinking, but noticed something else: "How much folks said what we *can't* do." She appreciated the concerns about appropriateness and hesitancy to offend and is careful in her own use of terminology. "We're being very deliberate about saying 'religion, spirituality, and ethical traditions.'" She added, "But if we're doing festival the right way, we're not saying to you, 'This is what you should be doing when you go to the Mall.' Instead, we are creating space. . . . We are seeking out people and bringing them together—and seeing what emerges from that coming together."

Banks, who was raised Southern Baptist, recalls that her grandparents had limited schooling. It was difficult for them to read the Bible; they understood their faith through practice. She adds, "That doesn't take away from the fact that their expressions of faith were profoundly beautiful. . . . That doesn't take away from what they bring to this tradition." While an academic perspective is important, she notes, "As we're running around in circles, the grandmother has baked the bread, and shared her story, and expressed her devotion. Meanwhile we're trying to define religion." For Banks, "It's really about that day-to-day experience, the quotidian." She continues, "The essence of the festival is really the culture-bearers and the tradition-bearers."

Together with her curatorial team, Banks began building the festival around "five interconnected themes that express how people employ religious and spiritual practices to construct community, find meaning, and transmit their worldviews."[6] These include:

---

[6] Smithsonian Folklife Festival, "2023 Folklife Festival, Living Religion: Creative Encounters in the U.S.," accessed February 28, 2023, https://festival.si.edu/.

Makers of Faith: material culture and placemaking;
Sound Religion: music and poetry for the soul;
Body and Spirit: dance as medicine and prayer;
Kitchen Theology: feeding the body, the spirit, and the ancestors;
Futurisms: constructing diverse visions for a shared future.[7]

As they began to sketch out the physical plan for the festival, it would be centered on a "world tree." Banks explains, "The world tree roots us, and it also connects us to the cosmos." She believes that the symbol connects across traditions, including those who might be more grounded in spiritual ecology—like Banks herself. Beyond the physical structures, they are also creating a soundscape of sacred music from varied traditions.

Curators are discussing how to honor the experience of, and emergence from, COVID-19: perhaps with a ritual, the tying of a ribbon, or writing names on paper. They are also discussing whether—and how—to consecrate or "clean" the space for the festival. But the team's primary focus is to reach out to artisans, culture-bearers, and tradition-bearers. As the curation process continues, Banks is regularly reminded of Braxton's powerful words about the potential of religion: "He regularly says that, when religion works, it is the most profoundly beautiful thing; and when it doesn't, it is the complete opposite." Considering the January 6 insurrection, she notes, "Being on the Mall is part of that—there's a really important sense that we are reclaiming that space, and we are opening that space and inviting folks inside."

The curation team imagines the festival as an opportunity to come inside and experience something from other faith traditions through "portals." She explains, "We won't build a mosque, a synagogue, or a church on the Mall, but we will build entryways." Banks continues, "As you enter one of the portals, you might find something different as the day progresses: a craftsperson, a musician, or people building drums. You might find a Gospel choir, or Taiko and Vodou drummers in conversation."

Banks elaborates: "The portals are meant to physically say, 'Come inside. Pass through.' These are the openings of these liminal spaces—and they're meant to be thresholds, portals, entryways."

---

[7] Ibid.

She observes, "A wooden gate could be a Buddhist temple, or it could be a Hindu temple. An archway could be a synagogue, a mosque, or a church. Nature is for some folks the Divine's first church, so that would be its own entryway." She added, "How often do people visit someone else's place of worship? That's what this festival is: an opportunity to witness some of the ways religion and spirituality manifest."

Part 2

Religion in the American City

Trouble in Troy

Troy, Michigan, like many other American cities, observed the National Day of Prayer (NDP) each year on the first Thursday in May. Here the observance took place on the steps of city hall. The event was well-attended, including the mayor, city council members, and community leaders. Often, the city of Troy would issue a proclamation, drafted by the local NDP Task Force, to mark the event. But when Padma Kuppa asked the local NDP Task Force to include a Hindu voice in the observance, she was rebuffed. Undaunted, Kuppa approached the mayor, who welcomed more diverse participation. The mayor granted part of her time for Kuppa to offer a prayer, and the words "Om Shanti" echoed across City Hall Plaza. The following year, Troy's NDP Task Force made a new request for a "National Day of Prayer–Troy Judeo-Christian observance" on the city hall steps. Would the city opt for two celebrations of the National Day of Prayer, move the observance, or cancel it? Is the Troy NDP Task Force coordinator correct that the committee shouldn't be forced to include other faiths? What options do the Mayor and Kuppa have? And what is the relationship between the NDP Task Force and the congressionally sanctioned observance?

(A) Case

By 2004 the National Day of Prayer observance had become something of a tradition in Troy, Michigan. For the prior ten years, it was held on the steps of city hall; since 2001 this area has been known as "Veterans' Plaza." Each year the local coordinator requested a resolution from the city council allowing for the observance of the National Day of Prayer—and for permission to display a large banner on the columns of city hall. The city pitched in for the event: staff offered practical assistance and

27

loaned sound systems, microphones, podiums, and chairs. The mayor and city council attended the observance and often offered remarks. But in May 2004 the mayor turned the microphone over to a Troy resident named Padma Kuppa, and for the first time, a Hindu voice was heard at the city's observance of the National Day of Prayer.

Until then, the event was presumptively—if not officially—Christian. The planners, the speakers, and the prayers were Christian. As Kuppa's prayers—"*Om shanti* ..."—echoed across Veterans' Plaza, some believed that the Day of Prayer observance had become more representative of Troy, Michigan's second-most-diverse city. To others, including Troy's National Day of Prayer coordinator, Lori Wagner, the forced inclusion of prayers from another faith altered the spirit of the event. Amid the differences of opinion, one thing seemed clear: the National Day of Prayer observance in Troy would never be the same.

The City of Troy

While some people think of Troy as a suburb of Detroit, it was formally incorporated as a city in 1955. Home to the corporate headquarters of many major US businesses, Troy is a relatively affluent city of just over eighty thousand people known for its award-winning public schools. Troy is regularly ranked among the nation's—and the state's—safest cities. At the time of Padma Kuppa's request to participate in the city's Day of Prayer, Troy's population was majority white, with the highest percentage of Asians of any city in Michigan: in the 2000 Census, 13.25 percent of the total population identified as Asian.[1] In 2004 the city had more than fifty places of worship, including large and influential Evangelical Christian churches, mainline churches, a range of Orthodox churches— Antiochian, Coptic, Greek, and Romanian—as well as one synagogue and one Hindu temple.

Troy's Observance of the National Day of Prayer

The National Day of Prayer was first observed in Troy in 1995, organized by the Troy NDP Task Force. It was affiliated with the national office of the NDP Task Force, based in Colorado Springs, which oversees thousands of

---

[1] "Troy, Michigan," Wikipedia, accessed February 28, 2023.

state and local events across the United States each year. In 1996 the city of Troy issued a proclamation for the NDP, as drafted by the local task force:

> WHEREAS, in 1775, the Continental Congress declared the first National Day of Prayer; and in 1952, both houses of Congress called on the President to set aside one day each year as the National Day of Prayer; and
>
> WHEREAS, on May 5, 1988, Congress passed a bill making the first Thursday of each May the National Day of Prayer; and
>
> WHEREAS, the United States of America is beset with a tidal wave of violence, both juvenile and adult, teenage pregnancies, dysfunctional families, and a host of problems which are tearing apart our societal fabric; and
>
> WHEREAS, it is no coincidence that these problems are occurring as values of faith are swept from the public square, replaced by postmodern moral relativism which rejects concepts such as right and wrong and personal responsibility; and
>
> WHEREAS, such a philosophy is at odds with the heritage of Americans, who historically have shared a broad consensus of religiously-inspired transcendent values, even while insisting on religious freedom; and
>
> WHEREAS, the power of prayer, and the power of God through prayer, have been at the core of the shared American experience throughout history;
>
> NOW, THEREFORE, BE IT KNOWN, that the City Council of the City of Troy hereby proclaims May 2, 1996, as the National Day of Prayer in the City of Troy and joins with our President and our Governor and other communities in encouraging our fellow citizens to join in prayer, asking that God's light might illuminate the minds and hearts of our people and our leaders, so that we may meet the challenges that lie before us with courage and wisdom and justice.[2]

---

[2] "Resolution #96-279 Request for Proclamation—National Day of Prayer, May 2, 1996," Troy City Council Minutes, March 25, 1996, Item D-13.

An "American Hindu," Padma Kuppa

At the center of the National Day of Prayer controversy was a thirty-nine-year-old mother of two. Padma Kuppa served as a Girl Scout co-leader and a Junior Great Books coordinator, and in PTA leadership at her children's school. She enjoyed being active in her local community and at the Bharatiya Temple. In 2002 she had been instrumental in forming Troy's Ethnic Issues Advisory Board.

Born in India, Kuppa came to the United States at the age of four. As the daughter of academics, she spent most of her childhood in a diverse and progressive college town in New York, with part of her high school years outside of Boston and the suburbs of DC. When she went back to India as a fifteen-year-old, she felt like an outsider; in the United States, she felt at home. Kuppa returned to New York for graduate school in engineering and began seeking out the Hindu tradition on her own. As one who grew up largely outside of a Hindu context, she always felt a pull toward the tradition. Perhaps it was genetic, Kuppa joked: she came from a long line of Vedic scholars.

When Kuppa moved with her husband and young children to Troy in 1999, she was pleased to be settling in a city with a large and active Hindu temple. While many who were part of the Hindu community in Troy came to the United States as adults, Kuppa related to the experiences of the second generation: children who were growing up in America. She understood what it was to be part of a minority group and also an American. She was proud to describe herself as an "American Hindu," as she felt that both her country and her faith were grounded in democracy: "Everybody's perspective is valid."[3]

Kuppa knew that Troy had faced previous controversies about public displays of religion: in 2003 the Ethnic Issues Advisory Board was asked to make a recommendation to the city council regarding holiday displays on city property. The board conducted an informal survey of local faith communities, and the results were telling: one-third wanted exclusively Christian displays, one-third wanted every religion to be represented, and one-third wanted no religious holiday displays at all on city property. For her part, there was no issue with Christmas trees and nativity scenes. "It's not a big deal as a Hindu to accept that Jesus Christ is also a valid path

---

[3] All quotes from Padma Kuppa in the (A) and (B) cases are from interviews with the author, March 28 and October 5, 2007.

to God. 'Truth is One; the wise call it by various names' (*Ekam Sat Vipra Bahudha Vadanti*). That is why I call myself an American Hindu."

Kuppa felt it was critical to be involved in service and helping others as a member of the Hindu community. Through the Ethnic Issues Advisory Board, she became active in a range of city events and served on a committee to organize Troy's annual Faith Community Prayer Breakfast: in 2004 the theme was "Let Freedom Ring." That April, she learned that a fellow committee member, Lori Wagner, coordinated Troy's observance of the NDP. Kuppa contacted Wagner to ask how the Hindu community might participate and recalled that Wagner told her that it was "too late"—the programs had already been printed. At the time, Kuppa knew little about the event but felt it was important for the growing Hindu community to be represented. She emailed the mayor, Louise Schilling, and Troy City Council members asking for help.

When Kuppa received a response from Mayor Schilling, who welcomed the participation of the Hindu community, she was thrilled. Schilling offered up time for Kuppa during the traditional mayor's opening remarks. After consulting with the temple's priest, Kuppa came to the steps of city hall to offer a simple prayer for peace: "Everybody should be well.... *Om shanti, shanti, shanti.*" It was the first time the National Day of Prayer observance on the steps of Troy's city hall included a non-Christian prayer.

January 2005, A Request to City Hall

In preparation for the 2005 event, Wagner initiated a request for the National Day of Prayer observance to city hall. Wagner worked part-time at city hall, so she knew many of the staff personally. She sent an email to a city staffer; her message was as friendly and casual as it was brief:

> Hi, there, Cindy!
>
> Hope this is a better time for you now that the ball field issue is settled!
>
> I am writing to request a spot on the agenda to obtain permission from the Council for the National Day of Prayer–Troy Judeo-Christian observance to be held at City Hall on Thursday, May 5, 2005, at noon. We appreciate the City's eleven years of support.
>
> Please advise when this will be scheduled. Thanks for your help![4]

---

[4] "F-06, National Day of Prayer Backup Material," March 7, 2005, Agenda Items, Troy City Council, Meeting Archive 2005.

In past years the city council was asked to issue a resolution for permission to hold "an observance for the National Day of Prayer"; the city council understood the clarification implicit in Wagner's email—and the dilemma that was now before them.

Before the request came in front of the city council on March 7, 2005, the city attorney prepared a memo outlining some of the critical legal issues.[5] One issue was whether the city needed to officially designate the area in front of city hall as a "public forum." This would recognize the past use of the space, which was not limited to city-sponsored events. Designating the area as a public forum would enable the city to resolve the dispute without further involvement: applications would be approved in the order of the date received, not based on their relative merits or inclusiveness. The city would not officially endorse any event held in the "public forum," but some wondered if the location—Veterans' Plaza, the city hall steps—carried with it an implicit endorsement. Further, a "public forum" would necessarily be open for use by any organization, including the Nazi Party or the KKK.

Researching and Reaching Out

In February, Kuppa began researching the National Day of Prayer and emerged with more questions than answers. She went online to "Ask the White House," directing her question to Jim Towey, then the director of the Office of Faith-Based and Community Initiatives:

> Padma, from Troy, MI writes: Is the National Day of Prayer only for those of Judeo-Christian faiths, or are all faith communities involved? What efforts will the President take to ensure participation by all faith communities in the United States?

*   *   *

> Jim Towey: Hi. The National Day of Prayer is organized by Dr. and Mrs. Dobson, who are Christians, but last year, for example, at the White House there were people from all different faiths. The President loves the fact that in America you are free to worship God in any way you choose, or to not have any faith at all. He loves the "freedom of religion" and the right to freely

---

[5] Ibid.

exercise one's faith, and the right of the individual not to worship. That is pluralism at its finest.[6]

In early March, Kuppa noticed that the National Day of Prayer was on the city council agenda for March 7. She was shocked to see that a formal request had been made for a "Judeo-Christian observance." On March 5, 2005, she wrote a letter to the city council. It cited her inquiry to the White House and noted,

> Ours is an inclusive nation, and so too our city must be an inclusive one. If the National Day of Prayer is for everyone, why can't the City of Troy's celebration of it also be for everyone? I would hope that your proclamation would be a celebration of what Troy is, instead of pitting us one ethnic or faith community against another.[7]

At the same time, Kuppa began to realize that this was an issue much larger than she had originally imagined and started reaching out. She recalled that Congregation Shir Tikvah offered warmth, responsiveness, and understanding: "They know what it is to be a persecuted minority." She called some of her friends in town—Baháʼí, Muslim, Jewish, and Christian—and contacted the National Conference for Community and Justice (NCCJ).

Branded a "troublemaker" by those who opposed her, she was pleased to find many in Troy who shared her view. She could only hope that the city council would feel the same way.

March 7, A Resolution Proposed

By March 7 the citizens who gathered at the city council meeting were sharply divided. During the meeting, Wagner commented, "Diversity is a wonderful thing, I agree. But diversity does not amalgamate us or make us one."[8] Some council members agreed that a Christian group should not

---

[6] Jim Towey, "Ask the White House, February 28, 2005," The White House, President George W. Bush, https://georgewbush-whitehouse.archives.gov/.

[7] Padma Kuppa to City Council of Troy, Michigan, letter regarding proposed resolution for "National Day of Prayer-Judeo-Christian Observance," March 5, 2005, in author's possession.

[8] Carol Marshall, "Prayer Group's Bid Draws an Outcry," Troy Eccentric, March 13, 2005, 1.

be forced to include participants from other faith traditions and suggested that other groups could hold events after the Christian observance was over. Another council member asked if several groups could gather separately, but at the same time.

During the meeting, Kuppa felt a range of emotions: disappointment, aggravation, anger, and disbelief. That night, she felt a strong sense that her ideal of America was being undermined. She had chosen to return to America in part because of the "rosy-hued" picture painted from the palette of her childhood. She knew she had to stand up not only for herself but for "the essential truths for America: that we are a country that is based on religious freedom and can engage in civilized dialogue and respect one another across all boundaries." Kuppa found strength from those who stood shoulder to shoulder with her: in addition to religious leaders, like Rev. Rich Peacock of Troy First United Methodist Church and Rabbi Sleutelberg from Shir Tikvah, she received support from members of the Islamic Association of Greater Detroit and the local Bahá'í community.

By the time the resolution came before the city council, the language had been changed: Rabbi Sleutelberg explained that the Jewish community wanted no part of an exclusive event. Mayor Schilling asked that the resolution omit the words "city of" when referring to Troy. She added, "If this resolution passes, I will not be attending this year. I think it is not a good idea for us to be segregated."[9] Ultimately the resolution was made to grant the request for "National Day of Prayer–Christian Observance" at Veterans' Plaza. The vote was three to two: the request was denied.[10]

Later that evening, Kuppa was stopped in the parking lot by a man who wanted to offer a word of thanks as well as a warning: "You have no idea what you're up against."

Letters to the Editor

After the meeting, Kuppa followed the coverage of the National Day of Prayer dispute in the press. She wrote a letter to the editor, offering a chronology of the events and clarifying her point of view. In doing so,

[9] Ibid.
[10] Ibid.

she quoted a *New York Times* editorial written on the disputes over public expressions of religion taking place across the nation:

> The founders may not have anticipated a country with many Hindu and Buddhist Americans, but they were wise enough to write a document that protects their rights. Our increasingly diverse nation must not appear to prefer some religions, and some citizens, over others.[11]

Lori Wagner also drafted a letter to the editor to outline the point of view of Troy's NDP Task Force, which stated (in part),

> Our position is that diversity does not amalgamate our faiths, forcing us to merge into one belief system on any subject—religion or otherwise. Instead, it allows the freedom to function within our subgroups while at the same time offering mutual respect for one another's beliefs.
>
> Diversity is something to be valued, but our Constitution and the Bill of Rights of the United States of America is a higher value. If citizens can't meet on the steps of City Hall, where has our freedom gone? If Veterans' Plaza is open to anyone, it must legally be open to all. Our state and national capitals have "first-come first-served" systems in place for any group to meet, the only restrictions being on the sound, litter, etc.—not the content of the message. This isn't about religion. It's about every citizen's right to peacefully assemble on public property and should be of paramount concern to all U.S. citizens.
>
> We hope that by working with the city in a spirit of compromise we can have a resolution in this matter pleasing to all.[12]

As Kuppa read the editorial, she wasn't sure what sort of compromise was possible, given the sharp divergence in their viewpoints. But she was certain that this issue was far from over.

---

[11] Padma Kuppa, "Prayer Celebration Should Reflect Ethnic Diversity of Troy," Letters, *Observer and Eccentric*, March 13, 2005, A7.

[12] Lori Wagner, "Is Council Legislating Faith in Troy?," Letters, *Troy-Somerset (MI) Gazette*, March 21, 2005, 8.

Questions for Reflection

- Under what circumstances, if any, is it appropriate for a government entity to endorse or participate in the National Day of Prayer? Or in other public prayer events?
- Should the city council approve the exclusive observance in front of city hall? What criteria should they use? Is the issue the exclusivity, the location, or the appearance of the city's endorsement of an event for one religious community?
- Is it appropriate for the city to "force" the NDP coordinators to be inclusive? What sort of compromise can you imagine that would be both constitutional and would meet the needs of all parties?

(B) Case

After the March 7, 2005, city council meeting in Troy, Michigan, the lines were clearly drawn. How would Troy observe the National Day of Prayer? Could a compromise be reached between those who advocated for an interfaith event and those who wanted to continue the tradition of a Christian observance on the city hall steps?

The Troy NDP Task Force and Lori Wagner found support from a range of Christian legal organizations, including the Thomas More Law Center, the American Family Association's Center for Law and Public Policy, and the American Center for Law and Justice. A number of area churches had also become involved in the effort for a Christian observance of the National Day of Prayer, and the Task Force circulated a petition in support of the observance.

At the same time, Padma Kuppa and those advocating for an interfaith celebration found support from the National Conference for Community and Justice (NCCJ). A coalition emerged, calling itself simply Troy Interfaith Group. It included members and leaders from the Islamic Association of Greater Detroit, the Bharatiya Hindu Temple, Congregation Shir Tikvah, Emerson Unitarian Church, First United Methodist Church, First Presbyterian Church, Northminster Presbyterian Church, St. Elizabeth Ann Seton Catholic Church, St. Anastasia Catholic Church, and the Bahá'í community.

March 28, Special Meeting of the Troy City Council

When Kuppa and the interfaith group learned that a special meeting was being called, they hastily wrote to Mayor Schilling and the Troy City Council to request a new resolution—or an amendment to the resolution—for the NDP observance: "The City of Troy authorizes the National Day of Prayer to be observed from 11 a.m. to 1 p.m. on Thursday, May 5, 2005." The request continued: "Furthermore, the Interfaith group shall conduct a one-hour Prayer Service open to all faith communities at the designated location."[13]

As soon as Kuppa and the interfaith group heard about the meeting, they prepared their talking points. What Kuppa was not prepared for, however, was the tenor of the debate. After she spoke at the meeting, she recalls, "I felt the hate." With the volleys of negative emotions and criticism toward her, she retreated to the ladies' room and cried. "I couldn't handle so much hate." As the meeting continued late into the night, Kuppa had to leave before a decision was made: her husband was in India caring for his seriously ill mother, and she needed to return home to put her children to bed. Kuppa had recently given up her bid for the Troy School Board: she wanted to focus on the needs of her family and on Troy's observance of the NDP.

Under pressure from both sides, the city council came up with a compromise: there would be two separate observances of the NDP on the city hall steps. After a series of resolutions and amendments, the language of the resolution read, "RESOLVED, That in 2005, the City of Troy authorizes the National Day of Prayer Task Force to hold a National Day of Prayer–Christian observance from 12:00 PM to 1:00 PM and that the Interfaith Group shall conduct a service from 11:00 AM to 12:00 PM on Thursday, May 5, 2005, at Veterans' Plaza." The resolution passed unanimously. After public comment, the meeting adjourned close to midnight.[14]

---

[13] Memo from the Interfaith Group to Mayor Louise Schilling and the Troy City Council, "Requested Resolution or Amendment," March 28, 2005; in author's possession.

[14] "E-02, Special City Council Meeting—Minutes Draft," April 4, 2005, Agenda Items, Troy City Council, Meeting Archive 2005.

An Email from a Veteran and a Response from the NCCJ

On March 28 a local citizen and veteran wrote the mayor and the city council members. Donald Schenk's email—included in the public agenda for the upcoming April 4 meeting—encouraged the designation of a limited public forum separate from city hall and the Troy Veterans' Plaza:

> An unregulated public display, observance, or demonstration—either for or against an issue—when conducted on the steps of City Hall could give the uninformed the impression that the City of Troy endorses the views espoused by demonstrators, whether this is true or not.... Troy Veterans' Plaza is a monument to our Veterans, their contributions, and the ideals and freedoms which they gallantly served, fought for, and in many cases died to protect. Key to their willingness to do this was their belief that America is a special place that includes all; that America is a place that celebrates and embraces diversity of culture, politics, and religion; and that America and its passion for liberty, justice, and equality is worth giving the last full measure of devotion to preserve and protect. This area is considered by most Veterans to be sacred ground.... We must speak for those no longer able to speak, and we must ensure their contributions are never relegated to a secondary position.[15]

On March 30, the NCCJ responded to the National Day of Prayer compromise with a statement, which began,

> We lament the decision by the Troy City Council to have two separate prayer services on the National Day of Prayer, one sponsored by an interfaith team with support from the Troy Ministerial Association and the other put on by an all-Christian group. This decision reflects poorly on Troy, a religiously and racially diverse community, which should reflect this diversity in a unified way.[16]

---

[15] "F-04, Designation of Limited Public Forums," April 4, 2005, Agenda Items, Troy City Council, Meeting Archive 2005.

[16] National Council for Community and Justice, "City of Troy National Day of Prayer Decision," press release, Detroit, MI, March 30, 2005.

An Organization Formed, a Decision Made

On April 3, 2005, many of those concerned about the NDP event in Troy gathered together, hosted by Rev. Rich Peacock at the First United Methodist Church. Representatives of many of Troy's diverse faith communities were in attendance. Together, they firmly established the name of the nascent organization: Troy Interfaith Group (TIG). Their membership included an attorney who threatened to sue the city for segregation. One of the first actions of the new group was a critical decision, marked by a press release that stated, "The Troy Interfaith Group has reevaluated our request for a time slot on Troy City property for Thursday, May 5, 2005, and we are withdrawing that request. We have decided that it would be appropriate to meet somewhere other than Troy City property for any religious purpose." The release noted that the group would gather for an NDP observance on the evening of May 5 "at a site to be determined." The press release ended with an invitation for local citizens to attend the next meeting of TIG—and their upcoming celebration.[17]

Kuppa was later quoted in a local newspaper explaining the decision: "I wanted to participate in something already existing, as in the National Day of Prayer. . . . But once we were out of the confines of something already existing, we thought we'd be better off in a place of worship."[18] Privately she felt good about the decision, having heard the voices of veterans who asked that the plaza not be made a public space. She was at peace with the decision: the emphasis could now shift from politics to prayers.

Two More Meetings of the City Council

The Troy City Council took on the NDP issue again at the April 4 meeting. Three limited public forum sites were established on City Hall property; the Veterans' Plaza and city hall steps were not among them. Any permits for use of these sites would be issued through the recreation department and would be handled on a first-come, first-served basis. The city council would no longer have to be involved in disputes about private events on city property.

---

[17] Troy Interfaith Group "National Day of Prayer," press release, Troy, MI, March 30, 2005.

[18] Shawn D. Lewis, "Day of Prayer at Troy City Hall Divides Religious Groups," *Detroit News*, April 6, 2005, C1.

On April 18 the city council met again. NDP Task Force members, together with a lawyer from the Thomas More Law Center, addressed the city council and argued for the constitutional rights of the Christian-identified group to hold a prayer event in front of city hall. After much discussion and debate, with a vote of four to three, the council approved the application for a Christian observance in front of city hall.

A Dispute Resolved

On May 2 the *Detroit News* reported on the resolution of the dispute:

> After months of contentious City Council meetings about who should worship where on the National Day of Prayer, a Christian group won the space it originally requested—on Veterans' Plaza in front of City Hall, where its members have worshipped for 10 years.... Thomas More lawyers on two occasions addressed the council and explained the constitutional right of Christians to hold their own prayer event in front of City Hall and stressed that it's unconstitutional to require a group to promote a message it did not want—in this case, non-Christian prayers.

The article went on to quote Wagner: "It is a win for everybody because the interfaith group has never had a prayer event before," she said. "And now, we get to meet where we've already wanted to, and we get to do what we've always done."[19]

While there was a resolution, for Kuppa, there was also a deep sense of disappointment. "I was disappointed in my fellow Americans.... They twisted what they were doing, from having a Day of Prayer, to having a Christian Day of Prayer, to needing 'free speech.' They're just trying to make sure that I'm not there, and that I don't count."

May 5, 2005, The National Day of Prayer in Troy, Michigan

At noon on May 5, 2005, Troy's NDP Task Force held a Christian observance in front of city hall. It took place in the Veterans' Plaza, now designated as a limited public forum. Two city council members participated in the event.

---

[19] Shawn D. Lewis, "Prayer Group Secures Plaza," *Detroit News*, May 2, 2005, B1.

At seven o'clock that evening, the Northminster Presbyterian Church hosted the Troy Interfaith Group's National Day of Prayer observance. The mayor and two city council members attended the multifaith gathering.

It was estimated that 250 people attended each event.

After the National Day of Prayer Controversy

In the years that have followed, the NDP-Christian observance of the National Day of Prayer continues to be held in front of Troy's city hall; the Troy Interfaith Group has held its annual NDP observance at a different local house of worship each year. Aside from a failed recall effort against Mayor Schilling and a city council member who opposed the single-faith observance—led by a group called The Troy Committee to Protect Free Speech—the controversy over Troy's National Day of Prayer faded from the headlines.

Since 2005 the National Day of Prayer–Christian Observance is celebrated on the city hall steps in Troy. The NDP Task Force uses the term "Judeo-Christian":

> We are the Judeo-Christian expression of the National Day of Prayer. The Task Force was a creation of the National Prayer Committee for the expressed purpose of organizing and promoting prayer observances conforming to a Judeo-Christian system of values. People with other theological and philosophical views are, of course, free to organize and participate in activities that are consistent with their own beliefs. This diversity is what Congress intended when it designated the Day of Prayer, not that every faith and creed would be homogenized, but that all who sought to pray for this nation would be encouraged to do so in any way deemed appropriate. It is that broad invitation to the American people that led, in our case, to the creation of the Task Force and the Judeo-Christian principles on which it is based.[20]

While the National Day of Prayer was the cause for the creation of the Troy Interfaith Group, the observance is now a small part of their wider activities. They are involved in a range of interfaith networking and outreach efforts, such as participating in unity walks and community events.

---

[20] Troy National Day of Prayer Task Force, "About Us," 2005.

After the controversy, TIG made an offering to the city of Troy: a tree of peace. The occasion was the city of Troy's fiftieth anniversary, and the motivation was symbolic: to bury the hatchet. The Interfaith Group hoped to move forward and put the prayer controversy behind them. Following the Iroquois practice of burying weapons beneath a pine tree to signify a path to peace, they donated a white pine tree to the city's Peace Garden. Versions of the Golden Rule from each of Troy's religious traditions were inscribed upon ribbons, and children of each community tied these ribbons to the tree's delicate branches. At the end, Rev. Peacock sent everyone on their way: "Just as we all entered this garden in peace, let us all go forward in peace."

After the controversy, Kuppa spoke with deep appreciation for those in the Troy community who have stood with her: from the early support of the Jewish community, to those who helped establish TIG, to her neighbors. For Kuppa, all of the events, service projects, and friendships formed are small efforts toward "making sure we are a pluralistic democracy." She adds, "We need to pursue our religious freedom. When you forget that, you become complacent. That kind of consciousness needs to be awakened in all of us."

Making an Impact; Coming Full Circle

The dispute over the National Day of Prayer forged new relationships in Troy and made an impact on individual communities. The Bharatiya Temple formalized an outreach committee for both inter- and intrafaith efforts; Kuppa visited houses of worship and participated in and organized many events.

In the early days of the controversy, Kuppa recalls that some in the local Hindu community were concerned about how outspoken she was over the observance of the NDP. Some felt that she was "waving the Hindu flag at city council meetings." She added, "Now they understand." Kuppa describes the inherent tension between the need to identify with one's minority group and the need to engage with the larger community: "It is a constant work, finding a balance between being a Hindu and an American, and that constant work is part of who I am. Not this or that, but both." While her children have felt some of the negative impact of their mother's activism—including the playdates and parties to which they were not invited—she notes, "They understand the need to stand up for what is right."

Kuppa reflects, "I'm not asking everyone to pray with me, but if you're going to have a city-sponsored Day of Prayer, then the city should come together." Kuppa adds, "If you don't want to pray with others, then you shouldn't be in the public space on the National Day of Prayer."

Postscript

Now known as the Troy-Area Interfaith Group (TIG), the organization has continued to expand; unlike many interfaith organizations born of crisis, TIG remains vital nearly two decades later. In addition to the NDP observance at a local house of worship and other annual events, TIG organizes Interfaith Workdays and educational programming. It is now even more diverse, including a Jain temple, a Sikh gurdwara, and the Ahmadiyya Muslim Center. Padma explains, "In this time of horrible political polarization and cancel culture from the left and from the right, it's those local relationships that have stood the test of time, that will continue to stand us and keep us in a positive space."[21]

While Padma Kuppa is proud of TIG's accomplishments, and participates in their events, she is no longer part of the leadership. Over the years she has become less engaged in formal interfaith activities and no longer volunteers at the Bharatiya Temple. One reason for her shifting engagements was a lack of time: in 2018 Kuppa was elected to the Michigan House of Representatives. She was the first Hindu, and the first immigrant from India, to serve in the Michigan legislature, and was reelected in 2020. For Kuppa, the NDP controversy in Troy "was a springboard for realizing that change could happen at the local level." She explains, "Being at the state legislature is one of the most powerful ways that I can have that impact."

Kuppa emphasizes,

We've got to work on issues *here*, where we are physically rooted. You may have passions about what's going on in another part of the world, but you need to put that aside and work where you can.... Unless you work on building understanding at the grass-roots, you're not doing a good job. You're not doing anything that's really going to be meaningful for real change.

---

[21] All quotes from Padma Kuppa included in the postscript are from interviews with the author, January 29 and December 2, 2022.

She helped draft resolutions and policies related to holidays in the state, developing language around Vaisakhi, Lunar New Year, and Diwali, together with people from other faith communities. Kuppa notes, "I'm glad that I'm able to be in the political space as a deeply rooted person of faith."

She especially enjoys issue-based advocacy work, such as her board service with the Religious Coalition for Reproductive Choice. Yet over the years she has become increasingly cynical about organizational interfaith work. While Kuppa cites a few notable exceptions, she asserts, "I really struggled trying to explain being Hindu in an Abrahamic setting. Everywhere I went, I was a square peg trying to fit into a round hole." And in some interfaith circles, Kuppa felt that "there were anti-Hindu strains coming through." She has also struggled with the ways in which religious disputes with their roots in South Asia complicate local interfaith relations.

Kuppa has also stepped away from her outreach role at the Bharatiya Temple. "I was just getting very frustrated with the Hindu community, because they weren't becoming advocates and understanding the fifty-thousand-foot view." Kuppa notes, "There's a great Will Rogers saying: 'I'm not from an organized political party. I'm a Democrat.' And I would say that about Hinduism: 'I'm not from an organized religion. I'm a Hindu.'" She emphasizes the vast internal diversity of the tradition, describing a tree with many branches. Kuppa explains, "I do still think two things: that Hinduism is pluralism, and that pluralism is the pathway to peace. It's active engagement with diversity, so it's not just living in your little silo." Kuppa reflects, "I think it's good that I'm not working within the Hindu world; instead, I'm working as a Hindu on issues that I care about. I think that it's more effective for me to be the public servant than to be the public Hindu."

Over the years, as a public figure, Kuppa has faced criticism: some take exception to her affiliation with the Hindu American Foundation; others have criticized some of the positions expressed in her writing;[22] moreover, she was sued by the Council on American Islamic Relations related to a zoning decision. A few make inflammatory claims, such as a website dedicated to "Exposing Padma Kuppa."[23] Kuppa notes, "For

---

[22] "Michigan State House Candidate's Writings Assailed as Anti-Christian, Anti-Muslim," *India Abroad*, November 13, 2018, https://www.indiaabroad.com/.

[23] Exposing Padma Kuppa, "Padma Kuppa Linked to Violent Hindu Nationalist Groups in India," accessed February 28, 2023, https://www.padmakuppa.net/.

people to think that I have some connection to Hindu nationalism is ludicrous." Padma describes the attacks as "anti-Hindu rhetoric." She explains, "I feel like I'm crushed because there's no one to protect me from Hinduphobia … and there's no one to protect me from the Christian nationalism and white supremacy." Kuppa reflects, "And I am the public figure, so I have to take it all.… But I'm human."

Looking back to her initial request to participate in the NDP, she recalls, "I was just like, 'Hey, what are you doing? You are not allowing everyone that's part of the community to participate?' I didn't realize that I was opening a Pandora's box." But she notes, "If anything, that incident deepened my desire to be more connected to the core of Hinduism than anything else." Before Kuppa raised the issue, few in Troy—or elsewhere—understood the connection between the NDP Task Force and Christian exclusivism. Kuppa recalled, "Many of them became involved in trying to recall Mayor Louise Schilling … which then turned into the Tea Party here in Michigan."

Today, the NDP Task Force's statement of faith makes its commitments clear. It begins, "We believe in the Holy Bible as the inspired, only, infallible, authoritative Word of the Living God." It ends with a reference to "the spiritual unity of believers in our Lord Jesus Christ." Each May, the NDP Task Force invites citizens to "Gather to pray in Jesus' name for our nation in front of Troy City Hall." It is one of forty events in the Troy area alone that is affiliated with the NDP Task Force.[24]

*   *   *

In late 2022 Kuppa narrowly lost her reelection to Michigan Senate District 9 by just 795 votes. Kuppa described the well-funded campaign against her as "rooted in attacks, lies, and propaganda"—including fliers claiming she is a Hindu nationalist distributed at a local mosque and Republican ads depicting her as a communist—with minimal support from the Democratic Party. For Kuppa, the margin of just .069 percent "speaks to my resilience." She added, "It also speaks to the people who did support me."

As she wrapped up her term after four "toxic" years in the State House, her emotions were close to the surface. Wiping away tears, she noted, "Right now it is more than hurt. It's anger. And sorrow. That I didn't live

---

[24] National Day of Prayer "Post or Find an Event," accessed February 23, 2023, https://www.nationaldayofprayer.org/.

up to the expectations of all those people who supported me." She brightened as she described the dedicated campaign volunteers, including two retired ministers who knocked on doors, wrote postcards, and donated to the campaign. One of these, Rev. Rich Peacock, was among those who stood with her in support of an inclusive National Day of Prayer back in 2005. Reflecting upon her time in office, Kuppa wrote,

> As a state representative, I had a difficult time as a minority in the minority—a Democrat in a majority Republican chamber, one of a handful of legislators serving a district with a lean Republican partisan tilt; the only immigrant at times (and that too, a brown woman new to partisan politics), the lone Hindu in the legislature, the highest-ranking Hindu woman elected in the state, and so on. The trails I blazed were not always rewarding: breaking glass ceilings left me with a lot of cuts.[25]

As she looks to the future, Kuppa notes, "I am glad to be done with partisan politics." She adds, "I need to find a place where I can build." Kuppa isn't sure of her next steps, but she may return to her original field of mechanical engineering, with a focus on alleviating climate change. "I want to build. I want to create."

---

[25] Padma Kuppa, "Beyond Building Magnificent Mandirs and Mosques, We Need to Strengthen Our Political Giving Muscle," American Kahani, November 18, 2022, https://americankahani.com/.

A Call to Prayer

Dr. Karen Majewski understood why the request for the call to prayer was challenging for her small community of Hamtramck, Michigan. As city council president, long-time resident, and scholar of immigration, she appreciated the divergent points of view in the small, diverse city. For some in Hamtramck, the call to prayer was a sound that connected residents to their faith and signaled they were home; for others, it was an unwelcome noise that was yet another reminder of the ways in which the city was changing. Once a majority Polish city, Hamtramck was transforming to a plurality Muslim city, with large Bangladeshi, Bosnian, and Yemeni populations, as well as a small but longstanding Black community and a newer Hindu community. As Majewski sought to help Hamtramck navigate the divisive issue over the call to prayer, she also faced calls from the press, contentious public hearings, and ongoing political opposition. Strictly speaking, she noted, it was a constitutional issue, and the city should not prevent free expression, but how might they avoid greater division? As a leader of a rapidly changing city, what resources might she seek? What, if anything, does she need to know about the call to prayer? How is sound different from—and similar to—visual expressions of difference? What is at stake?

(A) Case

As Dr. Karen Majewski (My-ev-ski) drove up to the small brick city hall building in Hamtramck, Michigan on April 13, 2004, she noticed a number of news trucks parked out front. "ABC, NBC, Fox News ... that's not a good omen, you know."[1] Just a few months prior, Majewski became president of the city council: she still considered herself a reluctant

---

[1] All quotes from Karen Majewski in the (A) and (B) cases are from interview with the author, Hamtramck, Michigan, August 11, 2014.

newcomer to politics. At the sight of the news trucks, Majewski recalled, "You want to keep driving and head over the Ambassador Bridge [to Canada]." Yet she knew instantly why the press had gathered in her tiny city: the broadcast of the call to prayer.

When Majewski moved to Michigan for graduate school, she wanted to find an ethnic urban neighborhood like her hometown of Chicago: a front-porch community where she would hear different languages spoken on the street. For a scholar specializing in immigration and ethnicity, Hamtramck was "the only perfect place." Her years in academia are often reflected in her speech, self-possessed demeanor, and her personal style: she wears her long hair in a stylish bun and carefully selects vintage clothing and subtle touches of ethnic jewelry. Just before Majewski was drafted to run for city council, she completed her PhD and published a book on Polish American identity. She had no political aspirations beyond her work on the city's historical commission, yet she welcomed being part of a shift away from "the Polish old guard" to a progressive, New Urbanism agenda.

Hamtramck is just over 2.1 square miles in area. In 2004 it was home to almost twenty-five thousand people: it is one of the most densely populated and most internationally diverse cities in Michigan. "It really is an old-school urban neighborhood ... with houses on thirty-foot lots, right next to each other. We live on top of each other." Hamtramck shares a zip code and most of its border with Detroit. Both cities grew and thrived along with the auto industry; today, both have deep financial woes. Majewski described Hamtramck as "gritty and hardscrabble," but added that the economic challenges of the city are long-standing: "We're down, but we're not out. That could be our slogan," she laughs.

One of the city's slogans is, "A Touch of the World in America." The city had seen earlier waves of German, French, and Ukrainian immigrants, and a well-established African American population, before the Poles began settling in Hamtramck. For more than five decades, the city has been predominantly Polish, from its churches and bakeries to its festivals: every mayor has been Polish. Newer waves of immigrants came from Yemen, Bosnia, and Bangladesh in recent years. By 2004 nearly one-third of Hamtramck's population was estimated to be Muslim,[2] with three mosques in the city's 2.1 square miles.

---

[2] Tim Jones, "Islamic Call to Prayer Stirs Tension," *Chicago Tribune*, April 21, 2004, W11.

Majewski heard the call to prayer regularly back when she lived just a few blocks over the Hamtramck line in Detroit. "It seemed like a nice thing. I liked hearing the call.... Really, I marvel at my naïveté now." When the city council received the request to broadcast the call to prayer from Al-Islah Islamic Center, a predominantly Bangladeshi mosque, Majewski thought it would be a "simple administrative process" to amend the existing noise ordinance. "I think, to most of us, it was already allowed by the Constitution, and the question was, 'How do we do this in a way that works for the community?'" Yet public hearings drew increasing numbers of residents, rising emotions, and the presence of the media. Some expressed concerns about unwanted noise and proselytizing; supporters compared the call to the sounding of church bells. She explained, "You know it's one thing for NBC to come in, and they have a story they want to tell, and they want drama and divisiveness, and conflict." But for people living in a small city, Majewski understood that the broadcast of the call to prayer was more complex than any sound bite.

> This is your street, and your house, and your window that's open that's hearing this. And your neighbors, the old Polish lady that you grew up with died and her kids sold the house to a woman in a burqa, you know. I have a lot of sympathy for the human drama, the individual drama, of dealing with those kinds of changes and issues. For the people who opposed the call, I had a lot of sympathy: individually, psychically, dealing with their world changing around them. That's a profoundly sympathetic position.

She added,

> And the immigrants coming in who want the community they live in to reflect themselves, and feel at home in that community: they are making their home literally in front of us, building a home and building a community and building an identity.... You come to a place where you don't know the language, the terrain is different, the houses are different.... Every little aspect of your life is changed. That is such a brave thing to do, and such a hopeful thing to do.

What she thought would be a "practical matter" had suddenly become national news. At the first public hearing on the noise ordinance, Majewski focused on staying calm and giving everyone a chance to speak. She recalled, "I felt profoundly challenged and stressed to do this right. Really, to do it in a way that brought honor to who we are as a city." She steeled herself for what would come next.

Abdul Motlib: A Request

In 2004 Hamtramck was home to three mosques: the primarily Yemeni Mu'ath Bin Jabal Mosque, the Bosnian American Islamic Center, and Al-Islah Islamic Center, a Bangladeshi mosque. Al-Islah, located in a modest two-story building with green awnings, faced the towering St. Ladislaus Catholic Church across Caniff Street, a busy commercial area with Polish bakeries and halal butcher shops. The bells of St. Lad's rang three times a day; at Al-Islah, the *adhan* was called five times a day inside. In Detroit and Dearborn, mosques have publicly broadcast the adhan, or call to prayer, for years. Yet when Abdul Motlib, Al-Islah's president, first made a formal request to the Hamtramck City Council in September 2003, it was refused due to an existing noise ordinance.

Motlib, like many others at Al-Islah, came to Michigan by way of New York, drawn by a lower cost of living and a vital Muslim community. A factory worker, Motlib has a quick smile and often wears a kurta and kufi. He found Hamtramck to be a welcoming place, and noted that the city, "with its cheap, small houses,"[3] reminded him of his hometown. Motlib soon emerged as a leader in Hamtramck's rapidly growing Bangladeshi community. He explained, "The prospect of broadcasting the call to prayer first crossed our minds when we first opened the mosque in 2003. It is a tradition that has been continued in mosques all over the world since the time of the prophet.... We wanted to continue this tradition."[4] Motlib sought approval from the city council out of a desire to be "considerate and respectful to our neighbors, both Muslim and non-Muslim."[5] With recent elections bringing in a new city council in Hamtramck, including its first Muslim member, Motlib decided to ask

---

[3] Isaac Weiner, *Religion Out Loud: Religious Sound, Public Space, and American Pluralism* (New York: NYU Press, 2013), 162.

[4] Abdul Motlib, email correspondence with author, November 2014.

[5] Ibid.

for permission again before beginning to broadcast the prayer. He sent a letter to the city council on December 28, 2003. It began,

> This letter is a request for an amendment to the City of Hamtramck's Ordinance No. 434, which prohibits unlawful noise and sounds. As part of the Islamic religion, it is our duty to "call" all Muslims to prayer five times a day. This is a short Arabic verse that takes approximately two minutes to complete. As an Islamic Center in the City of Hamtramck, we are requesting that this calling to prayer is permitted to be done on a loudspeaker at the five intervals during the day and night.[6]

Motlib explained that the Islamic Center would submit a new schedule each year, as the exact prayer times shift daily due to changes in sunrise and sunset. He added, "The Islamic Center is located on a very commercial street; therefore, few people will feel disturbed by the loudspeaker. This calling can be respected just as a Church's bells are."[7] After listing three mosques in the city of Detroit that broadcast the call, Motlib noted, "As a very culturally diverse community, by permitting this action it will build our city to become more united and familiar with each other's religion."[8] The letter concluded by pledging cooperation and thanking the council for its attention to the request. He was hopeful that soon, Al-Islah would soon broadcast the call from speakers mounted on the rooftop.

Members of the council indicated their support for amending the noise ordinance and scheduled a public hearing. When Motlib arrived at city hall on April 13, he was surprised at the number of people in attendance. "We went there, we saw a lot of people. So many people … against the call to prayer."[9] The next week, another hearing was scheduled: "We think that day, 'No problem.' Even myself, I go to my work, I say, 'This public hearing is finished.'"[10] But the crowd continued to grow,

---

[6] Alisa Marlene Perkins, "From the Mosque to the Municipality: The Ethics of Muslim Space in a Midwestern City" (PhD dissertation, University of Texas at Austin, 2012), 414.

[7] Ibid.

[8] Ibid.

[9] Sally Howell, "Al-Islah Islamic Center," Building Islam in Detroit: Foundations/Forms/Futures, video file, 2005, http://biid.lsa.umich.edu.

[10] Ibid.

and a third hearing was scheduled for April 27. Motlib recalled, "First floor, second floor, third floor, full! People coming from different states, different areas." Motlib explained, "They don't want to listen to the call to prayer in Hamtramck. But they tell their story, we tell our story."[11]

Three Public Hearings

Over the course of three public hearings, supporters and opponents of the amendment both spoke to the noise ordinance. Observers described the meetings as contentious but civil: the most notable exceptions, they explained, were comments from people who didn't live in Hamtramck. Many of those who supported amending the noise ordinance were members of the Muslim community:

> Today some people are saying that Hamtramck is being taken over by Muslims. But Hamtramck is not being taken over by Muslims. Hamtramck is being rebuilt by Muslims. Look at Conant five years ago, and look at it today. There was hardly any abundance of buildings there five years ago. There was just closed buildings, closed doors. And from then, Conant Street was being rebuilt by Muslims.[12]
> ...
>
> A gentleman before me mentioned that he is a citizen of this country. Well, he is not the only citizen of this country. We are all citizens of this country. I can recall that my grandfather served this country in WWII. And don't push this, "If you're not for me, you are against me." We are here to ask the honorable council to take a leadership role and to pass this amendment for the community. I have been here for 26 years ... and we ask you for a simple thing—to allow the call to prayer.... Now, we hear the bells every day, every hour, we never say nothing. We never say the bells call us to prayer. Now, we are citizens of this country. Just because of the way we look, you think we come in yesterday. But we contribute to this country, and we've been here in the city longer than some of you.[13]

---

[11] Ibid.
[12] Perkins, "From the Mosque to the Municipality," 274.
[13] Ibid.

. . .

Bismillah ar-rahman ar-rahim. . . . I recently moved to Hamtramck about six months ago and I have enjoyed being here in Hamtramck. . . . The adhan has been going on for many years, long before any of us were even here. It has been practiced for maybe 1500 years. So, for them to try and pass some kind of law that would hinder us from being able to practice that would cause a feeling of oppression in our hearts, that we weren't able to do this, and I think that if that kind of law were passed, that we couldn't do this in a country that claims freedom for everybody, I think that at that point we would all have to accept the hypocrisy of that statement. . . . I would ask our non-Muslim brothers and sisters to be tolerant of that, please, and to understand that it is not a call for you to cease worshipping what you worship, but a call for Muslims to come and pray together.[14]

Some of those who spoke in support of the amendment to the noise ordinance identified as non-Muslims:

I was born two miles from here. That gentleman there who has been a citizen for two weeks has the same rights as I do. . . . I have the right to make noise any time of the day. If I want to play my saxophone on my front lawn, I can do it. But I want to say, what is going on here is a true example of democracy. This is democracy in action, this is what we live in this country for. People are going to have differences of opinion. We are going to argue and disagree, sometimes vehemently. We are not going to get out our weapons, as someone suggested, we are going to leave this place, whatever the decision is, and we're going to try to live together, in peace and harmony. We have to get together and there is no other choice. . . . I'm proud that Hamtramck is going to set a precedent for the entire country. This is amazing that you guys have to decide something important. It's got to be done sometime, and even though I'm not a Muslim and I'm not a Christian and I have my rights, I want freedom for all religions.[15]

---

[14] Ibid., 247.
[15] Ibid., 279–80.

A larger number of speakers expressed concern about the amendment
to the noise ordinance:

> I am here because this hurts my heart, my soul, my inner spiritual
> being.... I respect the Muslims, their religion, their God, but I
> don't have to hear their God praised in my ear five times a day,
> seven days a week, 365 days a year. And where can I go, I am 68
> years old, and where will I go? ... You want me to go? No, I will
> not leave! It's my country, too, just as it is yours. I respect you; I
> have no malice for any of you, I just want my rights also, and that
> is to adore my God in my own home and not have to listen to a
> God I don't believe in—Allah.[16]
> ...

> And if this council passes this noise ordinance then you are going
> against the Constitution because you are not giving me the right
> to force my religion on somebody, you are forcing their religion
> on me. And I have no choice but to hear them five times a day,
> fifteen minutes out of every day, maybe two hours a week, maybe
> 1,000 hours a year, that I have to listen to them telling me about
> Allah, how great he is. My God tells me, "You want to pray, go
> into the silence of a room and close the door and talk to me
> there." I don't need any amplification through horns of anything
> telling me who Allah is. I know who God is.[17]
> ...

> Everyone keeps talking about their rights. The rights of Christians
> have been stripped from them for the last 30 years of this country.
> And you are doing the same thing. This [city hall building] used
> to be a Catholic hospital. With a cross. With the Ten Command-
> ments. Bibles, with prayers, but it's now a city building, and
> you cannot, by law, allow any religious artifacts, or any religious
> undertones to take place in this facility. Yet last week, there was
> Muslim prayer allowed downstairs, during the council meeting.
> I will guarantee you, that if Christians had tried to hold a Bible
> study downstairs, it would have lasted 15 [minutes]. I also guar-

[16] Ibid., 261.
[17] Ibid., 266–67.

antee you that if Christians were trying to do what Muslims are doing here, the ACLU would shut us down in 72 hours.[18]

. . .

I've lived in Hamtramck all my life over 81 years and I have this to say. . . . The Muslims are allowed to pray in their mosques, there are hardly any cities that face this problem. And I think that the grace belongs on the other side. If you really think about it, intolerance doesn't come from the few people who object to this, because they have a right to object, but it comes from the other side. Before this, everybody got along. They speak their own language in their homes, they teach their children the religion they want, freedom of religion is not denied to them. . . . Why agitate this entire community?[19]

At the end of the third and final public hearing on April 27, the council voted unanimously to approve the amendment to the noise ordinance. The new ordinance read: "The City shall permit 'call to prayer,' 'church bells,' and other reasonable means of announcing religious meetings to be amplified between the hours of 6:00 a.m. and 10:00 p.m. for a duration not to exceed five minutes."[20] It gave the city council "sole authority to set the level of amplification"[21] and stated that any complaints were to be filed with the city clerk. The ordinance would be effective beginning May 25, 2004. Al-Islah would begin broadcasting the call on Friday, May 28.[22]

Robert Zwolak: A Matter of Noise

From the beginning, Robert Zwolak explained, "It was a matter of noise."[23] Like many residents, Zwolak wasn't born in Hamtramck, and

---

[18] Ibid., 271.

[19] Ibid., 272.

[20] Isaac Weiner, "Religion Out Loud: Religious Sound, Public Space, and American Pluralism" (PhD dissertation, University of North Carolina at Chapel Hill, 2009).

[21] Ibid.

[22] Ibid.

[23] Unless otherwise noted, all quotes from Robert Zwolak are from interview with the author, Hamtramck, Michigan, August 12, 2014.

his first language wasn't English. He spent the first three years of his life in Detroit, under the care of his Polish grandmother while his parents worked in a factory. He would later move to California and learn English, but it took many years for him to fully master the language and he struggled at school: "We didn't have English as a Second Language [ESL] like we do today." Zwolak returned to Hamtramck to attend high school, marry, and raise five children. He is now a grandfather with white hair but appears younger than his age might suggest.

Zwolak, slight in frame with a deep voice, noted, "It was a different community back then." He explained, "You had parochial schools, you had a lot more church activity, a number of veterans; organizations, over one hundred bars in town. It was basically a blue-collar town of factory workers." He added that Hamtramck has always been a "springboard community" with earlier waves of Germans, Poles, Ukrainians, Italians, and Yugoslavians and later influxes of Yemenis, Bosnians, and Bangladeshis. "So when it occurred it was kind of subtle. It wasn't overly apparent other than when the Bangladeshis came in, the initial big wave, you would see their dress and their cultural garb. Very obvious." As the hall manager at the Knights of Columbus in Hamtramck, Zwolak witnessed these changes firsthand: "And I had a great experience with the Hindus, the Bangladeshis, the Yemenis, the Buddhists, who would rent the hall for their weddings and religious ceremonies, and baptisms, you name it—to really see a different culture."

When the call-to-prayer issue came up, Zwolak attended the hearings and listened to residents voicing their objections and resentment. He noticed that many Muslim men spoke in support of the call and many Christian women spoke against it. For those who opposed it, a few expressed prejudice, and some expressed concern about evangelization; Zwolak recalled that most simply didn't want to have to hear the noise. He added, "But then, as the controversy became more public, you could then see more charged feelings between people." For Zwolak, there was a simple way to resolve this: "Put it on the ballot and let the people decide." After the city council voted to amend the noise ordinance, Zwolak knew that he had a limited amount of time to get a petition circulated to put the issue on the ballot. He served as city clerk years before and knew this was his best recourse.

It took little effort to get more than six hundred signatures. Yet, he noted, "in facilitating the petition and getting the petition out there on the ballot, my name of course was attached as the ringleader, so to speak." Soon he was receiving phone calls from all over the country. "I was getting calls from radio stations for interviews. I was getting calls from a religious group that wanted to come in and do some type of a cultural statement. And my response: 'No. This is not a religious issue: it is a noise issue.' And I didn't want to get engaged in that type of situation."

Early in his political career, back in the 1980s, Zwolak led a successful effort to recall half of the city council due to mismanagement. "So I've had my share of conflicts. But again, it's always been, 'Let the people decide.' If you don't like it, then you have the choice to make a change. And if you need to make a change now, then make a change now. It's the democratic process."

Rev. Sharon Buttry: An Interfaith Concern

Small and gentle in speech and manner, Rev. Sharon Buttry had little interest in attending the hearings about the call to prayer or making political statements. An American Baptist minister working at an Evangelical church outreach center providing ESL classes in Hamtramck, Buttry noted, "I don't go to council meetings. I find them to be very dysfunctional."[24] She explained, "I knew there were plenty of articulate people who were going to be there, and I felt like my best option was to work behind the scenes." From the beginning, Buttry explained, it was an interfaith concern: "The problem was that the Catholic church across the street was amplifying the church bells from their tower, they were no longer ringing them by hand. So the Catholic priest and the leaders of the mosque came together to amend this ordinance to satisfy both the Catholic church and the mosque." She added, "[a] lot of people say, 'Well, you know, the Muslims just came in and then they wanted what they wanted, and pushed it through': that wasn't true at all."

She believed that most of the local people who opposed the call were struggling with changes to their community, complicated by difficult economic times. Yet for those who opposed the call and didn't even live or work in Hamtramck, she felt differently. "There were some really strident protestors [David's Mighty Men] who came up from Ohio.... That was embarrassing and very frustrating for me." She explained, "I feel ashamed

---

[24] Unless otherwise noted, all quotes from Sharon Buttry are from interview with the author, Detroit, Michigan, August 10, 2014.

when people act like that and say they are representing my faith. So that was very upsetting to me."

With tensions rising in the community, an informal local clergy group emerged with the help of interfaith leaders from neighboring communities. For Buttry, this was her first involvement in interfaith work and the first time she entered a mosque. "And I was very, very honored, and humbled to be invited into that space, where that was going to be worked out in our community." With rising media interest, Buttry was even called upon by leaders at Al-Islah to act as their spokesperson: she understood that Motlib and others didn't want to have to express something this important in a second language. Buttry explained, "Religious liberty is such a huge part of our Baptist heritage. It never occurred to me to not be for the call to prayer." Her church outreach center was not Baptist-affiliated, and some of her colleagues were critical of her involvement in the controversy. "I took some heat." Buttry, undaunted, continued her "relational work," and added, "I always feel like your life speaks more than your words anyway. I just continue to live my faith by my conscience, which is another Baptist principle: freedom of conscience."

While she was honored to take a public role as the leader of the newly formed Hamtramck Interfaith Partners, Buttry preferred private discussion and relationship-building. "I have a reputation over the years of being fair-minded and able to talk to people on both sides of an issue." She described herself as "a fairly close friend" of Robert Zwolak, who served with her on a nonprofit board. Buttry knew that some people wanted to demonize Zwolak and others who opposed changing the noise ordinance to permit the broadcast of the call. "I've known him to have an incredibly kind and compassionate heart towards people who are down and out. So I just think it is interesting, when you get into these polarized situations, how easy it is to cut off relationships, and I try not to do that. I try to reach out over those boundaries and maintain the relationships."

Buttry saw the controversy over the call as an issue of identity: "This community in Hamtramck had such a strong identity built around Polish values and culture, Polish Catholic values and culture: neat-as-a-pin yards, people going out and washing the sidewalk. There's this whole reckoning back to the old days when the city looked so beautiful and pristine." Yet she added that those were different times, economically and culturally. "It's hard to let go when they perceive that it's worsening rather than improving. Everyone wants things to improve rather than fall apart. So I think the call to prayer is a daily reminder, several times a day, that things are really changing. And it's not going back to the good old days, or whatever they thought it was."

A Pope, a Petition, a Public Vote

On May 12 Motlib and a small group of supporters of the call to prayer came together at what locals often call "Pope Park." A short walk from Al-Islah, the park features an elevated ten-foot-tall statue of Pope John Paul II, honoring the first Polish pope. At the fundraising event to help improve the park and statue, the call to prayer was not mentioned, but speakers directly referenced the pope's respect for Islam.

Less than one week later, on May 18, Zwolak submitted the petition to Hamtramck city hall. It included over six hundred signatures, more than was required, and asked that the city council rescind the amendment to the noise ordinance. Since the City Council would not agree to rescind the amendment, the matter would go to a public vote. Until that time, the existing noise ordinance would stand, unamended.

After months of discussion and debate, the issue would finally come to a vote in Hamtramck on July 20, 2004.

Questions for Reflection

- Should auditory public displays of religious identity be treated differently from visual ones? Should sacred sound be treated differently from nonsacred sound? Is there a difference between the sound of church bells and the call to prayer?
- Majewski, facing public hearings on the noise ordinance, wanted to "do it in a way that brought honor to who we are as a city." What were her biggest challenges in this regard?
- Was a public referendum an appropriate method to resolve the dispute over the adhan in Hamtramck? If not, how should the community have resolved the dispute?

(B) Case

More than six months after Abdul Motlib sent a request to the Hamtramck Common Council to amend the city's noise ordinance, the question of the call to prayer finally came to a public vote. The news trucks were once again parked outside of city hall on July 20, 2004, but this time Dr. Karen Majewski felt relieved. Of the 2,662 votes cast, only 1,200 voted to repeal the amendment to the noise ordinance.[25] She stated, "I think that it is to the credit of the residents of Hamtramck that they voted to uphold the amendment."

Majewski was angry that the issue had ever gone to the ballot: "We saw it as a constitutional issue, and that's not subject to a public vote." By the time of the vote in July, she recalled, tensions in Hamtramck diffused. She noted, "The mosque did a really smart thing, rather than waiting for the vote, they started doing the call. So by the time the vote came … people had already been hearing it for a month, six weeks. And the sky hadn't fallen in." She noted, "Without the ordinance in place, the mosque started doing what they always had the right to do anyway: to do the call, now without regulation." Majewski felt that one of "the ironies" about the controversy over the call to prayer was the fact that the amendment to the noise ordinance actually imposed regulation on the practice.

Al-Islah Islamic Center broadcast the first official call to prayer in Hamtramck on May 28, 2004. With the help of the Council of Islamic Organizations in Michigan and the state's National Conference of Community and Justice, Al-Islah hosted an open house and press conference beforehand: local clergy, council members, regional interfaith leaders, and members of the press filled the small mosque. After a series of speakers spoke on themes of unity, Majewski was presented with a key, giving her symbolic control of the amplification system. With a scarf draped loosely over her head, Majewski posed briefly for the assembled media with the key.[26]

Shortly after, the muezzin recited the call to prayer, broadcast from speakers mounted on the rooftop. Local residents noted that the first broadcast call could barely be heard over the traffic bustling along the busy street. For Abdul Motlib, the call to prayer brought with it many emotions, along with a sense of "accomplishment, relief, and most of all tranquility because of how beautiful the call itself is."[27] After the long

[25] Associated Press, "Mich. Town Upholds Muslim Call to Prayer," NBC News, July 21, 2004, https://www.nbcnews.com/.

[26] Perkins, "From the Mosque to the Municipality," 305–7, and reports from Majewski and Buttry.

[27] Motlib, email correspondence with author, November 2014.

months leading up to that day, Motlib explained that on May 28, 2004, he was "showered with joy and happiness."

Two days before the first call to prayer, a small group of Evangelical Christian protesters from Ohio, David's Mighty Men, held a demonstration outside of Al-Islah: the protest was punctuated by the blowing of the shofar, a ram's horn traditionally associated with the Jewish High Holidays. Yet on May 28, there were no protesters, just a large press presence. Rev. Sharon Buttry, representing the Hamtramck Interfaith Partners, spoke at the news conference: "In Hamtramck, my neighbor worships in the church, the mosque and the temple. . . . I am glad for the call to prayer, because not only is it a call to prayer, it is a reminder to all of us to live out our faith in love and mutual respect."[28]

After the first broadcast call in late May, Hamtramck Interfaith Partners (HIP) hosted a series of "relational" events, culminating in what they termed "A Day of Prayer" to coincide with the special election on July 20. Supporters and opponents held formal and informal gatherings, including fellowship meetings and press conferences. By the end of the day, representatives from the interfaith community gathered to celebrate, and Motlib recited the call to prayer. He told a reporter, "Now we truly have approval from the residents of the city. . . . It's a long time we are waiting for this." Motlib later reflected, "Muslim vote in Hamtramck city is like 4 or 500. So how we get 1462? Of course, other community people they are supporting us. They realize we can stand with them."[29]

Robert Zwolak, like many of Hamtramck's residents who had voiced concerns at the meetings, was disappointed in the results. He explained, "The wording wasn't clear: a yes meant no and a no meant yes. And that was drafted by the council itself. People that had been circulating the petition, who were opposing it, were calling me and asking, 'How do I vote. . . ?'" The text on the July 20 ballot read, "Shall Ordinance No. 503, which amended Ordinance No. 434, to allow the City to regulate the volume, direction, duration and time of Call to Prayer, Church Bells and other reasonable amplified means of announcing religious meetings, be repealed?"[30] Zwolak explained,

---

[28] Sharon Buttry to Interfaith Partners, case study regarding call to prayer organizing in Hamtramck, 2004; in author's possession.

[29] Abdul Motlib, from Howell, "Al-Islah Islamic Center."

[30] Weiner, *Religion Out Loud*, 189.

Again, it's politics: when you're allowing one group to do some-thing that the other group doesn't want, then let the community decide. You're going to have people, even amongst the non-Muslims, who are going to say, "Hey, I don't have a problem with it." And I can't honestly say, if the wording was different on the ballot, would it have come out the same way if yes was yes and no was no? I don't know. But we've gotten past that.

The first time Zwolak heard the call to prayer in Hamtramck in May 2004, he noticed it. But soon, he explained, "It is like having children. You learn how to tune it out.... Like living by the railroad tracks when the train comes by, or like living by a freeway."

Following the vote, Hamtramck's noise ordinance was amended to read, "The City shall permit 'call to prayer,' 'church bells,' and other reasonable means of announcing religious meetings to be amplified between the hours of 6:00 a.m. and 10:00 p.m. for a duration not to exceed five minutes." The amendment gave "sole authority to set the level of amplification" to the city council but noted that no level would be enforced "until all religious institutions receive notice of such levels." Complaints were to be filed with the Clerk and placed on the agenda of the next regular meeting of the city council.[31]

After the Call to Prayer: 2014

In the years that followed, the controversy over the call to prayer largely faded away; however, Hamtramck's economic challenges continue. Boarded-up storefronts and houses still dot the landscape of the tiny city. Just off I-75, the yard of a single-family home in a row of tidy houses is overgrown with weeds, the door boarded up. A spray-painted message covers the wooden planks: "Don't remember me like this.... Remember the way I used to be."

Many Hamtramck residents can't recall a time in which the call to prayer was not broadcast from Al-Islah. Standing in downtown Hamtramck when the adhan is sounded, it can be difficult to know exactly where it is coming from: locals explain that the sound can shift depending on the wind and weather. As of late 2014, there were seven

---

[31] Perkins, "From the Mosque to the Municipality," 413.

mosques in Hamtramck, and all broadcasted the call to prayer.[32] For Motlib, the sound evokes both "history and meaning," adding, "It is a whole-body experience because it forces us to drop what we are doing and listen. It also reminds me of one of the benefits of the call to prayer, which is when broadcasted, we believe that Satan runs away because he cannot stand the sound of Allah's name."[33]

Shortly after the call-to-prayer controversy, Majewski became the mayor of Hamtramck. She believes her training as a scholar of immigration has helped her in this role: "What I see is the patterns over time. Regardless of ethnic group, regardless of generation, regardless of the time period when this group formed its identity in the U.S., the patterns are pretty much the same. And it's really helped to have that perspective.... Knowing what I do about the Polish community, and seeing it continue to evolve; it's not like a done deal." This knowledge also helps her to deal with the emotional impact of these changes. For years, her own church, historic St. Ladislaus, was threatened with closure by the Detroit Archdiocese due to declining numbers and finances: it survived by merging with another church. Majewski welcomed the continued growth of the Muslim community and many new mosques, but was concerned that some are being established in commercial areas, taking prime real estate off of the tax rolls.

Majewski notes that her studies of immigration are also helpful in recognizing the internal diversity of each community:

> To the outsider, those communities look monolithic. On the inside, of course you see all of the fragmentation, all of the power struggles, all of the factions, all of the issues that don't get aired publicly.... There's a lot going on in those communities. We may judge one or the other from what we see in the newspaper, or this person that we know, or what we see at a council meeting, or in the political arena, but in reality, there is a world that they are living in that we have no idea of, and that's informing their decisions and their strategies as a community.

During the controversy, despite the evident diversity of ethnicity and language in Hamtramck's Muslim community, little diversity of opinion

---

[32] Buttry, Majewski, and Arif Huskic, interview with the author, Hamtramck, Michigan, August 2014.

[33] Motlib, email correspondence with the author, November 2014.

about the call to prayer was apparent in the public conversation. However, ten years later, discussion on local news websites includes comments from Muslims suggesting that the sound should be turned down; some directly questioned the use of loudspeakers. One comment, from a citizen who identified himself as a Yemeni Muslim, stated in part, "The prophet PBUH never used loudspeakers to call the Athan, people have watches they can use to know what [time] the prayer is. If anything, the Athan shouldn't be [called] outside the timeframe of work hours (10am–6pm) to avoid bothering non-Muslims with the sound when they are relaxing."[34]

Ten years after the controversy, the city council—like the city itself—was half Muslim. Majewski notes, "The city really is always changing." Yet Majewski held tight to her "ideal" vision of the city: "Of openness and welcoming, and working through difficult questions together."

Interfaith Activity after the Call

Looking back, Motlib acknowledges the formal and informal interfaith efforts that supported the call to prayer, whether the director of a local think tank who wrote op-ed pieces or the Catholic priest from St. Lad's across the street who was a steadfast ally. Motlib notes, "Despite the opposition, I felt a strong support from the interfaith community, and I believe that their votes of confidence and support had a huge role in the final outcome. I was very grateful for everything they did for us."[35]

Hamtramck Interfaith Partners continued bringing the community together for a couple of years after the controversy, including "A Celebration ... Moving on to a Call for Dialogue and New Community," held in the Bosnia and Herzegovina Association Hall. By then, it was no longer of interest to the local and international media. At that event, Abdul Motlib commented, "A crisis brought us together, but the richness of our faith traditions will keep us together." Yet over the years, interfaith activity in Hamtramck slowly faded. Buttry explains, "After a while, it became harder and harder to get people to come to meetings, because there was no focal point for us to dramatically gather around, and people just get busy."[36]

[34] Charles Sercombe, "Residents Complain That the 'Call to Prayer' Is Too Loud," *Hamtramck (MI) Review*, accessed October 2014, http://www.thehamtramckreview.com.

[35] Motlib, email correspondence with author, November 2014.

[36] Sharon Buttry to Interfaith Partners, case study.

Then, in 2008, new allegiances formed in a battle over a human rights ordinance (HRO): some understood the HRO as protection for LGBTQ people in housing and employment; for others, the HRO mandated special privileges to a fringe group. While the HRO was defeated in a public referendum, some friendships formed in the common cause of the call to prayer were lost.[37]

At Home in Hamtramck

Looking back, Abdul Motlib explained that the vote proved that "Hamtramck people can live, get together different culture, different religion, different community. They don't have problem with each other. So from that election still, we don't feel anything bad. We feel very proud of it."[38] Ten years after the call to prayer came to Hamtramck, Motlib and other leaders of Al-Islah were focused on developing a landmark mosque, just steps away from the original building. Fundraising materials for the project explained that "the community has grown considerably and the existing mosques are unable to accommodate all worshippers for Jummuah and Eid prayer."[39] The flier also mentions twice that Al-Islah "is the first mosque in America that is permitted by law, as voted by its citizens in the year 2004, to broadcast the call to prayer (adhan)."[40]

A decade after the call-to-prayer controversy, Robert Zwolak was elected to the Hamtramck City Council. Zwolak's view on the call was cemented by his experience living across the street from one of the city's seven mosques: he distributed a "mini-petition" regarding the call to prayer being broadcast from the new mosque. He explained, "The call to prayer there is absolutely blaring. Imposing, blaring, whatever." With the petition, he noted, "We didn't want to eliminate it, we just wanted them to tone it down. That's all it was, just tone it down." He explained that the police chief visited the mosque on more than one occasion, asking

---

[37] Alisa Perkins, "Negotiating Alliances: Muslims, Gay Rights and the Christian Right in a Polish-American City," *Anthropology Today* 26, no. 2 (April 2010): 19–24, https://doi.org/10.1111/j.1467-8322.2010.00723.x; Buttry, interview with the author, August 2014.

[38] Motlib, from Howell, "Al-Islah Islamic Center."

[39] Al-Islah Islamic Center, Hamtramck, MI, expansion project brochure, posted on Al-Islah website, August 2014.

[40] Ibid.

the sound to be reduced. But other than a few complaints about volume, Zwolak said, the controversy "has probably gone away." He added,

> It has always been a noise issue; it's still a noise issue. It's not anything where people are intolerant of the call to prayer or what is being said. The community has basically been accustomed to the call to prayer, and all the other activities, the Eid, and the Ramadan. Some people are more friendly in terms of wishing people happy Ramadan or happy Eid, whatever the case may be. So you don't see any real resentment or comments, other than a few people who are normally, naturally bigots and racists. You're never going to change them, which is unfortunate, but they are few and far between.

Although Zwolak has lived in Hamtramck since he was a child, he reflected that he no longer considers the city to be his "hometown."

> I'm beginning to lose some of that sense. Yeah, because my family, basically my entire family has left Hamtramck. And it's not just cousins, my classmates, and we have such a different population.... Life was entirely different in Hamtramck. Hamtramck is just a constantly evolving, springboard community.

Buttry, however, has embraced Hamtramck as her new home. When the call-to-prayer controversy began, Buttry lived nearby in Warren but chose to move with her family to Hamtramck shortly afterward. From her home today, she explains, "If the wind is just right, I can hear two calls to prayer." While the call to prayer is rarely discussed in Hamtramck ten years later, when Buttry hears it driving through downtown or sitting on her front porch, she often pauses to reflect, "This is my city. And it's just a reminder of the diversity that we have, and both the joy and the sorrow that comes with that. It's poignant for me."

Postscript

After serving for sixteen years as Hamtramck's mayor, Dr. Karen Majewski was voted out of office in 2021. Majewski was proud of her public service in Hamtramck: she was the first woman mayor, the second-longest-serving mayor, and, for years, a Catholic mayor in a majority-Muslim city. After the election she declared that she was likely to be Hamtramck's "last Polish mayor." Majewski was replaced by a Muslim mayor and, in a first for America, an all-Muslim city council. The city, home to three mosques in 2004, has thirteen two decades later.[41]

Majewski counts her support of the call to prayer as among her accomplishments in Hamtramck; however, she regrets having the government intervene in "the mechanics of the ordinance."[42] She explains, "I would have set it up differently so that city council was not like the arbiter of whether the ordinance was being followed.... That should have been just strictly an administrative issue."

She is proud of the narrative she helped to construct about the small city. Majewski reflects, "Really, the world in two square miles. Hamtramck's a place where folks from all over the world could have a voice and make a place for themselves and find community and create community together. Not without controversy, but on the ground, on your own street, with your neighbors." Hamtramck is, she explained, "what America could be, in all its messiness."

Yet when Majewski looks back at her time as mayor, she explains, the dispute over the human rights ordinance, intended to protect LGBTQ rights, remains "a very, very bitter memory." She comments,

> While the call to prayer brought together people from different faiths in support of each other and in support of constitutional rights and religious freedom and honoring each other's traditions and protecting each other's rights, this in some ways, brought together some of the same coalitions to defeat those same principles ... this time using religion as a weapon. And it's disgraceful what happened.

She describes how Catholic and Muslim communities "joined forces with right-wing fundamentalists from the west side of Michigan to spread just the worst of the stereotypes and fear mongering [about LGBTQ folk].... Just despicable, despicable."

---

[41] "Mosques Near Hamtramck, Michigan, United States," 2023, https://prayersconnect.com/.

[42] All quotes from Karen Majewski in postscript from Zoom interview with the author, February 24, 2022.

Majewski appreciated Alisa Perkins's book about Hamtramck, *Muslim American City*, which juxtaposed the debate over the call to prayer with the contested human right ordinance; however, Majewski recognized that the author was critical of her leadership. Perkins wrote,

> As with other narratives supporting the ordinance, Hamtramck is figured here as a model of diversity for the nation—provided it makes the correct choice about gay rights. This point resembles the hopes that call-to-prayer supporters had for the city in 2004, when they thought that the outcome of the vote would send a message to the rest of the nation about the inclusion of Muslims in the public sphere.[43]

Perkins noted that "[Some] supporters portrayed the Muslims as victims of false consciousness and as uncomprehending puppets of the [American Family Association of Michigan, a conservative Christian group]"[44] and that supporters "worked from an implicit set of beliefs about alliance formation that failed to take moral nuances into account.[45] In the end, supporters and opponents of the ordinance both "felt betrayed by their former allies."[46]

During Majewski's last mayoral campaign, a controversy emerged over flying the Pride flag at city hall. Since the HRO debacle, Majewski felt that there was greater acceptance of LGBTQ rights; however, she recognized that some opponents saw her support of the flag as a political opportunity. "It was really politicized around the next mayoral campaign and city council campaign. And used against me." She continues, "I don't want to sugarcoat any of this; the leadership should be ashamed of itself.... And they may find in this election, they could use it effectively, but that's not going to continue to serve them down the road."

During the debates, one of her major opponents, Amer Ghalib, was among those expressing disapproval of flying the Pride flag in Hamtramck. Ghalib, who would later be elected as mayor, referenced the battles over the HRO and said the flag "would only create tensions in the

---

[43] Alisa Perkins, *Muslim American City: Gender and Religion in Metro Detroit* (New York: NYU Press, 2020), 206.
[44] Ibid., 207.
[45] Ibid., 217.
[46] Ibid., 200.

city."[47] Five of the other candidates, including three Muslim candidates, signed a "Statement of Unity" that called for "unifying against hate in the community, and embrac[ing] marginalized communities faced with prejudice in order to increase compassion and understanding."[48]

During a Q&A with mayoral candidates, when asked about the Pride flag, Majewski responded,

> All sides should be listened to, but there is simply no room for compromise when it comes to recognizing and honoring human rights and the dignity of all our residents. The very term "diverse" includes people of all sexual identities and preferences, so to claim to champion diversity while at the same time seeking to marginalize whole categories of humanity is essentially hypocritical, undemocratic and immoral. I will continue to advocate for all Hamtramck residents, regardless of race, religion/spiritual practice or lack of it, gender/gender identity, sexual preference, ethnic background or immigration status. There is no wiggle room on this principle.[49]

Majewski would later cast the deciding vote on the Pride flag. On a warm day in Zussman Park, when the Pride flag was raised for the first time, only a small crowd gathered. Majewski offered brief remarks to reinforce her vision for the city—"whether or not it lived up to that vision."

While Majewski knows that her support of the Pride flag was used against her in the campaign, she isn't convinced that this cost her the election. She explained, "It's completely natural that people are going to vote for folks who they think represent them, or who tell their story, who speak their language. So, as the demographic changes, I can completely understand some people are going to vote for a '-ski' at the end of the name and some people are going to vote for what they perceive as an Arabic name. And that's human nature and it's completely understandable."

When Majewski looks to the future, she hopes that Hamtramck's cityscape, with its "old-school downtown," will be honored and protected.

---

[47] Simon Albaugh, "Candidates and Commissions Respond to Hamtramck Pride Flag Debate," *Yemeni American News*, June 17, 2021, https://yemeniamerican.com/.

[48] Ibid.

[49] Hassan Abbas, "Q&A with Hamtramck Mayoral Candidates," *Arab American News*, July 30, 2021, https://arabamericannews.com/.

More so, she hopes that an understanding of diversity "that includes everyone" will be honored in Hamtramck. She adds that "diversity" doesn't equate to an all-Muslim city council. She explains, "That also does not represent the reality of the Hamtramck demographic. If our population is 50 percent women, where's 50 percent of women on that council?" In 2022, the city council included one woman, a progressive Polish American convert to Islam; Majewski notes that the city's all-Muslim council includes diverse points of view.

> This is something that I've tried to stress, in all my years in elected office, is that Islam isn't a monolith. We wouldn't talk about Christians that way, that Southern Baptist is the same as Polish Catholic. And we've got different cultures, different languages, different experiences in the old country, different social systems, different family relations and different histories that brought them here, and different ways of worship. I mean, if you want to talk about diversity of Bosnian as opposed to Yemeni, yes, they're both Muslim, but their practices and their social worlds are completely different.

As a "cultural Catholic," Majewski rejects reductionist views about religion—including her own. She notes, "Despite all the problems with the church as an institution, I respect it enough to have found a tenuous space for myself at its margins." Drawn to the "fundamental principles of mercy and redemption, its marriage of humanity and divinity," she also hopes for the church's reform on issues such as LGBTQ rights. Majewski explains, "LGBTQ+ issues have been important to me since high school, when a dear friend and teacher was fired for his political beliefs, and warned not to contest his illegal firing under threat that his sexuality would be publicly revealed. He was also a devoted Catholic. For me, in 1972, that was a turning point."

She observes, "LGBTQ+ rights and identity continue to be a hot-button issue among certain elements of our community, especially some Yemeni American social media influencers and activists, who continue to use inflammatory language and share right-wing media reports to stir the pot." In 2022 a controversy arose when the Human Relations Commission raised the Pride flag on Jos. Campau, the town's main thoroughfare, alongside many of the international flags. Majewski explains, "These flags are paid for by community members, not by city funds, and are meant to reflect the diversity of our residents." Majewski explained, "Things got quite heated on this issue in 2022, resulting in the formation of a new community group, the Hamtramck Queer Alliance, of which I am a member."

With her political career behind her, Majewski is happy to return to her academic research and writing—and to running her vintage store. There is a Pride flag in the store's front display case; she used to fly the flag outside, but it was stolen—as were many throughout Hamtramck. In addition to ongoing debates over the Pride flag, another issue emerged on Hamtramck's political agenda in late 2022: proposals to ban books with LGBTQ content in school libraries. These proposals have been supported by the new mayor. For Majewski, this is "another issue that is being used by reactionary elements for political gain, against the interests and well-being of the city and its residents at large." She explains, "It does actual harm—not just to young people who are already marginalized and vulnerable—but to the continued progress of our democracy and, dare I say, our humanity."

Part 3

Fault Lines in Interfaith Relations

A Sign of Division

In Sharon, Massachusetts, an interfaith youth group, led by teens and coordinated by Executive Director Janet Penn, spent months planning an event at Temple Israel: "Sharing Sacred Seasons." That year, the Muslim month of Ramadan and the Jewish High Holidays coincided. It would not happen for another thirty years. Sharon, a town that for decades was majority Jewish, was becoming religiously diverse, with a large Muslim population. For many religious and community leaders in Sharon, their town was "a living laboratory" for interfaith relations. Events like an interfaith *iftar* at the synagogue were just one example of the vibrant and vital relationships being forged in Sharon. On the morning of the event, Penn, a member of the temple, walked by the large sign in the lobby that reads, "We Support Israel." That day, she viewed it through a different lens: How would it be received by their guests from the local mosque? Should she ask the rabbi to remove the sign, despite the community's deep commitments to Israel? How should the rabbi respond? Is their interfaith relationship strong enough to take on the subjects they avoid, the subjects that divide them, like Israel/Palestine? Are interfaith events like this truly meaningful if the toughest parts of the encounter are avoided?

(A) Case

The day finally arrived. After months of preparations, Janet Penn and a group of teenagers from Interfaith Action, a youth interfaith group, were busy cooking, making signs, moving tables, and readying Temple Israel for a special event. For the first time in years, the Jewish High Holidays and the Muslim holy month of Ramadan coincided; it would not happen again for more than thirty years. The teens from Sharon, Massachusetts, envisioned an interfaith event they called "Sharing Sacred Seasons." It would bring together Jews and Muslims, Hindus and Christians, and neighbors of other traditions in celebration. Some four hundred people were expected to attend, and the temple was buzzing with excitement.

The teens from Interfaith Action had planned the whole event: they would begin with Indian dancing to celebrate the Hindu festival of Navratri and continue with an educational program featuring youth speakers. The event would culminate with an iftar fast-breaking in the sukkah. The meal would be South Asian; it had taken some time to find kosher basmati rice, but like many obstacles, this had been overcome. Such details mattered, Penn explained, in an event that was meant to build trust. As the executive director of Interfaith Action, Penn observed that in Greater Boston and beyond, Jewish-Muslim relations had been a challenge in recent years. She and the teens viewed Sharing Sacred Seasons as a symbol of hope and possibility. Yet, as they made their final preparations, Penn saw something she feared would derail all of their plans.

As guests entered the synagogue, they would be greeted by a large sign, poised on an easel, which read, "We Support Israel." It occupied a central position in the entryway, and as Penn knew well, a central place in the identity of her Conservative Jewish community. For many, "Israel is absolutely essential to the survival of the Jewish people and therefore for their own survival."[1] Many had lost relatives in the Holocaust and felt that this wasn't merely a matter of politics; it was deeply personal. Yet, over the years of her own interfaith involvements, Penn had become aware of another, competing narrative: for many Muslims, Israel was seen as a symbol of oppression. She feared that the sign would be viewed as "an unbelievable insult: 'You bring us into your home, and then you're slapping this into our face?'" She added, "For Muslims now, in this country, they are dealing with incredible discrimination on an ongoing basis. So, there's fear, there's anger."

As a member of Temple Israel, Penn had walked by the sign a thousand times. But that night, standing in the entryway, she recognized that the sign represented everything that divided the Muslim and Jewish communities. In keeping with the philosophy of the youth-led program, she gathered a group of teens to ask their opinion: "Would this sign be a problem?" Their answer was a resounding "Yes."

---

[1] All quotes from Janet Penn in (A) and (B) cases are from interview with the author, Sharon, MA, September 2008.

Sharon's Religious Diversity

Sharon, Massachusetts, is a quiet New England town of eighteen thousand, located between Boston and Providence, Rhode Island. In 2007, when Interfaith Action was planning Sharing Sacred Seasons, Sharon was home to eight churches, seven synagogues, the Islamic Center of New England and its Islamic school, and a growing Hindu community. Yet the town's religious diversity is relatively new: until the early 1990s, the town was known for its predominantly Jewish population, including large Orthodox and Conservative communities. When the neighboring town of Milton, Massachusetts, opposed the development of a mosque there, the Muslim community came to Sharon. Here, they were welcomed by local clergy, who printed their endorsement in the local newspaper: "Sharon Welcomes Islamic Center."

Rabbi Barry Starr of Temple Beth Israel commented: "Very often the Bible reminds the Jews, 'In Egypt you were strangers, or aliens ... ,' and therefore, when you have your own land, you can't treat anybody as an alien because you know what it was like. So, in a sense, in America, we're all aliens."[2] Rabbi Starr continued, "You can use an American version of that: 'You have been aliens in America. How can you treat anyone else with less than absolute respect, because you know what it was like when you weren't treated with respect?'" He elaborated, "But unfortunately, you forget quickly. As the so-called Pilgrims did when they came here and did not extend religious freedom—for the very reason they came here, they then excluded others from their communities."

When the Islamic Center of New England broke ground in 1992, this celebration was attended by Father Robert Bullock from Our Lady of Sorrows Catholic Church, Rabbi Barry Starr, and Imam Talal Eid of the Islamic Center, among many others. In the years that followed, the clergy council remained active in interfaith work; indeed, Penn recalls that the late Father Bullock once described Sharon as a "living laboratory" for small-town interfaith relations.

---

[2] All quotes from Rabbi Barry Starr are from interview with the author, Sharon, MA, September 2008.

Penn and Interfaith Action

Inspired by the growing diversity of Sharon, in 1999 the Anti-Defamation League identified the town as the site for an interfaith youth group. Janet Penn, a silver-haired mother of two grown daughters, was selected to coordinate the effort. She spent her own youth as "secular but searching"; she came to be active in the Conservative Jewish tradition as an adult. Penn's parents were first-generation Americans and not particularly observant Jews: she grew up eating pork, and holidays were more an opportunity for family gatherings than religious observance. But she did have an awareness that her family could not join certain clubs because they were Jewish. Although she had no background in interfaith relations, she held an MBA and an MSW and had extensive experience in nonprofit management. "I was immediately hooked." Penn found that interfaith work resonated particularly with her values and her faith: "It goes back to the very basis in the Torah, Abraham and Sarah, of offering hospitality to the stranger in the tent."

In 2004 Penn established Interfaith Action Inc. as an independent entity and grew the organization to more than 50 student members. Known by the teens simply as "Interfaith," the program provides extensive training in compassionate listening and facilitating dialogue. With the motto of "Reflection, Connection, Action," the youth plan their own interfaith events, often participating as speakers or facilitators. For Penn, programs and events are important, but she noted, "The question is what's going to make this sustainable? And for the youth, I think it's about giving them the skills, and the opportunity, and the mentorship so that they can go off and do it themselves and own it."

In recent years, Penn had begun to develop a program that would build "a sustainable culture of pluralism" in the town of Sharon. While the clergy council and other civic partners were enthusiastic, she often found the work with the community adults to be challenging. Penn felt that Israel/Palestine had become the "elephant in the room" in interfaith relations: it was often unspoken, but its divisive presence was felt among many Jews and Muslims. Penn explained that with "competing narratives," neither group could really hear the other. Rarely, but painfully, the anger came to the surface; on more than one occasion, she had been the recipient. She was becoming weary and often felt like she was walking on eggshells.

Echoes and Local Woes

Penn noticed that conflicts happening elsewhere often seemed to echo in the Sharon community. In addition to the ongoing Middle East conflict, a protracted controversy over the Islamic Center of Boston Cultural Center had polarized parts of the local Muslim and Jewish communities. Just the year before, Sharon was shaken by the arrest and detention of the town's Imam. When Homeland Security took Imam Muhammad Masood and his son into custody, many were in shock: he was a well-respected religious leader, active in interfaith relations. While the investigation later cleared Imam Masood and his son of any links to terror, it was revealed that his brother was affiliated with a terrorist group in Pakistan. Imam Masood had violated the terms of his work permit by staying past the established dates and would now face deportation.

Throughout the crisis, clergy from Sharon rallied around Imam Masood, his family, and the Muslim community. Many in the Muslim community were first-generation Americans, still acclimating to their new context. Some had struggled with bias and backlash in a post/9-11 America and now were afraid of guilt by association. Temple Israel created a fund for the Imam's family, and both Rabbi Starr and Janet Penn were among those in Sharon who attended hearings and offered letters of support.

Yet Penn observed that for many in Sharon, the sense of fear and distrust grew. She knew that many Muslims and other community members saw the investigation as a frightening abuse of power and a pattern of raising suspicion. This, it seemed, only increased the sense of displacement for a relatively new immigrant community. For some in the Jewish community, the arrest brought into question their own safety: any link to terror was threatening and disturbing. Some in the Jewish community questioned Temple Israel's involvement and marginalized Penn for her efforts. Penn felt that her work was becoming more difficult—and also more critical. The need for healing and bridge-building was acute.

Reflection and an Awkward Position

As Penn stood in the entryway and looked at the sign, she reflected on the dedication and hard work that had led up to the event. She thought of the students—representing all of the town's faiths—who had been meeting every week, throughout summer vacation and into the fall, to plan Sharing Sacred Seasons. They had been trained through Interfaith Action to listen to another's view, to facilitate dialogue, and now to work collaboratively and creatively to bring the community together. They were concerned about the sign, as well as the success of the event.

She thought of Tanweer Zaidi, the interfaith coordinator at the Islamic center, and how eager he was to encourage participation from a sometimes-reticent Muslim community. Zaidi ensured that the iftar at the synagogue was the only communal option that evening: the mosque would be closed, and those who wanted to celebrate as a community would do so at Temple Israel. It was a bold decision, Penn felt, one that demonstrated Zaidi's commitment—and also perhaps the frailty of relations among the diverse communities of Sharon.

Penn felt uncomfortable approaching Rabbi Starr about the sign. After all, Interfaith Action was a guest at Temple Israel. Rabbi Starr had generously offered the facilities of the synagogue at no charge. After talking with the teens, she knew she had to raise the question but shuddered to think that she would have to place the rabbi in an awkward position. How could she ask him to remove the sign, given the community's dedication to Israel? Yet how could she invite people to observe their holiday at another house of worship and greet them with a sign they might read as hostile? Penn saw Rabbi Starr approaching down the hallway and with some hesitation asked if she could have a few words with him.

Questions for Reflection

- If you were Janet Penn, what would you say to Rabbi Starr? If you were Rabbi Starr, how would you respond to Janet Penn's concerns about the sign?
- What options are available? What are the risks and benefits of each approach?
- Based on the case, what does the sign represent to the temple? What might it represent to some of the interfaith guests? Are there ways to bridge this gap?
- Interfaith Action is a guest; Temple Israel is the host. How might their respective roles of guest and host, and ideas about hospitality, inform how to approach this dilemma?

(B) Case

Janet Penn approached Rabbi Starr and said that, in consultation with the teens of Interfaith Action, she wanted to speak about a matter of some concern. As they walked over to the front entryway of Temple Israel, Penn explained that she and the teens were worried about how the guests might react to the "We Support Israel" sign. Rabbi Starr looked at the sign and said simply, "Let's take it down."

Penn noticed with some relief that Rabbi Starr had barely hesitated in his response. He later explained, "It seems to me that when you invite someone into your home, you give them an opportunity to feel welcome." He described the principle of *hachnasat orchim*, a Hebrew phrase that Rabbi Starr translated as "welcoming the guest or stranger." For the Muslim community of Sharon to come to a synagogue for a religious observance was unprecedented. He recognized the fear and division between the two communities and saw the Sharing Sacred Seasons event as an important step. The sign, he thought, might shift the focus to politics: "I wanted everybody's mind focused on spirituality."

Rabbi Starr agreed with Penn that the issue of Israel/Palestine was the elephant in the room, noting that an Arab-Israeli problem had somehow become a Muslim-Jewish problem. "It really needn't be that, on either side. But the rhetoric, on both sides, makes it difficult." Moreover, he felt, the Sharon community wasn't ready to engage in a dialogue. "It has to be safe. You can't talk about this in a situation that isn't safe. Because everybody knows that it's going to be fraught with a lot of emotion, and nobody wants to wear that emotion on their sleeve. I think we're all afraid of it. When I'm talking about Israel, I get very emotional. I can get angry. And I think everybody's afraid of that, because then the human discourse breaks down."

As Rabbi Starr spoke about safety, he recognized the similarities between this situation and the advice he offers to couples. He explained that, in a relationship, it isn't a matter of subsuming your person and becoming a chameleon to suit the needs of the moment; that can destroy self-identity and self-esteem. Rather, he notes, "You have to create the safe environment in which real communication will take place—real listening and real hearing will take place—and that doesn't happen the day you get married. It sometimes never happens at all, but it certainly takes years of work to create that environment."

Rabbi Starr continued, "We're committed to Israel. We know that. And every Muslim who came here knew that. But for a religious moment in their lives, it was not necessary to rub it in their face." He recalled that a local hospital, Caritas Norwood, has a statue of Jesus in every room; however, patients of other faiths may request that the statue be removed. Rabbi Starr noted, "I know that the hospital is committed to its work with Jesus, and what it does for healing the world, and all of that, but there is respect for the individual patient."

In a diverse community, Rabbi Starr explained, it is important to address the challenges of pluralism. "One of our classic rabbinic ideas expresses this very well. There was an argument between two ancient rabbis about matters internal to the Jewish community. And indeed, the suggestion was made by someone in the community that, 'You know, people who follow those two rabbis' positions shouldn't even marry each other.' And the answer that our tradition gives is: 'Both views are the views of a living God,' which doesn't mean both are correct. You can choose one; you have to choose one." He continued, "That we all are part of a society in which we place our faiths in a living, moving, motivating God is what our view of pluralism is—my view of pluralism is. That it can happen between Jews and Christians and Muslims is part of my personal credo."

Looking back, Rabbi Starr and Penn agreed that what was most critical in this decision was the involvement of the teens in the discussion. "[Penn] presented it to these young people as a learning experience for them, to feel what it would be like, and to decide for themselves what they wanted to do in this situation." Penn was relieved by Rabbi Starr's openness to the concerns that the teens raised. She felt that too often in the American Jewish community there is no space for debate and discussion when it comes to the topic of Israel.

Rabbi Starr strongly cautioned, however, about taking this specific situation too far. He recalled that when the Muslim community was invited to the synagogue a few months later for a film, he did not take the sign down. "It was not a spiritual event." He explained, "It is our home, and we're going to support Israel, and we do, and very strongly." He underscored that the sign itself said nothing offensive: "I see a sign in support of Israel as a kind of neutral statement of my own commitment. But it's read elsewhere in a very different way."

Mike, one of the teenagers from Interfaith Action, recalled the discussion about the sign but couldn't remember the ultimate decision. What he did remember was the culminating event of Sharing Sacred Seasons: on a warm October evening just after sunset the Muslims of Sharon gathered in prayer next to a sukkah. Then Muslims and Jews, Christians and Hindus, and neighbors of other faiths entered the fragile structure to share a traditional iftar meal. "It is a powerful image that sticks with me, a powerful idea."[3] He continued, "There were four hundred people there, many of whom had never participated in an interfaith dialogue. It starts the ball rolling. While it is not going to create world peace or get everybody to love each other, it is a step, and it is important."

Postscript

In the years after Sharing Sacred Seasons, youth-led Interfaith Action grew and gained national recognition for its innovative approach. The teens, trained as facilitators, helped to fuel vibrant local dialogues and vital interfaith relations in Sharon, Massachusetts. Soon, Interfaith Action became Youth LEAD (Youth Leaders Engaging Across Differences), reflecting broader categories of identity, including race, culture, sexual orientation, and religion. After a few years, Executive Director Janet Penn sought to broaden the impact of Youth LEAD, forming new branches in other cities; however, the organization was difficult to sustain administratively and financially. In 2018 Youth LEAD found a new home at Boston's Emerson College, but—like Janet Penn, who moved to a town twenty minutes away—it no longer has a significant presence in Sharon.

In Sharon, another local interfaith effort established by Penn, the Sharon Pluralism Network, remains active today, as is the town's clergy group. And for years following the interfaith iftar at Temple Israel, robust relationships continued—especially between the Orthodox Jewish community and the Muslim community. Sharon residents came together for regular programs, including an interfaith Thanksgiving event at the mosque that drew nearly one thousand people.

One of those in attendance was a local religious leader and Sharon resident, Sam Smith.[4] Smith explained that, when the Muslim ban was

---

[3] All quotes from Michael (last name removed) are from email correspondence with author, September 2008.

[4] All quotes from "Sam Smith" (pseudonym) in postscript are from phone interview with the author, June 24, 2022.

announced in 2017, Sharon's Jews reached out to their Muslim neighbors; after the Tree of Life killings in 2018, Sharon's Muslims offered letters of kindness and concern. "There was support," he said simply. In recent years, however, such relationships have "atrophied."

Then, in May 2021, the war in Gaza brought Sharon's citizens to the streets. In the town's central Post Office Square, a group of Jewish community members gathered with signs supporting Israel. The next week in Post Office Square, a gathering twice the size took place: a pro-Palestine rally. With signs referring to Israeli "apartheid" and "genocide," Smith notes, "It was provocative in a town that is plurality Jewish." Counterprotesters shouted from cars; people yelled at each other on the street. Smith describes the signs raised in protest—on both sides—as an unnuanced form of communication. "These signs are a statement, not an invitation to dialogue." What was "painful" to witness in Sharon's town square turned "pugilistic" on social media. Smith later observed, "This level of communication is so bad, so hurtful."

He continued, "Sharon is a living laboratory, with striking diversity. . . . But things have atrophied. We could blame it on the pandemic. We could point to the ways in which Israel/Palestine has become more brittle." He cautions local leaders—in Sharon and elsewhere—not to be passive about relationships. "Don't just rest on relationships that are there. Grow them. In absence of clear lines of communication, reach out. We're neighbors here. We have to avoid harmful, hurtful communication."

Janet Penn, after learning about the angry words in downtown Sharon and social media, had an idea: invite members of the two communities together for a dialogue. Each could bring their respective signs and explain what they mean to them. Rather than shouting, she proposed, "Let's have a conversation."[5] She explained,

> Understanding pain points and what words mean to different people creates the safety Rabbi Starr mentioned [in Case B]. Dialogue builds a foundation for understanding the attachment that both peoples have to the land and helps develop the trust necessary to have more nuanced conversations about power, pain, fear, and ultimately hope. From that place of understanding, it's possible to find ways to advocate together for justice despite our differences.

---

[5] All quotes from Janet Penn in postscript are from Zoom interview with the author, June 16, 2022.

Yet the event never came together; phone messages were not returned.

From the sign of division in the synagogue lobby to the signs of division during the protests in Sharon's town square, the issue of Israel/Palestine continues to complicate local interfaith relationships. Smith will continue reaching out, yet he worries, "People don't have the muscle for these kinds of interactions to go well. They can get the muscle through actually meeting with each other and making mistakes and learning. They can also get it from training."

Although Penn no longer lives in Sharon or works with Youth LEAD, she remains active in interfaith relations. Prior to retiring in 2022 the focus of her work as a staff person at the Sisterhood of Salaam Shalom was developing skills for engaging in difficult conversations between Muslim and Jewish women. After three decades in the field, Penn notes, "I think Muslim-Jewish relationships are probably the most fraught that I've known them." She questions the merit of intermittent program-focused interfaith activity. "They have value, but they don't really change things." Too often, she asserts, interfaith efforts avoid the difficult issues. For Penn, it is a question of getting beyond, "You like hummus, I like hummus." She explains, "We need to build a skill set." Yet Penn notes that few training opportunities are available to talk across difference—whether at the community level or in colleges and universities.

After decades of local and national interfaith work, Penn observes, "I don't see a whole lot of movement. And I think that's where my deep sense of sadness and hopelessness comes in." More recently, she has shifted her emphasis overseas, working with Tagyheer, an organization she describes as "a nonviolent movement of Palestinians organizing Palestinians to strengthen civil society and end the occupation." She adds, "It is the first time I felt hopeful in a long time."

Reflecting back, Penn notes that her words years before about the sign at the interfaith iftar weren't strong enough: "It would certainly be viewed as 'hostile' and an 'insult' by most in the Muslim community." As for the Jewish community, she added, "The sign represents the temple's institutional support of Israel but doesn't account for the diversity of opinion among members or address the silencing of those who don't support Israeli policy regarding Palestine. This is a huge issue within the Jewish community."

Fliers at the Peace Parade

The Sikh community in El Sobrante, California, is vital and visible: the gurdwara, perched on a hillside with its distinctive domes, and the Sikh people, many of whom wear turbans—*dastaars* and *patkas*—or brightly colored scarves. On a warm summer day in July, the Sikh community gathered for a "peace parade." Devotional singing filled the streets as the Sikh Scripture, the Guru Granth Sahib, moved in festive procession through the center of town. Hearing the music and viewing the floats, Pastor Kent Brandenburg saw an opportunity to distribute his fliers, designed specifically for the Sikh population: "Please Consider these Words of Love My SIKH Friend." For Brandenburg, sharing his faith in Jesus Christ as the only path to salvation is central to his Evangelical Christian tradition. For the Sikhs, who practice no form of proselytization and who have experienced a surge of violence and discrimination in a post-9/11 America, the fliers are an affront. Is it appropriate to proselytize at a public religious event? How might both communities move forward? In the context of tolerance and interfaith understanding, is there space for proselytization?

(A) Case

On July 23, 2006, as services at the Bethel Baptist Church were ending, Pastor Kent Brandenburg heard loud chanting and drumming outside. When Brandenburg remembered that local Sikhs were holding a Peace Parade, he saw an opportunity; some years ago, he developed a flier to reach out to the growing Sikh community in El Sobrante, California. Brandenburg ran out to the parade route, where he saw large images of Sikh gurus moving by on flatbed trucks. He spent a few minutes handing out fliers while complimenting the Sikhs on their festive attire. Brandenburg later wrote about his outreach to the Sikhs on his blog:

Twenty years ago, when we started the church ... right away we began meeting many Sikhs while going door to door. Like with every other person in this area, we became concerned with the salvation of the Sikhs. The Bible teaches that there is salvation only in Jesus Christ, and that outside of Him is destruction (John 14:6; Acts 4:12; John 3:18, 36). This is not a new message. This message has been preached by Bible-believing Christians for two-thousand years.[1]

The flier, "Please Consider These Words of Love My SIKH Friend," cited biblical passages and Sikh Scripture. It began,

Mool-Mantar says, "God is the Eternal Truth." If we were to agree on this, even as in John 14:6, the Lord Jesus Christ said, "I am the truth," then neither of us would be afraid of hearing the truth. Bible Christianity and Sikhism contradict in doctrine. Both could not at the same time be truth.[2]

Toward its conclusion, the flier warned,

Without believing in Jesus Christ, you, my Sikh friend, will die in your sins, and in so doing, will be condemned to Hell forever. Receive Jesus Christ alone as your Lord and Savior today, turning from your sin and your religion.[3]

A week later, a reporter from the *Contra Costa Times* contacted Brandenburg regarding the Sikh community's objections to the flier. The subsequent article quoted Mr. J. P. Singh, the president of the El Sobrante Gurdwara Sahib: "To coexist in this country in love and peace, I think there has to be an acceptance of other people's religions."[4] Singh objected to the content of the flier and questioned the appropriateness of seeking converts during the Peace Parade, saying, "I feel it would be offensive, if

---

[1] Kent Brandenburg, "My Sikh Issue: Pluralism versus Relativism," What Is Truth, July 12, 2007, https://kentbrandenburg.com/.

[2] "Please Consider These Words of Love My SIKH Friend," *Contra Costa Times*, August 27, 2006; available at https://pluralism.org/.

[3] Ibid.

[4] Tom Lochner, "Sikh Leader Objects to Pamphlet," *Contra Costa Times*, August 27, 2006, via Lexis-Nexis, accessed January 2009.

the Christians were having an event, to pass out Sikh literature."[5] Singh added that Sikhs do not seek converts, as they believe in the equality of all religions.

In the days and weeks after the parade, Brandenburg received many negative responses to the fliers, including several letters from the Sikh community. He also was contacted by a local businessman who ran Bianco's Deli, adjacent to the church. Mr. Bianco, having learned that some of the fliers were distributed from the deli parking lot, wrote to the gurdwara leadership and Brandenburg. Describing the flier's content as "hate speech," Bianco wrote, "I want you to know that I strongly condemn such attitudes, and I'm embarrassed and disappointed that my neighbors would treat you (also my neighbors) in such a manner."[6] In addition, the El Sobrante Municipal Advisory Committee publicly condemned the church's distribution of fliers at the parade.[7]

In the wake of the controversy, Brandenburg posed a series of questions on his blog, "What Is Truth?" He questioned the definition of hate speech and wondered how the peaceful distribution of materials could be seen as bullying. He asked about the limits of free speech and whether it would be likely that the town would permit a parade in which Bible verses were broadcast over loudspeakers, particularly if it was in front of a gurdwara.

Brandenburg added, "Jesus said, 'I am the way, the truth, and the life: no man cometh unto the Father, but by me.' That's exclusive, yes. It is also something that has been preached here since the first Pilgrims got off the Mayflower." He continued, "We can't be intellectually honest and not judge important things like what we believe about eternity.... Jesus told believers to warn about Hell in his kingdom parables in Matthew 13. If rejection of Christ results in Hell, we can't be loving by saying nothing. If we love health, we must hate disease. Truth is antithetical."[8]

Questions for Reflection

- Is Kent Brandenburg merely exercising his legal rights? Is the "marketplace of ideas" a sufficient approach to religious diversity?

---

[5] Ibid.
[6] Brandenburg, "My Sikh Issue."
[7] Ibid.
[8] Ibid.

- How do Kent Brandenburg's and J. P. Singh's theological approaches to religious diversity differ? What are the implications of each approach for civic pluralism?
- Are the historical, social, and political experiences of Sikhs as a religious minority in the United States relevant here? If so, how, and to what degree?
- How should a society that values freedom of religion and freedom of speech respond to unwanted or aggressive proselytization? How does the context affect the analysis (public vs. private venue, minority vs. majority religion, etc.)?

(B) Case

After the fliers were distributed at the Peace Parade, a Sikh organization offered a written response: a flier titled "Please Consider These Words of Love My CHRISTIAN Friend."[9] Following the model of the Christian flier, it asks, "Can the Guru Granth Sahib and the Bible, your book, contradict when they promote truthfulness?" Citing biblical passages and the Guru Granth Sahib, the flier contends, "On learning deeply the meanings in the Guru Granth Sahib, as well as the Bible, one will come to the conclusion that there is no contradiction of what 'true and truth' are, and how to benefit from it."

The flier explained, "Although Sikhism does not accept idol worship and rituals in the attempt to bribe God, Sikhism believes all should be respected and treated equally.... God is the home for all things to exist. Hell starts in this life. Hell is the condition of the soul." Later, it states, "The Bible teaches 'The kingdom of God is within you' (Luke 17:21). The value of human life, regardless of one's faith is valuable and worthy of God's unconditional love.... Only God is the true judge."

After articulating a range of theological similarities—and differences—the flier notes, "The Guru Granth Sahib does not compete with the Bible, for there is no reason to do so, but agrees on the need to spread truthfulness to the world." The flier concludes, "Let us cooperate and inspire each other to live truthful[ly] and encourage one another to better care for ourselves and others towards salvation, tranquility and success."

---

[9] All quotes from "Please Consider These Words of Love My CHRISTIAN Friend," *Contra Costa Times*, August 27, 2006; available at https://pluralism.org/.

The following year, Brandenburg noted, the Sikh parade drew a larger crowd—and greater resistance to the distribution of fliers. The angry response from some Sikhs was later characterized by Brandenburg as "breaking the law and impeding our right to free speech."[10] He wrote in his blog:

> We believe that truth is absolute, but since they don't, it shouldn't matter to them. They should see our beliefs in their own relative fashion, since that is how they view the world, and we will look at things in black and white, since that is how we view the world.
>
> Pluralism says that religions may coexist peacefully and still contest each other [ideologically], spiritually, and philosophically. Pluralism is strongly defended by the first amendment. We can believe and practice what we want in this country. This is also an honest and consistent approach. Two positions that contradict cannot both be true. They shouldn't be treated like they are both true, just for the sake of the relativist.
>
> … If you are true relativists, you should be happy that we can believe and practice as we wish. You should not encourage our belief and practice to be "stopped."[11]

Postscript

In El Sobrante, Sikhs referred to their procession as a "peace parade": to Sikhs, this observance is more commonly known as Nagar Kirtan.[12] As part of Nagar Kirtan, the Guru Granth Sahib (the Sikh Holy Scripture), is processed through the local community. Sikhs host parades in cities across the United States: the largest of these is in Yuba City, California, less than two hours from El Sobrante. Each year, Sikhs gather for a three-day festival in Yuba City, with as many as one hundred thousand people in attendance. The Yuba City Nagar Kirtan is said to be one of the largest gathering of Sikhs outside of South Asia.[13]

---

[10] Brandenburg, "My Sikh Issue."

[11] Ibid.

[12] "Nagar Kirtan," accessed February 28, 2023, https://www.sikhiwiki.org/.

[13] "Yuba City Sikh Parade," Pioneering Punjabis Digital Archive, accessed February 28, 2023, https://pioneeringpunjabis.ucdavis.edu/.

Dr. Rucha Kaur is among those who has travelled to Yuba City for the event. She attends both as a proud community member and as a grassroots organizer from the Sikh Coalition, a civil rights organization born in the days following September 11, 2001. Formed in a "moment of emergency"[14] as hate crimes surged against Sikh Americans, one of the organization's first decisions was how to respond to the fact that Sikhs were targeted because some perceived them to be Muslim. The Sikh Coalition resolved to deliver a message that no one should be targeted for their appearance or for their faith. Kaur reflects, "It's an opportunity to step up, to educate, to create awareness. It's an opportunity to come together in solidarity and community."[15]

For those with a visible external identity—including a turban or head scarf—Kaur notes, there are unique challenges as well as opportunities. She emphasizes,

> For Sikhs, the external identity is on purpose: Sikhs are meant to stand out, we are meant to be called upon. There's a strong sense of being called to serve and being recognized in times of crisis, as someone that can be depended on. So that external identity in my mind should never become a burden for Sikhs. It is meant to be a blessing.

More than twenty years after 9/11, and more than ten years after the massacre of Sikhs in Oak Creek, Wisconsin, Kaur regularly receives the question "Are things better for Sikhs now?" She replies,

> It really depends on what you mean by "better." Are there more resources, are we better connected, is there more representation from Sikhs in different spaces, where that representation is really crucial and important? Yes. Have Sikhs continued to be in the top-five most targeted communities in the country? Yes. When you adjust for population size, that's really problematic.

---

[14] "About Us," Sikh Coalition, accessed February 28, 2023, https://www.sikh-coalition.org/.

[15] All quotes from Rucha Kaur are from Zoom interview with the author, June 23, 2022.

Yet Kaur notes that many in the Sikh community want to move beyond the "post-9/11" frame and reject a "victim narrative." Kaur explains that, as a community that has been part of America since the early 1900s, and for one that values optimism and resilience, "agency is important." She emphasizes Sikh values in her outreach, including the central role of *seva*, or "selfless service." Most gurdwaras in the United States offer a weekly *langar*, a community meal free to all. She explains, "It's not rooted in the traditional understanding of charity. It's rooted in the understanding of equality: giving back and making sure that what you have you are spreading equally."

While proselytization is unwelcome, she explains, it is hardly a central issue for the Sikh American community today. Kaur feels this way even though she, herself, has experienced it. In 2019, while Kaur was attending the Nagar Kirtan in Yuba City, she was handed a flier about converting to Christianity. Kaur quickly dismissed it, thinking it must be an "anomaly." She, like most people at the event, "just kept walking." Later, she reflected, "Nagar Kirtan is the celebration of Sikh values, Sikh faith, and it's Sikhs coming together, in community.... You're at a celebration of the values of the faith telling people that their faith isn't valid." She adds, "Now do they not understand that, or do they understand that and still use this as an opportunity?"

When people knock on the door at Kaur's home seeking to convert her, she reflects, "I will say, 'I'm very comfortable in my faith, thank you very much,' and I shut the door." Kaur welcomes opportunities for constructive interfaith conversations, noting, "In my personal experience, nine interactions out of ten with people from other faiths have been very pleasant—in general, if they don't know about the Sikh faith, they are open to learning more and having that conversation." But, she adds with a laugh, "What I'm not willing to engage in is you telling me all the ways I'm going to hell, thank you very much. I'm cool."

Kaur warmly remembers her first Nagar Kirtan in New York City: "It's Madison Avenue, where on a daily basis you're not encountering all these Sikhs." That day, Kaur scanned the street and noticed that almost everyone looked like her, with many men wearing turbans. "And that sense of belonging, in a space that is our adopted home, I think is particularly special for those of us who have chosen a different place to make our lives." Kaur has friends who grew up in the United States who have participated in the Sikh Day Parade for more than twenty years: "They

remember being children, boarding buses going to New York City, participating in the parade. And now they are going with their children." The
Sikh Day Parade in New York City is an annual event that draws up to
thirty thousand people to Madison Avenue. At Sikh parades—whether in
New York, Yuba City, or El Sobrante—Kaur explains, "It creates a sense
of belonging in a world where you don't see yourself reflected every day."

Kaur left her home in India at age twenty-three to come to the United
States, packing up her world in three suitcases. She worked in another
field before becoming an advocate within the Sikh community. "I felt
called to do more. I was truly unhappy with the way the world was and I
wanted to do more. Now, I have a fifteen-month-old daughter, so the call
to serve is stronger." She reflects, "I hope that my daughter never has to
question her identity and she never has to question whether she belongs;
I feel like that's what I work for every day now."

Some twenty years later, Rev. Dr. Kent Brandenburg now lives in
southern Oregon, where he established another independent Baptist
church. Brandenburg's efforts to convert Sikhs are not unique: In 2019
the Lausanne Movement—inspired by Dr. Billy Graham and focused on
coordinating efforts for the global mission of Christianity—convened a
global consultation on Sikhism. The consultation identified "the need
and opportunity to present the Gospel to 27 million Sikhs in Punjab,
India and around the world."[16] Their objectives are: "to share research,
share resources, intercede and mobilize the Global Church to engage the
followers of Sikhism—the fifth largest organized religion in the world."

Proselytizing is a complex and contested issue in local interfaith relations—whether the campus or the community. Many universities, such
as Northeastern, have policies that expressly forbid "[p]roselytizing,
witness, or ministry that negatively impacts students."[17] This includes
"approaching individuals who have not themselves initiated contact."
When a new interfaith center opened at Johns Hopkins, the chaplain
explained the adaptations to their sacred space—removing pews and
using frosted glass to cover images in the stained-glass windows. As she

---

[16] All references to the Lausanne Movement, "Lausanne Consultation
Addresses Reaching Sikhs," Global Diaspora Network, December 15, 2019, https://
www.global-diaspora.com/.

[17] Northeastern University Center for Spirituality, Dialogue, and Service,
"Student Groups," accessed February 28, 2023, https://spirituallife.north-
eastern.edu/.

described the Interfaith Council, the chaplain noted, "Our only rule is no proselytizing. Other than that, we talk about everything."[18]

A similar current is evident in grassroots interfaith groups. Interfaith Partners of South Carolina advises, "Interfaith occasions are never the place to proselytize for one's own religion. It's perfectly appropriate to invite others to visit your services and events, but advancing your religion as a preferred alternative is highly disrespectful."[19] From the earliest conversations at the Tri-Faith Initiative—an effort to co-locate a mosque, synagogue, and church in Omaha, Nebraska—the problem of proselytization was identified. Rev. Chris Alexander, former minister at Countryside Community Church, explained, "The primary agreement among the three faith traditions is that there will be NO attempts to proselytize between the faiths." Yet, Alexander added,

> Evangelism is different from proselytizing in that we are witnesses to, and messengers for, God's story from our own experiences. We are encouraged to tell the stories of our faith traditions to each other, but not for the purposes of conversion. Rather, our purpose is to share how each of our traditions brings joy to each of our respective communities.[20]

This distinction is one shared by Interfaith America, a national organization that has taken an intentional approach toward engaging Evangelicals in interfaith spaces. They note, "Christians play a critical role in shaping American civil society and culture, yet Evangelicals as an identity group are often stereotyped and weaponized in today's polarized discourse."[21] Amber Hacker, Interfaith America's COO, developed guidelines for campus interfaith groups seeking to bridge the gap to Evangelicals. These start with "Affirm[ing] the importance of evan-

[18] Michael Hill, "Religion Finds a Place on Secular Campuses: In Age of Diversity, Students Worship at Interfaith Centers," *Baltimore Sun*, November 30, 1998, 1A.

[19] Interfaith Partners of South Carolina, "Resources: Religious and Cultural Sensitivity," accessed April 19, 2023, https://interfaithpartnersofsc.org/resources/religious-and-cultural-sensitivity/.

[20] Chris Alexander, "The Tri-Faith Initiative," *Missiology: An International Review* 47, no. 1 (January 13, 2019): 25.

[21] Interfaith America, "Evangelicals and Interfaith Engagement," YouTube, February 22, 2022.

gelizing." Hacker, who identifies as Christian and was raised in an Evangelical family, writes,

> In the Christian Bible it says to "go into the world and preach the gospel to all creation" (Mark 16:15). Sharing the work and salvation of Jesus Christ is a key component of Christian belief and practices and recognizing this is important to understanding the values of evangelical students, staff, and faculty in interfaith groups. Indeed, many groups have a missional (or evangelizing) focus at times, including Catholics, Muslims, Mormons, and Baháʼís. All members of an interfaith group should respect the motivating values of each other, evangelical or otherwise, and avoid harmful stereotyping of certain practices.

While Hacker's guidelines affirm that interfaith work isn't an appropriate space for proselytizing, she offers an important reminder: "Indeed, interfaith cooperation exists not because people believe the same things, but because they don't."[22]

---

[22] Amber Hacker, "Evangelical Christians in Interfaith Cooperation," Interfaith America, accessed February 28, 2023, https://www.interfaithamerica.org.

Part 4

Mosques in the American Landscape

A Mosque in Palos Heights

Mayor Dean Koldenhoven didn't have much experience as a politician when he first heard about the mosque coming to Palos Heights, Illinois. He did not know much about the Al Salam Mosque Foundation community or their religious tradition, or why the residents of Palos Heights seemed to be so angry and afraid. He did know that his own tradition taught him to "love your neighbor as yourself." Koldenhoven, a down-to-earth former bricklayer, knew that he needed more information—and the help of local pastors. At the time, Palos Heights had eleven houses of worship: all of them Christian churches. With a petition making the rounds, it became clear that most in his small Illinois town opposed the sale of the church to a Muslim organization. What resources might be helpful to him as he navigates this controversy? How might he address the fear and anger? Is it appropriate for him to engage the town's pastors? What is at stake for Mayor Koldenhoven, and for the citizens of Palos Heights—including its Muslim citizens?

(A) Case

Dean Koldenhoven has the large, weathered hands of a former bricklayer; the long, distinct name of his Dutch ancestry; and the colorful bolo ties of a man who likes to do things his own way. Koldenhoven enjoyed being mayor in a city with a small-town atmosphere, where people know each other by their first names. Many people in Palos Heights, Illinois, referred to him simply as "Mayor Dean."

After many years of working in construction, Koldenhoven was appointed to serve as the city's zoning commissioner. He knew the construction trades and had a straightforward, no-nonsense attitude. After eight years working with an increasingly divided city council,

Koldenhoven ran for mayor. He was elected in a close race: the margin of victory was just 156 votes. But, Koldenhoven joked, "It only takes one vote to win."[1]

In March 2000 Koldenhoven started hearing some talk around Palos Heights, rumors mostly: "word on the street" was that Arabs were going to buy the Reformed Church of Palos Heights. It wasn't clear who exactly these people were, but it was clear from the rumors that they were not welcome in Palos Heights. Koldenhoven began receiving phone calls and letters from concerned citizens, asking, "What are you going to do about this?"

Palos Heights

Palos Heights, Illinois, is a small bedroom community in the southwestern suburbs of Chicago, with a population of just over twelve thousand. Bordered by a forest preserve, the small city is a grid of leafy neighborhoods with neat, upper middle-class homes. Many of the city's residents are of Dutch ancestry, affiliated with the Reformed Church of America and the Christian Reformed Church; in addition, a large and active Catholic parish serves the city's Irish American population. Unlike many cities in the southwestern suburbs of Chicago, including neighboring Bridgeview with its large Islamic Center and School, Palos Heights was not known for its diversity: in the year 2000, of the eleven houses of worship in the small city, all were Christian.

In the city's official publication, *View from the Heights*, Koldenhoven wrote a Christmas message to the city:

> Over the past several weeks, my wife and I have been worshipping in the eleven churches that are in the Palos Heights city limits. It has been a very enlightening experience. Although we all worship in a different manner, we have one thing in common, we all worship the same Lord Jesus Christ, whose birthday we celebrate on the 25th of December. I find it amazing that as a town of 12,188 people, we have eleven churches, what a blessing![2]

---

[1] All quotes from Dean Koldenhoven in (A) and (B) cases are from interview with the author, Palos Heights, IL, October 27 and 28, 2005.

[2] Dean Koldenhoven, "We Are Blessed," *View from the Heights* 12, no. 4 (Winter 1999): 1.

The Reformed Church of Palos Heights was one of the five churches situated along the city's main thoroughfare of 127th Street. The Reformed Church's ties to the city were long and deep: some residents say that the plans for the church existed before the city was incorporated in 1959. Palos Heights was home to other Christian Reform institutions, including Trinity Christian College and Back to God Ministries, a local media group. Many kids growing up in Palos Heights came to the Reformed Church for some of the city's recreational programs: with its central location and large gym, it was a natural fit.

Under the leadership of Pastor Peter Semeyn, the congregation at the Reformed Church had grown to over eight hundred parishioners. Their beloved brick church building had become too small, so the Reformed Church community made the difficult decision to sell the building. Before putting the property on the market, church leadership inquired with the city of Palos Heights to see if the library or recreation department could use the building. After many meetings and an informal feasibility study by the Parks and Recreation Department, the city chose not to pursue the purchase. The space wasn't ideal for their needs, and the city didn't have the budget to renovate the church property. After a year and a half of informal explorations, the Reformed Church of Palos Heights hired a real estate agent and listed the church for sale.

They received three bids and accepted the highest one. The Al Salam Mosque Foundation offered a purchase price of $2.1 million. As was common in major real estate transactions, it was contingent on funding; more unique, perhaps, was the contingency that the buyer would receive written verification from the City of Palos Heights that the building could be used as a mosque and a school. The Reformed Church signed the contract on March 15, 2000.

A Letter to the Pastors

Everyone in Palos Heights seemed to be talking about the sale of the church, and Koldenhoven didn't like the tenor of what he was hearing: much of it seemed to be rumor and fear. He received numerous phone calls and letters from citizens telling him to stop the purchase of the church. Koldenhoven didn't know much about the Al Salam Mosque Foundation and was unclear what religion the group actually practiced; he decided to do some research. He stopped by the offices of a local

Christian media group and picked up some copies of their introductory flier about Islam.

On April 11, 2000, Koldenhoven sat down and wrote a letter to every pastor in his town. Printed on City of Palos Heights stationery, the letter began, "There is the possibility that the Reformed Church on 127th Street (across from the Palos Heights Recreation Center) might be sold to an 'Arab' buyer." He expressed his interest in making "a peaceful transition" and avoiding any intimidation or violence. He wrote,

> What concerns me is all the negative racial and ethnic remarks I am hearing. I hear these remarks both on the street and by people calling me on the phone.... What is important is that as a people living in a blessed community, we must let these "new" people know that they are welcome to worship wherever they want to. That is the first amendment to the Bill of Rights (Free Exercise Thereof).
>
> More importantly is when something of this magnitude comes to our community (an Arab religion that is anti-Christian in nature) I ask myself, "What would Jesus do?" The Jesus I know would say, "Welcome to Palos Heights." There is a hymn that is worded, "They will know we are Christians by our love, by our love." I believe that if we live up to these words, God will bless us for treating these newcomers as welcome neighbors. This could be a time that as Christians we will be put to the test as to what it means to live our Christian faith and beliefs.

He asked the pastors to preach sermons on this matter, and reminded them, "Palos Heights already has many 'Arabs' living here and nothing has changed."[3] Enclosed in each letter was a flier about Islam.

At the same time, Koldenhoven wanted to reach out to the leaders of the Al Salam Mosque Foundation. He spoke with Father Cronin, the new priest at St. Alexander's Catholic Church, and together they extended an invitation to the leaders of Al Salam to meet at the city hall. The meeting was brief, but friendly; Koldenhoven shared some of the fliers he had sent out to the pastors and was pleased to have the opportunity to extend a hand to the Muslim community.

---

[3] Dean Koldenhoven to the Pastors of Palos Heights, letter regarding sale of the Reformed Church, April 11, 2000; in author's possession.

A Meeting at City Hall, May 16

After many weeks of rumors, and amid rumblings of opposition, residents were eager to voice their concerns at the May 16 city council meeting. Before the meeting, one neighbor commented to a local newspaper: "I think our town is being taken over by the Mideastern people. I think our town is going downhill, not prospering."[4]

The mayor opened the meeting as he always did: "Each in their own way, ask for guidance," followed by a moment of silence. Alderman Julie Corsi noted that she received a certified letter regarding the contract for the sale of the Reformed Church. Rouhy Shalabi, legal representative of the Al Salam Mosque Foundation, requested written verification that the church's special-use permit to operate in a residential area would transfer with the building. Corsi explained that the city would not issue such a letter: "As in other instances, let the buyer beware."[5]

Koldenhoven read the minutes from Recreation Committee meetings held in 1998, which mentioned the sale of the church property, reviewed the feasibility, and stated the decision to not pursue the purchase. He wanted this to be a matter of record. After extensive discussion, Corsi inquired if the city could make a bid to purchase the church property with a contract for sale pending. The city attorney advised against this course of action. Corsi asked about the process of condemning the church property, and the city attorney replied that this suit could be filed if the property in question is required for a public purpose. Corsi moved to authorize the attorney to draft an ordinance that would call for the condemnation of the Reformed Church for public benefit, but the motion failed.

After a brief recess, citizens spoke: one resident addressed the council directly, saying, "I've got to be honest, folks, I don't want a mosque in my neighborhood.... I've seen what [it's] done to other neighborhoods, and I don't want that [to] happen to my property values."[6] He then asked that the city rescind the special-use permit for the church. A prominent local lawyer, and neighbor of Koldenhoven's, offered praise for what he described as the "energy and creativity" in evidence at the meeting. He

---

[4] "Proposed Heights Mosque Packs Council Meeting," *The Reporter* (Palos Heights, IL), May 18, 2000, 3.

[5] Minutes of the Regular Meeting of the City Council, City of Palos Heights, May 16, 2000.

[6] "Proposed Heights Mosque Packs Council Meeting."

added that the city might look at Al Salam's request to use the building as a school as one means to question the special use. An executive session was called to discuss litigation and acquisition of property, and the meeting was adjourned less than twenty minutes later.[7]

Planning and Zoning Committee Meeting, May 23

Koldenhoven was increasingly concerned that some aldermen, with whom he had long-term conflicts, saw the issue of the mosque as a political opportunity. The vast majority of those in Palos Heights were expressing strong opposition. Given the tone of the May 16 council meeting, Koldenhoven called Shalabi to ask him to attend the next zoning meeting and suggested that he bring members of the Muslim community. Koldenhoven believed that his role was to run the meetings according to *Robert's Rules of Order*, not to offer comments on the content; however, he wanted to be sure that Muslims were being represented, so that they could respond directly to the issues that were being raised.

Planning and Zoning Committee meetings in Palos Heights were occasionally contentious, but rarely well-attended. Meetings generally drew a few citizens from Palos Heights, but on May 23, the small brick city hall was overflowing. Alderman Corsi invited Shalabi to speak about Al Salam's plans for the building. Shalabi explained, "The mosque is a church whose members are Muslim and it's like any other church. People come there to worship." He explained that there would be weekend schools, but they would not have a full-time school. "There already exists a structure there. There's a church there, and we would be using that same property to practice our religion."

In response to concerns about traffic and parking, Shalabi added, "Our busiest days are Friday afternoon from 12 to 2 p.m. That's our Sunday. That's the day that Muslims gather to pray together generally. There are two holidays in the year." He explained that one of the contingencies in the contract with the church was a letter from the city of Palos Heights indicating that the church could be used as a mosque and school.

Alderman Corsi opened the discussion to the committee, and Shalabi began fielding questions. Some aldermen encouraged Shalabi to make a

---

[7] Minutes of the Regular Meeting of the City Council, City of Palos Heights, May 16, 2000.

formal application for a special-use permit. Alderman Murphy noted that his main concern was not related to the mosque, but rather that the city didn't have an opportunity to purchase the church to meet local recreational needs. He explained that those who opposed the purchase of the church shared this concern. "That's what most people here were talking about last Tuesday night. That was their main concern. I don't think anyone spoke out against you."

When Corsi opened the discussion to the citizens, diverse concerns were raised: How would this impact traffic on 127th Street? What is the size of your congregation? Where is the $2.1 million coming from? Would a call to prayer be broadcast? As the comments began to take on a more accusatory tone, Shalabi's replies became more defensive. Shalabi explained that there were already Muslims in Palos Heights, and said, "By the way, you have twenty churches here and I'm not sure you need twenty churches here but that's not my business. But we don't even have one mosque here for a large Muslim community that's entitled to have a place of worship if it so chooses. I don't see anyone questioning the traffic when it comes to the churches in this community."

One resident, who stated at the previous meeting that he didn't want a mosque in his neighborhood, pursued the traffic issue: "That noon to 2 p.m. period when there would be worship at the mosque is actually one of the busiest times ever in the Rec Department. . . . As for the traffic situation, you are looking at a different entity as far as the influx of traffic from the mosque as compared to the other churches which worship on Sunday." Another resident raised the issue of changes to the exterior of the building: "Right now that building fits in well with the neighborhood. It doesn't stand out." Although Shalabi offered assurances that there would be no dome, and that "we want to fit in," another citizen weighed in: "Everyone is kind of sugarcoating. There's obviously a little opposition. . . . Two million dollars is a lot of money. I think that's a risky investment."

Corsi stated that Al Salam would need to have a public hearing for the special-use permit. "I think we are dealing with a big difference. We are not really going from a church to a church. We are going from a church to something different." When Shalabi asked how the mosque was different, Corsi replied, "I think, when we look at Palos Heights, we do have other churches. You are absolutely correct. . . . However, just about all of them practice on Sundays." She argued, "What you are proposing is, like, upside down. . . . It is kind of like comparing apples and oranges.

I believe that you are still looking for a house of worship, that you are not looking for a church per se, you are looking for a different kind of entity that I think should be ruled on its own merits."

Shalabi responded, "Those who worship in synagogues, their big day is Saturday as opposed to Sunday. I think we need to be sensitive to religions that are other than our own and respect them, and I don't believe that's a basis for you to say that we are any different than any other religious institution that's in this village."

Corsi replied, "I don't think I meant to say that you per se were any different in your belief than anyone else's. I think the usage is a different type of usage." She explained, "If your congregation was coming and going on Sunday, this wouldn't even be an issue." She affirmed that his faith was as important as any other faith, but also that he would need to apply for a special-use permit. Corsi noted, "I have been chairman of this committee for seven years. I have never issued a letter to anyone one way or another. That is why we have public hearings. You schedule a hearing. You get your opinion right then and there."

Shalabi inquired as to whether other churches in the community have had to apply for a special-use permit, and Secretary Larson indicated that all of the churches became special uses from 1985 on, and there hasn't been a new church since that ordinance was changed. Shortly after, the meeting was adjourned.[8]

Meeting of the City Council of Palos Heights, June 6

Two weeks later, on June 6, hundreds of people once again packed Palos Heights' city hall. The council chambers were full, and people spilled out into the hallway. The mood was tense. After a moment of reflection and brief city business, citizens began addressing the council. One of the first to speak was the prominent local lawyer who had spoken at the previous city council meeting. He said that it was inaccurate to describe the people of Palos Heights as bigoted, citing the "legitimate"[9] concerns about the size of the mosque and traffic. He presented a stack of petitions to the clerk that urged the city to purchase the Reformed Church property by whatever

---

[8] All quotes from the Transcript of Planning & Zoning Committee Meeting, City of Palos Heights, May 23, 2000.

[9] Minutes of the Regular Meeting of the City Council, City of Palos Heights, June 6, 2000.

means are available to them, including the power of eminent domain. If the city purchased the church, he added, they could rent the sanctuary to the mosque. He noted that the freedom of religion is our most important freedom, but that the issue at hand was the need for recreation.

Another citizen, who had walked door to door with petitions, said that residents of Palos Heights want the church for recreational purposes. He encouraged the council to act with the majority, not according to their own personal views. He emphasized that the mayor should pay particular attention to the views expressed in the petitions. After some talk of the traffic impact, a tall, lanky, and soft-spoken English professor made his way to the microphone. Michael Vander Weele asked, "I have a simple question for us all, and that is where was the energy, where was the eloquence, where were we before we learned that the church might be turned into a mosque?"[10]

Alderman Healy suggested that the attorneys for the city, the church, and the mosque meet to discuss how they might resolve the matter. The council voted, and the city attorney was authorized to enter negotiations. After more discussion, Murphy made a motion to authorize the city attorney to offer the Al Salam Mosque Foundation reasonable attorney fees if it would withdraw its contract to purchase the Reformed Church. The motion carried. Finally, Murphy made a motion to move the next city council meeting to the Recreation Center gym; the motion carried. Shortly thereafter, the meeting adjourned.[11]

A Column by Phil Kadner

After the June 6 meeting, a local newspaper columnist interviewed some of the key players in the dispute. The *Daily Southtown* published Phil Kadner's column, "Battle over Mosque Puts City in Spotlight" on June 9, 2000:

> Discrimination and religious bigotry exist in the best of communities. Sometimes the signs of prejudice are evident. More often, people hide behind excuses that almost sound legitimate on the surface. In Palos Heights, the Al Salam Mosque Foundation has signed a contract to buy an existing church building for $2.1

[10] Janice Neumann, "Council Pursues Purchase of Church: Mosque on Hold in Palos Heights," *Chicago Tribune*, June 7, 2000.

[11] Minutes of the Regular Meeting of the City Council, City of Palos Heights, June 6, 2000.

million. More than 1,700 residents signed petitions urging city officials to buy the church and turn it into a recreation center. Some city officials in response are threatening to use the city's powers of eminent domain to take possession of the land if the Mosque Foundation attempts to enforce its contract.

In the piece, Kadner asked Murphy if the use of eminent domain was fair. Murphy replied, "If someone had intervened early on to stop Adolf Hitler, there might not have been a world war." After this quote, the reporter added, "I told the alderman he had used a very poor analogy. But he did not retract his words." The column quoted Koldenhoven: "They're [opponents of the mosque] hiding behind a veil of hypocrisy, because there was no interest at all until the mosque came in." Corsi commented, "A political leader should not add fuel to the fire. . . . The mayor has unjustly labeled this entire community racist. He's wrong." Kadner's column ended with a challenge: "City residents claim they are not motivated by bigotry and prejudice. Now is the time to prove it."[12]

Second Letter to the Pastors, June 12

Since the crisis began, Koldenhoven had been in conversations with local pastors, including Reverend Hamstra from his own Christian Reformed Church, Reverend Semeyn from the Reformed Church, and Father Cronin from St. Alexander's, each of whom was actively teaching and preaching within their own communities on this issue. After the most recent council meeting, with tensions mounting in Palos Heights, Koldenhoven sent a second letter to the pastors on June 12, 2000:

> I implore you to preach a sermon or sermons on this scripture that I am enclosing with this letter. The community of Palos Heights is going through a rough time right now because of the impending sale of the Reformed Church of Palos Heights. Because of fears, ignorance, and bigots spreading their hate-filled words to their neighbors, and yes, even aldermen of this City . . . the hatred is spreading. I believe this is because they are not

---

[12] Phil Kadner, "Battle over Mosque Puts City in Spotlight," *Daily Southtown* (Chicago, IL), June 9, 2000.

hearing the Word of Jesus Christ as found in Matthew 22:35–40: ["One of them, an expert in the law, tested him with this question: 'Teacher, which is the greatest commandment in the law?' Jesus replied, 'Love the Lord your God with all your heart and with all your soul and with all your mind.' This is the first and greatest commandment. And the second is like it: 'Love your neighbor as yourself.' All the Law and the Prophets hang on these two commandments."]

Koldenhoven's letter continued, "I personally feel that we are being tested as a basically Christian community as to how we will welcome our new neighbors."[13]

A Letter to the Editor, June 18

In the spring of 2000, at every Little League ball game, church picnic, and community event in Palos Heights, the Reformed Church purchase was a topic of conversation. Most residents focused on the need for recreational facilities in the city; few dissenting voices were heard. On June 18, 2000, local newspapers printed a letter to the editor from a longtime citizen of Palos Heights, Sandy Broadbent. She noted the irony that local citizens were arguing to block Al Salam in front of Norman Rockwell paintings on the wall of city hall, depicting the "four freedoms"—including the freedom of religion. Her letter stated, in part,

> Residents seem to have completely disassociated themselves from any issues of racial or religious bias. And disassociation from the truth is a terrifying reality.
>
> There is a larger issue here than the issue of a mosque in Palos Heights. Democratic principles are at stake as well as the future of the world we want our children to inherit. While we cannot always be responsible for our thoughts, I believe that we ought to be responsible for how we behave and we ought to behave in accordance with ethical principles. If we lose our vigilance regarding freedom of expression, we just may lose our freedoms.[14]

---

[13] Dean Koldenhoven to the Pastors of Palos Heights, letter regarding suggested sermon on Matthew 22:35–40, June 12, 2000; in author's possession.

[14] Sandy Broadbent, "Palos Issues Clouded," *Chicago Sun-Times*, June 18, 2000.

Meeting at the Recreation Center, June 20

The next meeting of the Palos Heights City Council was held on June 20 at the Rec Center, across the street from the Reformed Church on 127th Street. The venue had changed to accommodate the growing crowds, but the mood remained similar to that of previous meetings: tense, charged, and sometimes hostile. That night, there were some 450 people in attendance, including a large contingent of media. The story was beginning to attract national attention, and the small city of Palos Heights was becoming known as "Palos Hates."

Walking into the meeting that summer evening, Koldenhoven heard a string of insults and felt the stares like "shooting daggers." It had been the same for weeks. The former bricklayer had a thick skin and had heard plenty of rough language when he worked in construction; he knew better than to show that they were getting to him. Koldenhoven was aware that the Muslims coming to the meeting were receiving the same threatening glares. He arranged for a plainclothes police officer to be in attendance, as he had for the previous meetings. Years before, he had taken a course on *Robert's Rules of Order* and knew that contentious meetings can suddenly become violent.

The meeting began with regular business and moved to communications from the aldermen. Corsi said that she had received many calls and letters from citizens and felt that the city needed to purchase the Reformed Church to meet its recreational needs. She added that members of all religions are welcome in Palos Heights. The first citizen to address the council noted that the church has been for sale for two years and wondered about the city's "sudden"[15] need to purchase the property. She also offered an analogy: in Lorraine Hansberry's play, *A Raisin in the Sun*, the neighbors of a Black family try to buy them out as a means to prevent integration in their Chicago neighborhood. Perhaps, she wondered, something similar was happening in Palos Heights.

An array of speakers from the Muslim community added their voices, including the president of the Mosque Foundation of Bridgeview and Shalabi. A Muslim resident of Palos Heights stated, "We are not going to create any problems. We are here to stay. We have full rights and are going to enjoy them. We are living in the United States of America."[16]

---

[15] Minutes of the Regular Meeting of the City Council, City of Palos Heights, June 20, 2000.
[16] "Heights Offers $200,000 to Make Mosque Go Away," *The Reporter* (Palos Heights, IL), June 22, 2000, 1.

Sandy Broadbent, a longtime resident of Palos Heights who had written a letter to the editor, addressed the council wearing an "I love Palos Heights" T-shirt. She emphasized the need to speak the truth about the conflict. She reminded those gathered about the discrimination that Irish immigrants faced just a few generations ago, and concluded, "I don't know what the solution is for the Recreation Department needs. I do know that I'd rather raise my kids in a community with no recreational facilities than in a community that obscures the truth and disallows the right to freedom of religious expression. What about you?"[17]

The majority spoke against the mosque. One woman raised the issue of assimilation: why, she asked, do Muslim women dress in that way? Another citizen said that the people of Palos Heights are not bigots and racists and blamed the mayor for this perception in the media; the issue is recreation. Others echoed this concern, saying it was unfair to cast this dispute as racist, when the real concerns were about recreation, parking, and traffic.

One speaker expressed his concern that Palos Heights now has a bad name, just because they are concerned about what type of people come into town. He noted that, as a born-again Christian, he doesn't force his beliefs on other communities, and doesn't believe "these people" should come into his community and tell him what to do. He stated that he would not come into a community if he wasn't wanted there. The speaker's concluding comments included the phrase, "Go back to your own countries."

Corsi called an executive session at 10:45 p.m. When the meeting reconvened, discussions turned to plans for the city's July 4 celebrations, authorizations for block parties, and road repairs. Then a motion was made to authorize the city attorney to offer the Al Salam Mosque Foundation two hundred thousand dollars to cover its expenses and allow the city to purchase the Reformed Church. The motion passed: the vote was five to three.[18]

The meeting, which began at 8:00 p.m., finally ended close to midnight. Koldenhoven was depressed. He got into his truck, drove home, and went to bed, but he couldn't sleep. He simply couldn't believe

---

[17] Sandy Broadbent, written speech delivered at the Regular Meeting of the City Council, City of Palos Heights, June 20, 2000; in author's possession.
[18] Minutes of the Regular Meeting of the City Council, City of Palos Heights, June 20, 2000.

what had happened at the meeting that night: so many hurtful things were said. He felt the two-hundred-thousand-dollar offer was an insult, and that, as mayor, he owed the Muslims an apology for the way the council had voted. This was not the only matter keeping Koldenhoven awake: his thirty-five-year-old son, Don, diagnosed with terminal cancer a few months earlier, was increasingly ill. Koldenhoven tossed and turned.

A Letter to the Al Salam Mosque Foundation

The next morning, Koldenhoven went into his office before 6:00 a.m. to compose a letter of apology. He wrote, "Please convey my thanks and also my apologies to all Islamic faith people. To you and to all of your Islamic people, you have my highest respect." He praised those who spoke out at the council meeting for their eloquence and courage, and continued,

> The formal offer to your Mosque Foundation of $200,000 to step aside was not only an insult but a disgrace. Please forgive us, I would encourage you to proceed with the sale of this property. I can't wait for the day you take ownership! I welcome you into our City and hope that I can address your congregation with that welcome. It would be an honor to be with your Islamic people.
>
> My apologies for the insulting remarks that some residents made, and also for the council's action.[19]

Responses from Local Clergy

On June 29, a local newspaper, *The Reporter*, contacted Palos Heights' pastors to inquire about the impact of the mosque controversy on congregations. Most noted that it wasn't a matter of open discussion within their community but affirmed that, as Christians, they have a responsibility to love their neighbors. Others described the mosque as an opportunity to share Christ with new Muslim neighbors.

Father Cronin of St. Alexander's Catholic Church stated that he was working within his community to address fears and, more widely, to build interfaith bridges. He noted, "We should welcome and honor diversity, because that's the reality of the world. I would think Christ's

---

[19] Dean Koldenhoven to Rouhy Shalabi, letter regarding an apology following an offer made by the City Council, June 21, 2000; in author's possession.

prayer is more realized, that we start living together as one, when we welcome people who are different. We don't have to agree with them, but we should welcome them."[20] Together with Koldenhoven, Cronin was working on "relational meetings" between Christians and Muslims in the area. Father Cronin explained, "We have to lead the way.... We have to show that Christianity is not about closing the door."[21]

Adding Fuel to the Fire: A "False Religion"

On June 26, 2000, with the controversy making national news, Koldenhoven, Shalabi, Murphy, and Karen Hayes were invited to discuss the issue on *Chicago Tonight*, a public television program. Hayes, the coordinator of the National Day of Prayer in Palos Heights, was among those who openly opposed the mosque. Hayes stated that she does not object to individual Muslims living in Palos Heights, but she does object to "false religions" coming into Palos Heights. She explained, "Theologically, I'm a Christian, and that means there's only one God, and I do believe that.... So, obviously, if a false religion is coming to town, I would be a hypocrite to say I didn't have stirrings of concern there."[22]

Those statements drew an outraged response from many observers. Koldenhoven later said, "How much do these people have to take? That's not representative of the Christian faith. 'Love God and love thy neighbor' are two of the greatest commandments from Christ. That's Christianity in a nutshell." Alderman Murphy defended Hayes, while affirming the right of all people to worship. He stated, "That's Karen's deep-felt belief.... I don't believe she means anything malicious by it. She believes Christianity is the one true religion." Edward Hassan, a longtime Muslim resident of Palos Heights, commented, "I think people like [Hayes] have so much love for their religion that they just turn against other religions.... We have fanatics in our religion too. But, in fact, God is one god for all religions, and nobody can prove otherwise."[23]

---

[20] "Local Clergy Reacts to Mosque Controversy," *The Reporter* (Palos Heights, IL), June 29, 2000, 26.

[21] Darlene Gavron Stevens, "Churches Act to Heal Rift: Christians and Muslims to Meet," *Chicago Tribune*, June 30, 2000, 1.

[22] Stanley Ziemba and Janice Neumann, "TV Comment Adds Fuel to Mosque Controversy: Palos Resident Calls Islam 'False Religion,'" *Chicago Tribune*, June 28, 2000, 1.

[23] Ibid.

The Passing of Don Koldenhoven, July 10

Koldenhoven's son Don passed away on July 10, 2000, at the age of thirty-five, following a short but intense battle with cancer. The Koldenhoven family was devastated: Don left behind a young widow and two small children. For Dean Koldenhoven, the loss was even harder to bear at a time of great personal and professional crisis. Many times, his wife, Ruth, had encouraged him to resign from his duties as mayor. But Koldenhoven, who took much solace from his son during the dispute, wanted to follow his son's example: if Don could show such bravery, calm, and clear thinking in the face of death, Koldenhoven thought, he could handle the dispute over the mosque.

The Koldenhoven family held Don's funeral at the Palos Heights Christian Reformed Church. Reverend Sam Hamstra led the service, which was attended by many of the key players in the mosque dispute, including Shalabi. Father Cronin spoke at the service: he had become a friend to the Koldenhoven family in their personal crisis and a support to the mayor in his efforts to welcome the mosque to the city. In Palos Heights, for a Catholic priest to speak at a Christian Reformed church was not just unique, it was groundbreaking. In a time of considerable sadness, the service offered some solace: it seemed as if bridges could be built across difference, and that coming together was more important than anything dividing the community.

An Offer Accepted, July 13

On July 13, 2000, Shalabi sent a letter by fax and regular mail to the city's clerk, mayor, city council, and city attorney, which stated, "Please be advised that on behalf of the Al-Salam Mosque Foundation, your June 20, 2000, offer of Two-Hundred Thousand ($200,000.00) Dollars is hereby accepted."[24] A copy of this letter was sent to the lawyer for the Reformed Church. Shalabi held a press conference in front of city hall to announce Al Salam's acceptance of the offer; his tone was conciliatory.

---

[24] Rouhy J. Shalabi to Dean Koldenhoven et al., letter regarding acceptance of offer, July 13, 2000; in author's possession.

Special Meeting Convened, July 14

At 1 p.m. on Friday, July 14, the city council convened a special meeting: they were joined by hundreds of citizens and members of the media. Koldenhoven wasn't in the mood for any "shenanigans," so close after the death of his son. He felt that the timing was no mere coincidence: the meeting had been called by those who wanted the offer to go through. If Koldenhoven were absent, there was no risk of a veto: an alderman would be named as mayor pro tem and the council would approve the two-hundred-thousand-dollar payment to the Mosque Foundation. Koldenhoven said, "They didn't figure on me showing up."

Still deeply grieving, he came to the meeting but made no remarks about his recent loss: he wanted to get down to business and get the meeting over with. Koldenhoven knew that, according to the rules, any decision about the offer could only be made at the next scheduled meeting. As he entered the room, he saw Michael Vander Weele, who had spoken up at a previous meeting. Vander Weele looked directly at him, raised his fist in the air, and said, "*Sterkte!*" Koldenhoven understood the meaning and the intent: it was the Dutch word for strength.

Alderman Murphy stated that a special meeting had been called to move forward with the offer, rather than waiting until the next regular meeting, because the attorney for Al Salam was going out of town and they were eager to have the matter settled. Alderman Fulkerson moved to defer, and Alderman Kamarski seconded: the motion would be deferred to the next regular council meeting.

The first citizen to address the council was Omar Najib, who offered condolences to the mayor on the death of his son and expressed his dismay that this meeting was called so soon after the funeral. He asked the council to make a statement to disassociate itself from the comments about Islam being a "false religion," and described the offer to Al Salam as a "bribe." Najib asked the council to vote its dignity, and for Al Salam to not accept the money.

A range of comments followed: some blamed the mayor, saying he shouldn't have spoken negatively about the city. Others argued that the offer wasn't a bribe, because there was a real need for recreation. Others praised the aldermen who had spearheaded the effort to buy the church and called upon the council to settle the matter that day. In addition, some of the aldermen addressed the council as private citizens: Murphy apologized to Shalabi and the Muslim community for making an analogy to Hitler. Corsi refused to address Koldenhoven as "Mayor," stating that he had spoken badly about the citizens of Palos Heights.

Unlike the earlier meetings, most of the citizens were now expressing embarrassment and dismay: some spoke out in support of the mayor and against those who had made bigoted remarks; others questioned the fiscal responsibility of the decision. One citizen stated that children didn't need expensive facilities for recreation and asked that the city "cut the baloney." Others argued for the right of Muslims to have a place of worship. One woman said that the calls for recreation were a "smoke screen," and urged the mayor to veto the offer.[25]

Toward the end of the meeting, Edward Hassan spoke. He explained that, as a Muslim and a resident of Palos Heights for thirty years, he was embarrassed—not to live in Palos Heights, but for Palos Heights. He voiced concerns about the finances, the potential for a lawsuit, and the ways in which personal and political agendas had fueled the dispute. He reminded the aldermen of "the silent majority" and the fact that some five hundred Muslims already lived in Palos Heights. Hassan described the offer from the city as an insult to the Muslims. He said, with sadness, "If you look deep in your hearts, you don't want a mosque here."[26]

The special meeting adjourned just over an hour after it began; they would reconvene for the regularly scheduled meeting in just four days. On July 18, 2000, a decision would need to be made.

A Postcard Received

Awash in grief and controversy, Koldenhoven hit his lowest point when he received a postcard at city hall a few days after his son's funeral. The picture on the front was nondescript; the message on the back read, in part, "They buried the wrong Koldenhoven." He closed his office door, put on Aretha Franklin's Gospel music loud enough to drown out the sound, and cried. He told himself, "'Toughen up Dean, get through this,

---

[25] Minutes of the Special Meeting of the City Council, City of Palos Heights, July 14, 2000.

[26] Michelle Mullins, "Mosque Says It Will Accept Buyout," *The Star* (Tinley Park, IL), June 16, 2000, A1, A4.

'cause you don't make any examples by crying. You gotta lead the town; you're the mayor.' ... Maybe it's the hard-nosed Dutch in me, but you just gotta plug on."

Questions for Reflection

- What do we know about Palos Heights as a community? Do you think it deserves the moniker "Palos Hates?"
- Some participants in the Palos Heights dispute, including Mayor Koldenhoven, speak as people of faith and also as citizens or public officials. Is it appropriate to bring a religious or theological voice to bear on public issues? Is it effective?
- What is the fundamental issue in the Palos Heights controversy? Does your perception of the issue differ from what various participants might identify as the fundamental issue?

(B) Case

Dean Koldenhoven described how his years of working in construction prepared him for his term as the mayor of Palos Heights: "When you've got bad weather, you don't complain about it, you deal with it. You either work through it or you don't work that day. You make a decision." He continued, "If it is ten degrees you're not going to work 'cause the mortar will freeze. If it is thirty-two degrees, the mortar won't freeze. If it's a thirty-mile-an-hour wind, you say, 'Get tough, let's finish this job.'" He explained, "It toughens you up to make decisions that you make your living on. And at the same time, you're not afraid to face things."

"No-Brainer"

For Mayor Koldenhoven, the decision before him in Palos Heights was a "no-brainer." His decision to veto the two-hundred-thousand-dollar offer—like his position throughout the controversy—was firmly grounded in his understanding of the US Constitution and guided by his Christian faith. For Koldenhoven, freedom of religion was a guarantee, not a decision; and the message of loving your neighbor didn't require much interpretation. He credits his seventh-grade teacher, Mrs. Niewenhuis, for teaching him about the First Amendment. He often recalled those lessons while listening to the discussions in city council meetings: "That is what this meant by 'everybody has the freedom of religion, even if it is a faith that you don't agree with.' And then the fact that Jesus said, 'Love your neighbor.' Those two things are what made my decision."

Although many citizens of Palos Heights had told him that, as their elected representative, it was his job to act according to the will of the people, Koldenhoven believed that his job was to act according to the good of the people. In a "republic," he explained, leaders have the responsibility to make the decisions; they do not simply act according to the majority or heed the calls of the loudest voices.

Many thought Koldenhoven should have vetoed the buyout offer when it was first made on June 20. Some saw stubbornness in his decision: although it was permitted by law to wait until the next scheduled meeting, it was not legally necessary to wait. Koldenhoven explained that he saw the offer as an insult and never thought that the Al Salam Mosque Foundation would accept it. Moreover, he felt strongly that the city of Palos Heights could not afford to buy out the contract and purchase the church. He had long been prepared to veto the offer but had never believed it would be accepted. As the next scheduled meeting approached, he felt confident that his veto would stand: one of the aldermen who originally supported the buyout had since indicated that he had changed his position. Koldenhoven sat down to draft his veto letter, disappointed but resolute.

A Veto from the Mayor, July 18

On July 18, 2000, at the next regular meeting of the city council, Koldenhoven read from his prepared text: "The power to veto is the Mayor's opportunity to express his opinion on an issue."[27] He explained that he listened to residents on both sides of the debate, but that "One of the very first things a Mayor, or any elected official learns, is that no matter what position, issue or decision one makes, at least someone will not approve. However, I cannot go against my own determination of what I believe is in the best interests of the City." He noted that the city did not have the resources to buy the property. After formally declaring his veto, Koldenhoven included a message for the Al Salam Mosque Foundation:

---

[27] Dean Koldenhoven to City Council of Palos Heights, memo regarding veto of offer to Al Salam Mosque Foundation, July 18, 2000; in author's possession.

It was also my hope that the Mosque Foundation would have rejected the proposal to buy out its rights under the contract, and I would not have to veto the Council action. Based upon conversations and statements made in the media I was of the opinion that their desire to move into Palos Heights to pursue their religious principles would not have been so easily compromised by their willingness to accept a monetary offer to walk away. It is my hope that the Mosque Foundation would reconsider and move forward with its purchase. For whatever reasons they may have the obligation to terminate their purchase agreement remains with them. Government has no place in this issue.

The statement concluded, "I believe that the vast majority of citizens of Palos Heights and myself would welcome the Mosque into our community."[28]

After the veto was read, Alderman Corsi apologized for her comments at the previous meeting when she refused to address Koldenhoven as "mayor"; Alderman Murphy explained that the meeting was called just a few days after the death of Koldenhoven's son because Shalabi was leaving town. Alderman Fulkerson brought forth a proposal to look at a private tennis facility for sale in the town to meet the recreation needs. Then Alderman Phillips explained that he had originally voted for the buyout offer because he felt it was his duty to respond to his constituents. For weeks, he had received emails, calls, and petitions from local residents urging the city to purchase the church; however, many constituents had contacted him since the vote to say the buyout was "morally wrong." Accordingly, he stated, if there is a vote to override the mayor's veto, he will not vote in the affirmative.

When it was time for citizens to address the council, the first person to speak was Kenith Bergeron from the US Department of Justice's Community Relations Service. Bergeron explained that his department responds to racial and ethnic tensions in US communities, offering a mechanism to begin dialogue. The response was mixed: some citizens thought Koldenhoven had "brought in the Feds"; others were encouraged that something was being done to heal the divisions and conflict.

Bergeron was followed by Father Cronin, who addressed the council on behalf of a group of Palos Heights pastors. The statement affirmed

---

[28] Ibid.

that every person is created in the image of God and deserving of respect. It also affirmed the constitutional right of Al Salam to buy, and the Reformed Church to sell, property in Palos Heights; the need for recreational space in the community; and the right to express legitimate concerns without being called a bigot or racist. Finally, pastors encouraged the city to engage in dialogue and work to heal the wounds caused by the bitter public debate.

As the meeting continued, there were statements of praise and condemnation for Koldenhoven: some congratulated him for his stand, others asked him to resign because of his comments that characterized the people of Palos Heights as bigots. A couple of citizens accused Koldenhoven of having a financial interest in the dispute, alleging that he was selling the bricks to build the new Reformed church, a charge he denied.

Ray Hanania, a well-known Chicago journalist of Christian Arab background, said, "This is not about Palos Heights being racist, but about those who have used racism to oppose something they did not want." Many from the Muslim community thanked the mayor, including Omar Najib, who also urged Al Salam to move forward with the contract. He said that if Al Salam walks away, they should do so with dignity: "Muslims are not for sale."[29] After 11 p.m., the meeting adjourned. The veto would now stand, with four aldermen publicly stating that they would not over-turn the mayor's veto. Koldenhoven was relieved. The issue, it seemed, was over. The contract between two private parties could now move forward.

Letters and Emails to Mayor Dean

Throughout the dispute, phone calls, letters, and emails streamed into the mayor's office: in the beginning, most were from citizens of Palos Heights asking Koldenhoven to support the purchase of the church. Some wrote to express their concerns about the controversy. One Palos Heights resident wrote, "When I went away to war in 1943, I had assumed that one of my enemies was bigotry and it was soundly defeated. It didn't stay down too long. It is alive and well and residing in Palos Heights."[30]

---

[29] Minutes of the Special Meeting of the City Council, City of Palos Heights, July 18, 2000.

[30] S.J.P. to Dean Koldenhoven, letter regarding bigotry in Palos Heights, July 27, 2000; in author's possession.

After the veto, the stream of correspondence increased dramatically: people of many faiths wrote from across the United States. Overwhelmingly, they wrote in support of the veto. The mayor also received a letter from Ray Hanania, who had spoken out at the July 18 meeting, inviting Koldenhoven to a dinner to be held in his honor by a group of Arab American organizations. Hanania's letter noted, "The issue is not just about a building or the sale of a building. The bigger issue is much more important, and it has to do with fighting discrimination and opposing those who would use bigotry as a political weapon to achieve their ends."[31] He received letters from fellow mayors and organizations, but most of the communication came from individuals. One was from a Dutch Reformed pastor in Iowa. "I'm sorry that you have had to bear the brunt of so much conflict, but sometimes we need to bear that burden as we 'seek justice, love kindness, and walk humbly with our God.'"[32]

A Lawsuit Filed, a Contract Expired

Ten days after the veto, Koldenhoven received a phone call from a reporter: "Will you be at the press conference in Oak Lawn today?" He was not surprised to learn that Al Salam had filed a suit against the city of Palos Heights and the aldermen; he was surprised, however, to find that he had been named individually as one of the defendants in the case.[33]

The lawsuit's first count was the violation of Al Salam Mosque Foundation's First Amendment right. The First Amendment states that "Congress shall make no law respecting an establishment of religion, or prohibiting the free exercise thereof; or abridging the freedom of speech, or of the press; or the right of the people peaceably to assemble, and to petition the Government for a redress of grievances." The complaint stated that the "actions and inactions" of the city resulted in the inability of the Al Salam Mosque Foundation to purchase the property, and that the city's refusal to provide zoning approval was "based on religious prejudice and an invidious discriminatory animus against Muslims." Other counts included

---

[31] Ray Hanania to Dean Koldenhoven, letter regarding dinner honoring stand, July 18, 2000; in author's possession.

[32] Email from Pastor Leon Aalberts to Dean Koldenhoven, July 30, 2000; in author's possession.

[33] Complaint, *Al-Salam Mosque Foundation v. City of Palos Heights et al.*, US District Court, Northern District of Illinois, Eastern Division.

conspiracy, tortious interference with contractual relations, breach of contract, and violation of the Religious Freedom Restoration Act.[34]

The Al Salam Mosque Foundation requested a trial by jury; they asked for a cumulative judgment, including compensatory and punitive damages, of $6.2 million, plus attorneys' fees. The Judge assigned to the case was James B. Zagel in the U.S. District Court, Northern District of Illinois, Eastern Division. At the same time, the real estate contract between the Al Salam Mosque Foundation and the Reformed Church of Palos Heights—the impetus for the controversy—simply expired.

A Dialogue Group Forms, September 2000

Legally, the dispute over the mosque continued; however, at the same time, some citizens of Palos Heights took their first tentative steps toward healing. Koldenhoven and a dozen local citizens met in the library of Trinity Christian College; they were joined by Kenith Bergeron of the Department of Justice (DOJ), who would facilitate the formation of a dialogue group. Participants praised his leadership but rejected the DOJ's "One America" curriculum as a format for dialogue: in this framework, religion would not be a topic for discussion. Yet many of the people of Palos Heights who came together for dialogue felt that religion could not be left out of the conversation. They agreed to bring their religious commitments to the table, and to work together to learn about each other's faiths, forming the Christian-Muslim Dialogue Group.

Koldenhoven was an eager participant in the first couple of meetings but was advised by the city's lawyers that—due to the pending lawsuit—it would not be prudent for him to participate. While Koldenhoven was disappointed, he was pleased that something positive had grown out of the controversy and made a point to attend their public events. Koldenhoven knew and respected those who were participating, including Michael Vander Weele, Sandy Broadbent, and Omar Najib. He was proud that this group would begin to model a new kind neighborliness for Palos Heights.

---

[34] 2005 Illinois Code—Chapter 775, "Human Rights 775 ICLS 35 / Religious Freedom Restoration Act," Illinois General Assembly.

*A Referendum to Pursue the Purchase
of the Reformed Church, November 2000*

While the contract between the Mosque Foundation and the Reformed
Church had expired and a lawsuit was pending, some of the aldermen
wanted to pursue the purchase of the Reformed Church property. A referendum was held in November 2000 to decide if the City of Palos Heights
should go ahead and pursue this purchase: it was rejected by nine votes:
2,856 to 2,847.[35] This referendum was but one indication that Palos
Heights was still a sharply divided city.

A Reelection and a Rejection, April 2001

Koldenhoven ran for reelection as mayor of Palos Heights in 2001; to
some, he was a hero, and to others, he gave the town a bad name. Koldenhoven felt he had more to contribute, and he ran a campaign focused on
leadership and revitalizing the city of Palos Heights. In the end, fewer
than six hundred people in Palos Heights voted for Koldenhoven. Overwhelmingly, there was the sense that, for or against the mosque, the
citizens of Palos Heights wanted a change. The political battles of the
city council were entrenched and had worsened during the previous four
years. Observers noted that Palos Heights residents were ready to start a
new chapter: everyone who was involved in the dispute was voted out of
office, including Koldenhoven, Corsi, and Murphy.

After 9/11: A Hate Crime and a March

Shortly after 9/11, Koldenhoven received a phone call: "What do you
think of your Muslims now?" In the Chicago area, as elsewhere in the
United States, the climate was charged. Hate crimes were being reported
against immigrants; there were rumors of Arab teenagers in Bridgeview
publicly celebrating the attacks. In Palos Heights, on the afternoon of
September 11, 2001, a Moroccan gas station attendant was attacked
with the blunt end of a machete. On September 12, crowds gathered
and marched along Ninety-Fifth Street toward the Bridgeview Mosque.

---

[35] Sabrina Walters, "After Ballot, Palos Hts. Mosque Debate Goes On," *Chicago Sun-Times*, November 11, 2000.

Palos Heights officers were among the first to respond. They came in riot gear and, with other local police, were able to disperse the crowd before they entered the mosque building—and before anyone was hurt.

Motion for Summary Judgment Filed and Denied

The city of Palos Heights filed a motion for summary judgment on January 4, 2002. They moved to dismiss the complaint, arguing that the city did not have authority to provide written authorizations and was not a party to the real estate contract. The city cited the intracorporate conspiracy doctrine to preclude the claim of conspiracy and argued that the Tort Immunity Act provided the city with immunity from the count of tortious interference. The city argued that there was no breach of contract, as the two-hundred-thousand-dollar offer had been vetoed by the mayor and was no longer valid.[36]

Four months later, Judge Zagel denied the city of Palos Heights motion for summary judgment. His ruling explained that "the free exercise clause prohibits local governments from making discretionary (i.e., not neutral, not generally applicable) decisions that burden the free exercise of religion, absent some compelling governmental interest."[37] The ruling noted that if the city interfered with a religious group's ability to establish a place of worship, this would indeed constitute a burden on the free exercise of religion. Judge Zagel dismissed three of the other counts, but noted,

> Dealing with a city on zoning matters is a delicate business, especially when religious conduct is at issue. Municipalities owe their religious institutions a constitutional duty to tread carefully once involved in zoning issues, and outright hostility to or shameful ignorance of religious faiths is unacceptable. At the same time, however, the business of governing requires municipalities and their employees to be out of reach from most private civil litigation.[38]

The case would be tried by a federal jury.

---

[36] Motion for Summary Judgment, January 4, 2002; in author's possession.

[37] *Al-Salam Mosque Foundation, Plaintiff, v. City of Palos Heights, et al., Defendants*, No. 00 C 4596 United States District Court for the Northern District of Illinois, Eastern Division, 2001 U.S. Dist. LEXIS 2208, February 20, 2001, Decided; March 1, 2001, Docketed. Lexis Nexis.

[38] Ibid.

Profile in Courage Award, May 2002

At home in his La-Z-Boy one afternoon in early spring of 2002, Kolden-hoven heard the phone ring. His wife, Ruth, picked up the phone and passed it to him: "It's Caroline Kennedy." The voice on the other line said, "I just wanted to let you know that you are the recipient of the John F. Kennedy Profile in Courage Award." Koldenhoven was shocked. After the conversation, he sat in silence, stunned. "My wife said, 'I've never seen you speechless.' I said, 'This is one of those times.' I got an award for just doing what comes naturally?"

The Profile in Courage Award, established in 1989 in honor of President John F. Kennedy, is given annually to an elected official who demonstrates "political courage." Koldenhoven brought his family to Boston to accept the award, including nine grandkids; some at the event joked that the Koldenhovens outnumbered the Kennedys. In his acceptance speech, Koldenhoven stated,

> I remember what JFK said to the nation after the confrontation with the governor of Alabama over court-ordered desegregation. He said, "We are confronted primarily with a moral issue. It is as old as the Scriptures and it is as clear as the American Constitution. The heart of the question is whether all Americans are to be afforded equal rights and equal opportunities; whether we are going to treat our fellow Americans as we want to be treated."[39]

Koldenhoven thanked his friends and family for their support and recognized the efforts of the Christian-Muslim Dialogue Group. He praised Father Cronin, who attended the ceremony, for his help and leadership; finally, he accepted the award in honor of his late son, Don. "As Caroline Kennedy has said, 'I have come to believe, more strongly than ever, that after people die, they really do live on through those that love them.'"[40]

Senator Edward Kennedy also offered remarks at the award ceremony, noting, "There was a time in our own city of Boston when there were signs in the windows offering jobs, but with the warning that 'No Irish Need

---

[39] John F. Kennedy Presidential Library & Museum, "Dean Koldenhoven—Acceptance Speech," Remarks by Dean Koldenhoven, former Mayor, Palos Heights, Illinois, on receiving the John F. Kennedy Profile in Courage Award, May 6, 2002, https://www.jfklibrary.org/.

[40] Ibid.

Apply.' In 1960, many people said that a member of the Catholic faith should not be President of the United States or live in The White House." He stated, "We hear again the dark rumblings of some who say members of the Islamic faith cannot be good Americans and should not live and worship in our neighborhoods. Again today, we find we must struggle to rise above intolerance and remember our historic values." He continued,

> Mayor Koldenhoven held firm to his principles with unwavering resolve and honored our history, his own deep faith and our Bill of Rights. This man of such fundamental decency has been a member of the bricklaying profession all his life. He has built many strong walls. But as he showed us, the dangerous walls of religious intolerance between our fellow citizens are walls that must be torn down. He is truly a Profile in Courage.[41]

Lawsuit Decided and Motion for a New Trial Denied, May 2005

After a series of continuances, the case of *Al Salam Mosque Foundation v. City of Palos Heights, et al.* was finally tried in front of a jury in May 2005. Koldenhoven, Shalabi, Murphy, and Corsi were among those called to testify in the federal trial. Four days of testimony were followed by brief deliberations and a verdict in favor of the defendant, the city of Palos Heights. Al Salam filed a motion for a new trial, which was denied by Judge Zagel. No further complaints would be heard in the case.

After the Controversy

The building that was once the former Reformed Church of Palos Heights remains a Christian church: since 2014 it has been home to the conservative, Evangelical Anchor Church Palos. Aside from a new sign, the building appears to be unchanged; a large silver cross adorns the side of the brick structure.

Koldenhoven, who once joked, "Brick is my life," is now retired. Since the controversy, when he is invited to speak, he challenges the audience to

---

[41] John F. Kennedy Presidential Library & Museum, "Dean Koldenhoven: Remarks by Senator Edward M. Kennedy," May 6, 2002, https://www.jfklibrary.org/.

identify the five freedoms of the First Amendment. Very few are able to do so, but those who do win a prize: a John F. Kennedy pin.

The US State Department invited Koldenhoven to speak overseas; he emphasized the Constitution and American democracy. Koldenhoven recalled, "You've got to practice your freedoms. . . . You can't just say you've got freedoms; you've got to use them. You've got to speak up, if you see discrimination, you can't just sit there. You've got to speak up.'"

Many years after the mosque dispute in Palos Heights, Koldenhoven looks back without regret. He explains, "I think a lot of people learned from mistakes that we made."

Postscript

In 2004, just a few years after the mosque dispute in Palos Heights, the Orland Park Prayer Center secured land to develop in nearby Orland Park. Much of the opposition was the same, related to traffic, parking, and what was characterized as a different use than a Christian church. Just a few years after 9/11, opponents now added fears of extremism and the risk of terrorists among them—including shouts of "September 11" as supporters of the mosque spoke during village council meetings. Opponents of the mosque wanted the mayor and board to put the issue to public referendum. Rev. Vernon Lyons from the Ashburn Baptist Church said, "As a Christian, a Baptist, and an American, I am a firm believer in religious freedom, but when any group jeopardizes our national security and liberty, they are not deserving of our tolerance."[42]

Supporters of the Orland Park Prayer Center included some familiar faces from Palos Heights. Edward Hassan offered pointed comments at the May 26 meeting: "We pay taxes here. We go to school here. We shop here. But we cannot pray here?"[43] He said, "We are your neighbors, your doctors, your soccer coaches. It truly is a sad day for America and for the Constitution." Hassan later explained that he had "no hesitation"[44]

[42] Stanley Ziemba and Tribune staff reporter, "Orland Park Officials OK Mosque," *Chicago Tribune*, June 22, 2004.
[43] Quotes from Edward Hassan at the May 26, 2004, Orland Park Council Meeting, "Amidst Protests, Orland Park Mosque Moves Closer to Opening," *Daily Southtown* (Chicago, IL), May 27, 2004.
[44] Unless otherwise indicated, all quotes from Edward Hassan in postscript from phone interview with the author, September 9, 2022.

about speaking before the angry crowd. As a community leader and a prominent businessman, he knew the mayor and many members of the village council; a few years earlier, Hassan was in regular communication with Dean Koldenhoven about the proposed mosque in Palos Heights.

Hassan was pleased to see Koldenhoven at the June 21, 2004, Orland Park council meeting, which was moved to the Civic Center to accommodate the growing crowds. Many of those gathered opposed the mosque and favored a public referendum; it was standing-room-only, and the atmosphere was tense. Koldenhoven came to the wooden podium and introduced himself as a resident of Palos Heights. He reminded the audience that, in a republic, officials are elected to make decisions for the people. Speaking directly to the council, without notes, he said, "That means you have the decision to make tonight. And do it."[45] Koldenhoven continued,

> The First Amendment is one sentence long. It has three commas, a semicolon and a period. That's five freedoms listed in the First Amendment. The first one is what we're here tonight for. "Congress shall make no laws regarding the establishment of religion or the free exercise thereof." So that's what you should base your decision on.

Koldenhoven added, "And also … Jesus said, 'Love your neighbor.' Thank you." Unlike many of those who spoke in support of the mosque that night, Koldenhoven received no boos or shouts, only applause.

The Orland Park Prayer Center did not go to public referendum. It was approved unanimously by the village council in June 2004; they broke ground in October and opened its doors in June 2006. Started by prominent area Muslims with strong local ties, the main building is modeled on the Dome of the Rock in Jerusalem.[46] A second building later expanded the capacity of the Prayer Center, which now draws some eighteen hundred people for Friday prayers. Known for its vibrant youth programming, the center works with local police on any traffic

---

[45] All quotes from Dean Koldenhoven at the June 21, 2004, Orland Park Council Meeting: Ray Hanania, "Eyes of the Beholder: The Orland Park Mosque Battle (Fahrenheit 60462)," YouTube, May 13, 2012.

[46] For a history of the Orland Park Prayer Center, see Monique Parsons, "An American Mosque: Blending 7th-Century Revelations with Midwest Suburbia," WBEZ, February 2, 2017, https://www.wbez.org/.

concerns—and occasional incidents of vandalism. In March 2014, the center called to report that a bullet pierced the dome during morning prayers. The bullet holes were patched up, but the sniper was never found. Some say that the bullet is still lodged in the dome; Edward Hassan believes that the bullet moved through the structure, just as the community moved on.

Yet this would not be the only new mosque in the southwestern suburbs to experience opposition. Sixteen years after the controversy over the mosque in Palos Heights, the Muslim American Society purchased a former church building in neighboring Palos Park. As the events unfolded in a tiny village of fewer than five thousand residents, this wasn't a matter of national news; however, a local resident reached out to the Pluralism Project with concern. He wrote,

> What I hope does not happen is a repeat of the sad episode that occurred in neighboring Palos Heights almost sixteen years ago. In today's increasingly troubling climate of Islamophobia, I fear that may rear its ugly head in this case, but I am hopeful it does not. I do not want my hometown torn apart the way Palos Heights was, and I do not want my hometown to earn an embarrassing reputation. Personally, as a faithful Catholic, I view Islamophobia as a sin against Jesus.[47]

A "Save Palos" flier appeared in local mailboxes announcing in bold, all capital letters that a Muslim organization had purchased the former First Church of Christ [Scientist]. Arguing that Palos Park / Palos Heights does not have a large Muslim community, it outlined some of the change that would come to the local community. There were familiar concerns, such as traffic and noise "from non-residents, and property values decreasing as people move out." Other bullet points included the following:

- NON-RESIDENTS USING FACILITIES THAT <u>OUR</u> TAX DOLLARS PAY FOR.
- LARGE MUSLIM FAMILIES MOVING INTO YOUR NEIGHBORHOOD. SOME OF THESE FAMILIES HAVE 20 PEOPLE LIVING IN A SINGLE-FAMILY HOME.

---

[47] Email from [name removed] to the author, February 4, 2016.

- MORE WOMEN AT THE PALOS HEIGHTS POOL WITH BURCAS [*sic*]. THESE WOMEN GO IN THE POOL WITH THESE GARMENTS ON. THIS IS AGAINST POOL RULES, HOWEVER, IT STILL TAKES PLACE.

The flier listed upcoming village council meetings in Palos Park and neighboring Palos Heights, stating, "Voice your opinion if you have any pride in the Palos community and want to keep Palos the best community in the [Chicagoland] area."[48]

On February 8, 2016, when the Palos Park Board of Commissioners meeting opened for public comment, the first speaker referenced the flier.[49] In a departure from meeting protocol, the neatly dressed man refused to state his name and address. He began by explaining that he was a lifelong Palos resident. "I'm here to elaborate on some of the points raised in the flier regarding the mosque." In addition to traffic and property values, he explained that he was concerned about radical Islam. He added, "I'm not anti-Muslim. I went to school with many Muslims and played football and other sports side-by-side my whole life.... I don't really have any specific problem with them at all, in my entire life, or their religion. I admire their—the way the Muslims stick together as a people. However, I feel that at this time a mosque would not be a good addition to the Palos community."

After he spoke, applause rose up from the room, as did the tensions. One opponent, who was cautioned by a council member for shouting when others spoke, was later escorted from the building. Edward Hassan was disappointed that this episode was playing out again; he also noticed that many of the opponents appeared to be from outside of Palos. For the third time in twenty years, Hassan had to speak out in support of a local mosque.

Hassan began by stating that he had been a resident of Palos Heights for forty years and attends the mosque in Orland Park. He suggested that, rather than fear and accusations, people simply ask questions. After identifying himself as a veteran, Hassan expressed disgust that some at the

---

[48] "Fliers Circulating in SW Suburbs Fighting New Mosque," ABC7 Chicago, February 2, 2016, https://abc7chicago.com/.

[49] All quotes from February 8, 2016, Palos Park Village Council Meeting, recording of council meeting received from Palos Park Village through FOIA request, May 6, 2016.

meeting were accusing fellow Americans of terrorism: "Instead of reading your silly notes and standing here, you should read either your Bible, because I know that your Jesus is a man of peace, just like Muhammad and Moses—or read your Constitution." Hassan, who is married to a Catholic and has raised his children in both faiths, later explained that he didn't take the few "loudmouths" who opposed the mosque too seriously. "It's just unfortunate how uninformed they are."

Hassan observed that the crowd that gathered in 2016 in Palos Park wasn't nearly as large as the standing-room-only meetings in Palos Heights and Orland Park in prior years. And this time around, Hassan noticed, a larger percentage—Muslim and non-Muslim—were there to support the mosque. One non-Muslim community member explained how upset he was by the flier: "When I got this, it really affected me. . . . To me it is just blatant fear, bigotry, racism, whatever you want to call it." Right after he received the flier, he explained, "I had to go across the street, just in case this was placed in my neighbor's mailbox, and kind of apologize—that I think that Palos Park is better than this."

The former Christian Science church in Palos Park was zoned for use as a religious building: no approvals were necessary for the Muslim American Society, and the opposition did not convince the Palos Park Board of Commissioners that they needed to intervene. In 2020 the Palos Islamic Center finally opened its doors. When a reporter asked former mayor Dean Koldenhoven about the Palos Park controversy, nearly two decades after the opposition to a mosque in Palos Heights, he commented, "I can't believe it; it still rears its ugly head."[50]

Koldenhoven, who is now in his eighties, still resides in Palos Heights. He reflects, "When I meet people in town, their minds have not changed. Prejudice is a hard thing to erase."[51] Koldenhoven still gets an occasional angry look from those who opposed the mosque; when he meets someone who is Muslim, he enjoys offering a warm greeting of "As-Salaam-Alaikum."

---

[50] Angie Leventis Lourgos, "Opposition to Mosque Sad, Muslims Say," *Chicago Tribune*, February 23, 2016, 1.

[51] Unless otherwise noted, all quotes from Dean Koldenhoven in postscript from phone interview with the author, December 15, 2022.

Center of Dispute

For Daisy Khan, Cordoba House represented the natural evolution of Muslim life in America. Modeled on Jewish Community Centers (JCCs), this would be a center for recreation, education, worship, and interfaith engagement in Lower Manhattan. The name came from the Spanish city of Cordoba, where Christians, Muslims, and Jews once lived together in peace and harmony. Yet the newspapers, angry opponents, and some politicians called it by another name: the "Ground Zero Mosque." The response was swift and angry: many, including some who might otherwise be allies, suggested that Khan and her husband change the location. Yet others suggested that giving into these demands would only empower the hateful voices. As Khan searched for answers, sought allies, and tried to manage a coming crisis, the vitriol intensified and hate incidents against mosques began to rise. The "Ground Zero Mosque" dominated the head-lines and the public conversation. With pressure continuing from all sides, including those in the Muslim community who felt burdened by the crisis, Khan believed she only had two options: to stay in the fight or walk away. What advice might you offer to Daisy Khan? What resources—communal, spiritual, and practical—might she access? And how might she contend with the emotional toll of being at the center of a national firestorm?

(A) Case

On the evening of May 5, 2010, Daisy Khan was in a festive mood. Khan and her husband, Imam Feisal Abdul Rauf, together with colleagues and friends, celebrated the first formal presentation of their plans for a Muslim community center in Lower Manhattan. As the plates of tandoori chicken, biryani, and saag paneer were passed around the restaurant table, they discussed how warmly the local community board received the proposal: "All fifteen members were in favor of this; they were glad a center like this was coming to their neighborhood."[1] The center promised to bring jobs, vitality, and cultural events to an area near the World Trade Center site. In a neighborhood that had more commerce than community—and many empty storefronts—they would build a place for recreation, education, prayer, and interfaith engagement. After more than ten years of imagining the project, even small steps forward were a cause for celebration. There was still much to be done, from fundraising to developing a board, yet she and Rauf were elated that their vision was finally becoming a reality. It would be called "Cordoba House," taking its name from the Spanish city in which Christians, Muslims, and Jews once "lived together in peace and harmony."[2]

Yet Khan's mood changed the next morning when she came into the Upper West Side offices of the American Society for Muslim Advancement. A staff member gave Khan a copy of the *Daily News*, which reported that Cordoba House was "a 13-story mosque" located "steps from ground zero."[3] Khan was stunned. At the presentation the night before, they identified the prayer area as a small part of a larger project. Yet, she recalled, "There it was, in black-and-white: 'a 13-story mosque.'" Khan put down the newspaper and braced herself for what would come next.

From Cordoba House to "Ground Zero Mosque"

Online, the dispute over the center had just begun. Pamela Geller, a blogger and executive director at Stop the Islamization of America (SIOA), led the opposition against the project. The day after the presentation to the civic association, Geller posted, "What better way to mark your territory than to plant a giant mosque on the still-barren land of the World Trade Center? Sort of a giant victory lap." Calling it an "insult," she asked, "What's wrong with these people? Have they no heart? No soul?"[4] The next day, Geller announced the launch of a "Campaign Offensive" called

---

[1] All quotes from Daisy Khan, unless otherwise noted, in (A) and (B) cases from interview with the author, New York City, NY, May 27, 2011.

[2] Cordoba Initiative, "About Us," https://cordobahouse.com/about-us/, July 2011.

[3] Joe Jackson and Bill Hutchinson, "Plan for Mosque Near WTC Site Moves Ahead," *New York Daily News*, May 6, 2010, 12.

[4] Pamela Geller, "Monster Mosque Pushes Ahead in Shadow of World Trade Center Islamic Death and Destruction," May 6, 2010, pamelageller.com.

"Stop the 9/11 Mosque!" Geller's blog posts about Cordoba House generated emotional responses:

> Disgusting!!! This is an insult beyond comprehension.... I would rather not see any more mosques built here, but guess that can't be stopped.... This cannot be allowed to happen.... When are we as a people going to open our eyes and see the creeping infestation by this vile cult?[5]

News coverage quoted those who questioned the sensitivity of the project: one 9/11 family member said, "That's sacred ground." Some characterized Cordoba House as a "slap in the face" or an "insult"; others found it "despicable."[6] One week later, a *New York Post* piece, "Mosque Madness at Ground Zero," quoted Geller, who asked, "What could be more insulting and humiliating than a monster mosque in the shadow of the World Trade Center buildings that were brought down by an Islamic jihad attack?"[7] Later, the piece quoted Khan: "For us, it's a symbol, a platform that will give voice to the silent majority of Muslims who suffer at the hands of extremists. A center will show that Muslims will be part of rebuilding lower Manhattan."[8] The columnist raised a host of issues, from appropriateness to funding, and concluded, "There are many questions about the Ground Zero mosque. But just one answer. Move it away."[9]

Khan considered how to respond. Their goal was to improve understanding and build trust, yet now she and her husband found themselves in the middle of a heated dispute. Khan noted, "And then we saw the people behind it, and then we began to see who was driving the opposition. Stop the Islamization of America is an organized group, and this is now going to be a big fight." She explained, "So, either we were going to stay in the fight or we were going to withdraw completely. We decided to stay in the fight."

---

[5] Comments on Pamela Geller, "SIOA Campaign Offensive: Stop the 911 Mosque," *Centurean2* (blog), May 8, 2010.

[6] Jackson and Hutchinson, "Plan for Mosque Near WTC Site Moves Ahead."

[7] Andrea Peyser, "Mosque Madness at Ground Zero," *New York Post*, May 13, 2010, 17.

[8] Ibid.

[9] Ibid.

Daisy Khan and Imam Feisal Abdul Rauf

Khan has a penchant for embroidered jackets and silk scarves, and a proud and purposeful bearing. Born in Kashmir, she moved to Long Island as a fifteen-year-old. She is known today by her childhood nickname, "Daisy." Khan sometimes speaks of a "kinder, softer Islam," and for many in the interfaith movement, she and her husband seem to be an embodiment of that idea. Rauf has a charming, engaged manner that seems well suited for a self-described "bridge-builder." After the publication of his book, *What's Right with Islam: A New Vision for Muslims and the West* (2004), Rauf was in great demand at high-level interfaith meetings and in international diplomacy efforts for his accessible and hopeful message:

> We have two powerful tools with which to bridge the chasm separating the United States from the Muslim world: faith in the basic goodness of humanity and trust in the power of sincerity and dialogue to overcome differences with our fellow human beings.[10]

Khan and Rauf were married in 1996 and soon established the American Society for Muslim Advancement (originally named the American Sufi Muslim Association). A friend of Khan and Rauf, speaking to a journalist, characterized their partnership: "He is the thinker; she is the doer."[11] By 1998 they began planning for a center, which brought together Rauf's observations about the evolution of religious traditions in America with Khan's training in architectural design. She recalled,

> He said, "You know, in America, religions evolve and they Americanize over time." He had observed the Americanization of the Christian community, the Americanization of the Jewish community, and what institutions they had to build in order to be ... truly considered to be part of the American fabric. And it was largely going from places of worship to places of service: creating those kinds of institutions that served the larger community.

---

[10] Imam Feisal Abdul Rauf, "What's Right with Islam," CNN, TEDTalk Tuesdays, September 12, 2010.

[11] Michael M. Grynbaum, "Daisy Khan, an Eloquent Face of Islam," *New York Times,* November 12, 2010.

Their center would be modeled on the YMCA, the Jewish Community Center (JCC), and New York City's 92nd Street Y, "a proudly Jewish institution"[12] open to all as a cultural and community center. It was also inspired by the Chautauqua Institution in upstate New York, which brought together fine and performing arts, lectures, recreation, and worship. Their planned center would have a dedicated space for Muslim worship, given the lack of available prayer space for Muslims in the city.

Khan recalled that when they started envisioning the center, it was well before texting and email made virtual communication the norm. Together with young, creative congregants, they would meet at lunch after Friday *Jum'ah* prayers and at dinners that stretched late into the night. They dreamed, discussed, and planned the center they hoped to create. There were numerous business plans and hand-drawn sketches over the years, but the core concept was consistent: "pods" would be dedicated to worship, recreation, culture and the arts, and education. Each pod would have a corresponding Qur'anic reference: "So for education," she offered as an example, the motto would be: "God increase my knowledge." Khan brightened as she described it: "Everything had a strong meaning to it." It was, she explained, "building from within, from our Scripture, and letting it become alive."

From Inreach to Outreach

Khan and Rauf were both well aware of the challenges of establishing a center. As a young adult, Khan's family mosque was the Islamic Center of Long Island (ICLI), established by her uncle Dr. Faroque Khan. When still a student, she was brought into conversations with the architect; Khan designed the carpets that line the floors to this day. Khan laughed as she remembered the differences in vision: the architect wanted to create a Spanish-style terra cotta mosque; the largely Indo-Pakistani community wanted a "little white marble Taj." She added, "We settled somewhere in between the two." When Khan studied the floor plans, she identified another issue: the women's section was to be located in the basement, away from the main prayer hall. The architect, who was not a Muslim, applied a template from another mosque. "And I know all of

---

[12] 92NY, "About Us," https://www.92ny.org/.

the women who are behind this mosque: they are all heads of medical departments, they sit at the highest levels of their profession, and I remember telling some of these women, 'Do you know that you're going to be in the basement?'"

The layout of the Islamic Center was subsequently changed, but the negotiations were not over. There were members of the community who felt that the prayer hall should be separated, so an accordion door was installed between the men's and women's sections. Khan noted, "And that accordion door became everybody's nemesis." She continued, "Because a certain group of people who were very conservative started coming to the mosque, and just when the prayers would begin, the women who would wear *niqab* would get up and they would close the door. And the women who had built the mosque would go and open it again. Open, close, open, close." Khan added, "These are the kinds of things you deal with when you have different interpretations, when you have people with different schools of thought. We've seen this, we've seen this over and over again, and we've learned great lessons from it."

They later applied those lessons to their planned center, which would serve as a form of "inreach" to the Muslim community:

> There was so much that needed to be done within the Muslim community. Even doing culture and the arts within the Muslim community was like a big thing, because there was so much conservatism, and people thought, "Oh this is forbidden, this is forbidden." So we were even trying to promote, and project, the kind of Islam that we understood to be an Islam that encompasses all these different expressions.

People of other faiths would be drawn in through programs, but the primary audience was fellow Muslims. In 2000 they found the ideal site: the McBurney YMCA in Chelsea. "We got several supporters lined up, and the dot-com bust happened, and that was the end of that project.... And then the next year, 9/11 happened."

Khan explained, "All of a sudden, all of this work that we had planned for ourselves just literally got shelved and we went into doing massive outreach into the American public." She added, "And so we went from being an inreach organization to an outreach organization overnight." Khan offered another reason for the shift: "We were also a community

138   MOSQUES IN THE AMERICAN LANDSCAPE

that was being challenged, especially post-9/11, from outside. So some of that natural infighting got diffused ... because we have to be united right now, and we have to remain united."

"Come, Come, Whoever You Are"

After 9/11, Khan explained, "Our new mandate began." Through interfaith outreach, "We got to know the most amazing people that we would have never gotten to know if 9/11 hadn't happened." They built coalitions and learned about the complexities and internal diversities of other faiths. They heard about the challenges that other communities had experienced before them, whether Catholic or Jewish, Japanese or African American.

"So we're the latest kids on the block and we are going to have to face these challenges." She and her husband spoke at churches, synagogues, think tanks, and schools. "We were speaking to as many people as we could." These interactions led to the creation of new initiatives: Khan developed a global initiative for women, in part due to the questions about the status of women in Islam. In response to the persistent question "Why don't more Muslims speak out against extremism?" she created Muslim Leaders of Tomorrow to bring new voices into the public conversation. Questions about the role of democracy in Islam led to the Islamic Governance Project, which looked at ethics and law. "And so," Khan said, "we basically just put the [center] idea on the back burner."

Yet Khan and Rauf still held tight to the idea of a Muslim community center. When they established the Cordoba Initiative in 2004, they began referring to the center as "Cordoba House." The vision would now reflect their new emphasis on outreach: "We knew that there would have to be a strong multifaith component to this because Americans wanted to know more about Islam, and because we had started building coalitions with our faith communities. So after 2004, when we restarted thinking about this we said, 'Okay, this has to have a multifaith, pluralistic component to it.'"

In 2009 Khan met with a new congregant of Imam Rauf's, Sharif el-Gamal, a real estate developer. Khan remembered, "Gamal showed us the property that had been purchased for potential development." She recalled that his original plan had been to build condos, perhaps with one floor dedicated to a Muslim prayer space. "Gamal shared the vision of the Cordoba House and decided to dedicate the site to realizing the dream."

The former Burlington Coat Factory building was damaged in the 9/11 attacks and had been vacant for almost eight years. "It was the right size, the right footprint, and we could build upwards." It was also in the right place, not far from Rauf's Tribeca mosque. Soon they would start using the lower level as an overflow prayer space. As the leaders of the center, Khan and Rauf together established the mission and vision:

> Our guiding principle was always pluralism, because it is extremely important that we stay true to the highest, highest Islamic values of pluralism. Which is pluralism within the faith, because God has created this diversity; and pluralism among the faiths, because God has created all of these religions.... No one can challenge that, if you say that that is your guiding principle. It's like the Rumi poem, "Come, come whoever you are, the worshipper and wanderer. Ours is not a place of despair. Just come."

Indeed, their original plans for the center called for these words from Rumi's poem to be etched in stone outside, as a form of invitation. But throughout May 2010 Khan and Rauf continued to receive a very different message in the growing opposition to Cordoba House: "Leave."

From Muslim Community Center to "Ground Zero Mosque"

The first protest rally against the center, sponsored by SIOA with assistance from Stop the Islamization of Europe, took place on June 6, D-Day. More than one thousand people participated, many carrying flags or dressed in red, white, and blue. They gathered at the corner of Church Street and Liberty Street and carried signs such as, "A mosque at Ground Zero spits on the graves of 9/11 victims—Stand up America!" and "Why Cordoba? Cordoba is the place in Spain where [the] first Islamic Caliphate was established in the West."[13] Some held copies of a printed sign with the word "Sharia" in dripping red paint, evocative of blood. An older man wearing a New York Yankees cap and a flag T-shirt held up a handmade sign that said simply: "Everything I wanted to know about Islam I learned

---

[13] SIOA, "No Mosque at Ground Zero" June 6 Rally (Videos and Pictures)," No Mosques at Ground Zero, June 7, 2010, https://nomosquesatgroundzero.wordpress.com.

on 9/11."[14] Supporting groups included Jihad Watch, the Manhattan chapter of ACT for America, the Center for Security Policy, the New York Tea Party, and a number of grassroots groups.[15] Newt Gingrich and Geert Wilders, a controversial Dutch politician, were among the political figures in attendance.

The tenor of some of the opposition was troubling, not just for Khan and Rauf, but also for their supporters and advisers. One radio talk-show host said, "I hope the mosque isn't built, and if it is, I hope it's blown up. And I mean that."[16] An advertisement by a Republican PAC called Kill the Ground Zero Mosque was so "inflammatory" that a media strategist told Khan directly that if it was televised, they would have to leave the country. While major networks refused to air the ad, they regularly invited Pamela Geller to speak on her opposition to a project that was now widely known, and understood, as "the Ground Zero Mosque."[17]

Khan, Rauf, and their small staff scrambled to keep up with the growing crisis as well as the heightened emotions and ongoing threats and accusations. There were also practical matters: in mid-July, based on recommendations of the new PR team, Cordoba House was renamed "Park51"; Khan later added, "This was without our consultation." The organization remained "The Cordoba Initiative." Khan explained that once the controversy began and the opposition came out, "everything spun out of control.... We didn't know what happened to us." She remembered,

> I was so busy going day by day, and surviving, and trying to stay strong for everybody else that was looking at me.... I didn't have those moments where I said, "You know what, it's not worth it," because I know the stakes are very high. I just couldn't afford to have those moments. I used to walk in here, and I had twenty-year-olds who were managing the biggest crisis of this decade. So I was doing it for them; I was doing it for our community. I was

[14] Peach, "The No Mosque at Ground Zero Protest," YouTube, December 12, 2010.

[15] Ibid.

[16] Moises Mendoza, "Talk Show Host Calls for Bombing of Mosque; He Apologizes Later for Remarks on New York Plan," *Houston Chronicle*, May 28, 2010, B1.

[17] Christine Schwen, Justin Berrier, Eric Schroeck, and Kate Conway, "TIMELINE: Nine Months of the Right's Anti-Muslim Bigotry," Media Matters for America, September 10, 2010, https://www.mediamatters.org/.

doing it, like a good mother does: you don't show your children your vulnerability when you are being attacked. You just try to embrace and calm everybody down.

Khan also drew upon her spiritual resources. She noted that all of those who try to "change the status quo" are persecuted, and remembered the prophetic history from Moses to Muhammad. Khan remembered one hadith (a story from the life of the Prophet Muhammad intended as an example) that she kept in her mind so constantly, so vividly, "as if it was an image." She recounted that when the Prophet Muhammad first brought a new message, of One God, many people didn't like it. At the time, Khan explained, the Ka'aba was filled with idols, and people worshiped hundreds of gods. "Talk about bringing the opposite message of what people believe!" She continued,

> So he used to walk by an alleyway, and there was a woman who would always throw entrails and garbage at him.... We're talking loose entrails. And a couple of times he got hit, and after a while he got used to it, and he would duck. And then one day, there were no entrails.

Khan explained that when the Prophet inquired about the woman, he was told she was sick. He went to visit her, and the woman—who was once full of hate—was transformed by the profound act of kindness and became one of his followers. Khan remembered,

> I was always imagining myself walking down the alleyway, and entrails are being thrown at me. And I would imagine, every time I saw a newspaper article or blog, I would just say "Entrails!" ... I would come in here and say, "Guys, these are just entrails. Remember the Prophet's story of the entrails. Just duck.... File them away. Don't even read them. Hate mail: handle them; send it to the police. You have to protect yourself. These people will recognize their own mistakes in due time. Not right now." And that's how I survived.

Khan, Rauf, and their partners received violent threats and graphic hate mail. Her voice trailed off as she explained, "It is unbelievable. It's so bad, it's so ugly....." Khan preferred to focus on what they called "great mail." She explained, "Whatever negative was out there, it was always outweighed by the positive—and this huge embrace that was coming out of America."

Interfaith Support

Khan survived by drawing upon spiritual resources and, she explained, because of the "well" of interfaith support. Pamela Geller and other bloggers referred to her as "Khan the Con" and continued to ask, Was this a "victory mosque"? Would they impose Shariah law? Was the funding from extremist sources? Were they pretending to be moderates, using *taqiyya* (translated by SIOA and Jihad Watch as "Muslim deception"[18])? Khan responded,

> I also knew that the opposition didn't have anything on us. They were just going to fabricate things. There was nothing that I was concerned about. What are they going to do? And we had assets that they didn't have. Our assets were all our relationships. Our relationships came out so strongly.

From the beginning, Khan and Rauf received support from their interfaith allies. Some worked behind the scenes as consultants to the project; others stepped into the media fray or stood by their side during public events. At one charged and contentious community meeting, Khan recalled seeing Rev. Dr. James Forbes, an esteemed Senior Minister Emeritus of the Riverside Church, sitting on a staircase outside the crowded meeting room. She thanked Rev. Forbes for his support but encouraged him to go home, as it was getting late. Khan recalled,

> And he said, "Oh no, no, no, I'm not missing this, this is a historical moment, this is like I'm back in the old days [of the civil rights movement]." People saw many parallels within their own faith communities; especially in the African American community, they saw some very, very strong parallels with what they had gone through.

---

[18] Robert Spencer, "How Taqiyya Alters Islam's Rules of War," Jihad Watch, January 6, 2010, https://www.jihadwatch.org.

Khan explained that Rev. Forbes was one of many people to go "over and above the call of duty." She added, "They were not getting paid to do this; they were just doing what they thought was the right thing to do."

Yet not everyone working in interfaith relations supported the proposed center. On July 28 the Anti-Defamation League (ADL) issued a statement about the project, which read in part, "The controversy which has emerged regarding the building of an Islamic Center at this location is counterproductive to the healing process. Therefore, under these unique circumstances, we believe the City of New York would be better served if an alternative location could be found."[19] Khan was shocked. "It took the rug from underneath our feet." While some found the position of the ADL sensible, for others the statement seemed contradictory to the ADL's mission. Khan believed that the ADL's stance served to galvanize support for the center. She explained that, as the controversy continued, the voices of support from the Jewish community proved especially critical.

On August 4, two days after the Landmarks Commission ruled against making the former Burlington Coat Factory building a protected landmark, a group of rabbis and Jewish activists convened at the site of the proposed center. Rabbi Arthur Waskow and Rabbi Ellen Lippman were among those who offered Khan traditional housewarming gifts: a candle, bread, salt, and honey. At the event, Khan read a prepared statement but didn't take questions from the media. Many of the rabbis stepped up to express their support. Khan remembered that it was 104 degrees that day:

> It was blistering! Sweating, the sun was pouring, and there they are giving me honey, and honoring me, and doing a press conference.... There are *lots* of people that did things that no one ever expected of them, and they changed the discourse because of that.

As the controversy continued, many individuals stood up in support of the project, but Khan preferred not to state their names. Some had already received hate mail; others had lost donations from their congregations after taking a stand. "People had to pay a hefty price."

---

[19] Anti-Defamation League, "Statement on Islamic Community Center Near Ground Zero," press release, July 28, 2010, https://www.adl.org/.

Pressure from the State Department and
Hostility on the Homefront

While many in the interfaith community provided support, the State Department represented another source of pressure. Khan and Rauf were scheduled for a diplomatic tour of the Middle East to begin in August, but as the crisis wore on, they thought it might be better to stay in New York City. From the highest levels of government, the message they received was clear: Imam Rauf, who was speaking on behalf of the administration, could not cancel the trip because of a small opposition group. Yet, at the same time, Khan felt, "There was no way we could leave the house burning." Together they decided that Rauf would go on the three-week trip, and Khan would stay behind to advocate for the center. "I knew it would be a lonely journey, that it would be tough, but I had to do it." Yet once Rauf left on the trip, Khan stated, "That created suspicion: 'Where's the Imam?'"

By early August the national media began reporting that the "Ground Zero Mosque" might be fueling anti-Islam sentiments, with reports of incidents at mosques across the United States. Islamic centers in Michigan, Texas, Wisconsin, and Washington experienced vandalism; a New York mosque received a bomb threat; and a pipe bomb was detonated at an Islamic center in Florida. And in late July the Dove World Outreach Center announced an "International Burn the Qur'an Day." New and expanding Islamic centers in Tennessee, New York, and Wisconsin faced opposition and strong rhetoric.[20] While local opposition to mosques was a common occurrence, as Dr. Ihsan Bagby observed in the *New York Times*, "What's different is the heat, the volume, the level of hostility.... It's one thing to oppose a mosque because traffic might increase, but it's different when you say these mosques are going to be nurturing terrorist bombers, that Islam is invading, that civilization is being undermined by Muslims."[21]

During the month of August, reports of incidents were on the increase. A toy pig with the message "No Mosque in NYC" was left at a mosque in Chico, California. The Islamic Society of Wisconsin faced harsh opposition

---

[20] Center for Race and Gender at the University of California Berkeley and the Council on American Islamic Relations, "Same Hate, New Target: Islamophobia in the United States, January 2009–December 2010," accessed July 2011, http://crg.berkeley.edu.

[21] Laurie Goodstein, "Across Nation, Mosque Projects Meet Opposition," *New York Times*, August 7, 2010.

at a Green Bay City Council meeting. Demonstrators appeared outside a Bridgeport, Connecticut, mosque. Signs reading, "No Temple for the God of Terrorism at Ground Zero," were left at an Islamic center in Madera, California. And at the Islamic Center of Murfreesboro in Tennessee, shots were fired near the construction site of a new mosque.[22]

As Khan read media reports of the attacks against other Muslim centers, she said, "That's when we knew this was bigger than just us. Move it? You've now moved on to California, Tennessee, Florida." At her family's mosque on Long Island, over the years they had encountered occasional local opposition based on parking or traffic, "but not placards protesting Shariah. Not a national, organized opposition."

Mounting Tensions, Mounting Criticism

With tensions mounting, as the controversy continued into its third month, it was no longer merely a matter of those who supported the project and those who opposed it. The *New York Times*, which had been largely favorable in its coverage of the project, published a piece in early August that was critical of Khan, Rauf, and the real estate developer Gamal. The article noted that while planners may not have realized that it would be called "a victory monument to terrorism," they failed to engage with those who might oppose the project, did not consult with experienced Muslim organizations, and didn't hire a public relations firm until after the controversy ensued.[23]

> How Ms. Khan's early brainstorming led to today's combustible debate, one often characterized by powerful emotions and mistaken information, is a combination of arguable naïveté, public-relations missteps and a national political climate in which perhaps no preparation could have headed off controversy.[24]

A *Washington Post* column pointed criticism at Khan's husband, Rauf: "At the center of a global firestorm of debate, Rauf is absent, sticking to his commitment to lecture for the State Department in Bahrain about, of

---

[22] Center for Race and Gender at the University of California Berkeley and the Council on American Islamic Relations, "Same Hate, New Target."

[23] Anne Barnard, "For Mosque Sponsors, Early Missteps Fueled Storm," *New York Times*, August 13, 2010 (corrected version), A1.

[24] Ibid.

all things, 'how we emphasize religious tolerance in our society.'"[25] The August 23 article added, "Rauf's wife said he would not be available for an interview until next month."[26]

In August, a number of Muslim individuals and organizations publicly expressed concerns and criticism. The Muslim Canadian Congress wrote a letter to Rauf, dated August 10, which "urg[ed] the Cordoba House Initiative to abandon its proposed Ground-Zero Mosque in New York in the face of outrage expressed by large segments of the American population." The letter stated:

> Many Muslims suspect that the idea behind the Ground Zero mosque is meant to be a deliberate provocation, to thumb our noses at the "infidel." We believe the proposal has been made in bad faith and, in Islamic parlance, is creating "fitna," meaning "mischief-making," an act clearly forbidden in the Qur'an.... The Qur'an commands us Muslims to, "Be considerate when you debate with the People of the Book"—i.e., Jews and Christians [chapter 29, verse 46]. Building an exclusive place of worship for Muslims at the place where Muslims killed thousands of New Yorkers is not being considerate or sensitive; it is undoubtedly an act of "fitna."[27]

Mustafa Stefan Dill developed a three-part analysis of the project, which characterized the "failures" of the Cordoba Initiative's social media and PR approach as "exhaustive and severe." More than two months into the controversy, he noted, "there still appears to be some confusion in the public perception over whether ... the project is a community center, an Islamic center, a mosque, or a mix, which got stuck with the label "Ground Zero Mosque."[28]

---

[25] Michelle Boorstein, "The Absent Imam at the Storm's Center; Interfaith Advocate Has Been Mostly Silent in N.Y. Mosque Debate," *Washington Post*, August 23, 2010, C1.

[26] Ibid.

[27] Muslim Canadian Congress, "Muslim Canadian Congress Urges New York's Ground-Zero Mosque Imam to Abandon Project," press release, August 9, 2010, www.muslimcanadiancongress.org.

[28] All quotes from Mustafa Stefan Dill, "Cordoba House 'Ground Zero Mosque': PR & Path Forward Part-1: Public Relations Analysis," Muslim Matters, August 17, 2010, https://muslimmatters.org/.

Hussein Rashid, long active in interfaith affairs, posted a piece titled "The Leadership Failure of Park51," which cited a lack of media planning or ability to articulate the center's goals:

> Many people are speaking out against the Islamophobes, but we should not conflate this with support of the center. The organizers of the proposed Park51 project lacked the vision that could have foreseen both the fabricated "controversy" of the Islamophobes and the discontent of the Muslim community that was not included in the planning process. Because the project's planners failed to foresee the former, the Muslim community has been forced to defend a project about which it is otherwise ambivalent.[29]

One young Muslim commentator described the project as "dangerously naïve." Despite the "noble intentions" of Khan and Rauf, Abed Bhuyan asked why they did not consult with other American Muslims who became "bystanders in what has become an attack on our religious freedoms."[30] Blogger Aziz Poonawalla echoed the concern that the Muslim community was being "dragged into" the controversy on his BeliefNet post: "In some ways it would be a relief if the issue went away. However, if the project does fail, then I think that the message that will be sent is that bigotry and fear of Muslims is not just permitted, it is effective."[31]

Khan described strong support from most Muslim individuals and organizations, despite a few vocal detractors. For some, Khan argued, it was a matter of "getting their fifteen minutes of fame." For those who said they should have consulted the Muslim community, Khan countered, "Who is 'the Muslim community'?" She explained that every Muslim center, whether in Long Island or Los Angeles, grows out of a small group in its own context: the Muslim community is diverse, complex, and ultimately local. As to the persistent criticism about the center's public relations approach, Khan laughed. As soon as the crisis broke, she noted,

---

[29] Hussein Rashid, "The Leadership Failure of Park51," Religion Dispatches, August 22, 2010, https://religiondispatches.org/.

[30] Abed Z. Bhuyan, "Park51: It's about the Community, Stupid," Patheos blog, August 25, 2010, https://www.patheos.com.

[31] Aziz Poonawalla, "My Final Word on Park51," Beliefnet, City of Brass (blog), August 18, 2010, https://www.beliefnet.com/.

they engaged some of the best media and communications firms available, but this crisis was something they had never seen. They hired one
of the top PR people in the city, who had worked with major banks and
knew how to handle a crisis: even she was stumped. Khan offered an
explanation: "You're dealing with Islam. Islam is a brand that has been so
tarnished in the past ten years. That is at the root of this."

Polls and Politicians' Perspectives

In the summer of 2010, opinion polls clearly indicated that the majority
of Americans opposed the proposed center, an important fact given the
midterm elections in November. As the controversy wore on, Mayor
Michael Bloomberg was among the few political figures to consistently
affirm the right for the center to be built. In early August, Bloomberg
went one step further. Standing on Governor's Island, with the Statue of
Liberty in the background and a group of diverse religious leaders at his
side, Bloomberg spoke:

> This nation was founded on the principle that the government
> must never choose between religions or favor one over another.
> The World Trade Center site will forever hold a special place in
> our city, in our hearts. But we would be untrue to the best part
> of ourselves and who we are as New Yorkers and Americans if we
> said no to a mosque in lower Manhattan.
>
> Let us not forget that Muslims were among those murdered
> on 9/11, and that our Muslim neighbors grieved with us as New
> Yorkers and as Americans. We would betray our values and play
> into our enemies' hands if we were to treat Muslims differently
> than anyone else. In fact, to cave to popular sentiment would be to
> hand a victory to the terrorists, and we should not stand for that.
>
> For that reason, I believe that this is an important test of the
> separation of church and state as we may see in our lifetimes, as
> important a test. And it is critically important that we get
> it right.[32]

---

[32] Michael Bloomberg, "Mayor Bloomberg Discusses the Landmarks Preservation Commission Vote on 45-47 Park Place," The Official Website of the City of
New York, press release, August 3, 2010, https://www1.nyc.gov.

On August 11, 2010, CNN released a poll regarding Americans' attitudes about the "plan to build a mosque two blocks from the site in New York City where the World Trade Center used to stand": 68 percent opposed, 29 percent supported, and just 3 percent held no opinion.[33] A Marist Poll indicated that 53 percent of New Yorkers opposed the project; however, only 31 percent of Manhattan residents disapproved.[34]

While Newt Gingrich and Sarah Palin had weighed in earlier to express their opposition, President Barack Obama did not comment on the issue until the White House iftar (a shared meal to break the fast during Ramadan) held on August 13. He began by acknowledging the trauma of 9/11, and continued,

> But let me be clear: as a citizen, and as President, I believe that Muslims have the same right to practice their religion as everyone else in this country. And that includes the right to build a place of worship and a community center on private property in Lower Manhattan, in accordance with local laws and ordinances. This is America. And our commitment to religious freedom must be unshakeable. The principle that people of all faiths are welcome in this country, and that they will not be treated differently by their government, is essential to who we are. The writ of the Founders must endure.[35]

The next day, President Obama was asked follow-up questions about his support of the project, to which he responded, "I was not commenting and I will not comment on the wisdom of making the decision to put a mosque there."[36]

A range of political figures soon weighed in, and in late August one politician raised the stakes: New York governor David Paterson asked Khan and Rauf to meet with him to discuss moving to another location:

---

[33] CNN/Opinion Research Corporation, "CNN/Opinion Research Corporation Poll—Aug 6 to 10, 2010," question 41, p. 11.

[34] Thomas Rhiel, "Poll: 68% of New Yorkers Oppose So-Called 'Ground Zero Mosque,'" TPM Live Wire, August 10, 2010.

[35] The White House, Office of the Press Secretary, "Remarks by the President at Iftar Dinner," press release, August 13, 2010, https://obamawhitehouse.archives.gov/.

[36] John Hudson, "Obama's 'Ground Zero Mosque' Two-Step," *The Atlantic*, August 16, 2010, https://www.theatlantic.com/.

"If the sponsors were looking for property anywhere at a distance that would accommodate a better feeling among the people who are frustrated, I would look into trying to provide them with the state property they would need."[37] He noted further that a move would be "a noble gesture to those who live in the area, who suffered after the attack on this country, and at the same time would probably, in many ways, change a lot of people's minds about Islam."[38] For months, Khan knew the center had become a "wedge issue," and the question of a move had been with them from the beginning. "Advisers came out of everywhere: 'Don't move it; stay the course.' 'Move it; you'll be heroes.' 'Don't move it: it will show you have buckled.'" Khan said, "There is no rule book on what to do when you're in a national crisis."

"Everybody Is a Stakeholder"

By late August, Ramadan was well underway, and the controversy had now extended more than three months. On August 22, with Imam Rauf still overseas on a State Department tour, protesters and supporters faced off at the site of the proposed center. The same day, Khan appeared on ABC News, together with Rabbi Joy Levitt from the JCC in Manhattan, on a program titled *Debating the Ground Zero Islamic Center*. The host, Christiane Amanpour, asked if Khan was going to "seek a compromise and move it." She replied,

> Well, what we are doing is we are meeting several stakeholders right now, because we understand the pain and the anguish that has been displayed throughout the country with the polls that are represented out there. And we want to build bridges. We don't want to create conflict. This is not where we were coming from. So, this is an opportunity for us to really turn this around and make this into something very, very positive. So we will meet. And we will do what is right for everyone.[39]

---

[37] Stephen Nessen, "Where New York Leaders Stand on the Islamic Cultural Center," WNYC.org, September 10, 2010.

[38] CNN Wire Staff, "Paterson Proposes Finding Compromise Site for Islamic Center," CNN Politics, August 18, 2010, http://www.cnn.com/.

[39] ABC News, "Town Hall Debate: Should Americans Fear Islam?," *This Week*, YouTube, October 3, 2010.

Amanpour asked if Khan planned to meet with the governor and consider his offer of another location, and Khan explained that, first, she would need to meet with their New York stakeholders. Khan outlined the many considerations: the sentiments of their supporters, their constitutional right to build the center, the extremists who are seizing this moment. Khan noted, "We have to be very careful, and deliberate, when we make any major decision like this."[40] Khan later reflected,

> The Muslim world is a stakeholder because they all want to see if you're going to be allowed to build a mosque. The Muslim community is a stakeholder, because everyone's saying, "Oh, let's see what happens with this Islamophobia." The whole interfaith community is a stakeholder, because they want us to succeed. The civic associations are all stakeholders, because they really want to make sure that the Constitution is being upheld. Then, the 9/11 families ... the whole thing came out because of them. And then you have the American public that seems to have also weighed in.

She emphasized, "Everybody is a stakeholder."

Questions for Reflection

- Khan observes that "Everybody is a stakeholder." Do you agree? How might you prioritize these stakeholders in order to guide her response?
- For Khan and Rauf, the mosque is "a symbol, a platform" for the "silent majority of Muslims." What risks are inherent in such "symbolic" projects? What are the risks of speaking of— or *for*—the larger Muslim community?
- From the very beginning, the "Ground Zero Mosque" name was used more regularly than either "Cordoba House" or "Park51." How is the name a critical part of the narrative? What do you think about the decision to rebrand? Was it effective?
- What is the significance of the ADL's position? How does this speak to the internal diversity of the Jewish community? How does the case reference the internal diversity of the Muslim community? Why is this significant?

---

[40] Ibid.

(B) Case

While Ramadan was set to end on September 11, 2010, the dispute over the "Ground Zero Mosque" showed no signs of resolution. In early September, Daisy Khan's husband, Imam Feisal Abdul Rauf, returned from his State Department tour and rejoined the outreach and media efforts. Each day, for Khan and Rauf, there was something new. The Anti-Defamation League launched an "Interfaith Coalition on Mosques," citing "a disturbing rise in discrimination against Muslims trying to legally build or expand their houses of worship."[41] Donald Trump offered to buy the Park 51 building, with the requirement that any future mosque was "at least five blocks further from the World Trade Center site."[42] Pastor Terry Jones offered to cancel his plans for "International Burn a Qur'an Day" if they would move the center.

For months, Khan heard criticism and calls to "move the mosque," as well as steadfast support for a Muslim community center. She later emphasized, "There was nothing to move." Khan explained it was a vision for a project in a privately owned building. Neither she nor Rauf were convinced that the problem was, in fact, the location: "The opposition was frightened of the vision itself."

For organizations like Stop the Islamization of America (SIOA), Khan believed, a Muslim community center threatened their narrative about Muslims. "That is their modus operandi: that's what they've been doing, that's what they've been saying for years. They wanted to keep the fear of Islam alive." She added, "And all of a sudden this center comes along, with culture, and arts, and food, and integration. 'Come, everybody, experience Muslims, and you don't have to be scared.'" If they had taken their vision elsewhere, Khan thought, the opposition would follow them. And so, Khan explained, they moved forward:

> People were watching us. We had an obligation to people; we couldn't cave in.... We were just standing tall. We hadn't done anything wrong. Our intention was good. Somebody misunderstood and

---

[41] Anti-Defamation League, "Interfaith Coalition to Assist American Muslim Communities Facing Opposition in Building Mosques," press release, September 7, 2010, https://www.adl.org/.

[42] Sumathi Reddy and Tamer El-Ghobashy, "Trump Offers to Buy Out Islamic Center Investor," *Wall Street Journal*, September 9, 2010.

misconstrued our intentions, but that doesn't mean our intention was bad. So we stood on that ground.

At the same time, SIOA planned for the "9/11 Rally of Remembrance" at Ground Zero. The 2010 rally was a memorial for victims of 9/11 and a protest against the "Ground Zero Mosque." It was expected to be even bigger than previous rallies. Supporters of Park51 planned a candlelight vigil on September 10. Meanwhile, Khan and Rauf continued their outreach—including, more recently, to 9/11 families and others who opposed the center. Khan described to a reporter what they had learned in these conversations: "We've discovered that there really has not been a national dialogue since 9/11. And that's what this project has done: it sparked a lot of discussions that should've been had after 9/11. We went to war; we've never had a proper discussion."[43]

September 10, 2010

On September 10, 2010, a newly formed group, New York Neighbors for American Values, held a candlelight vigil at the site of the planned center. Just two weeks before, more than forty civic, interfaith, and religious groups established the coalition "in support of religious freedom and diversity and to rebuff the increasingly strident opposition to a proposed Islamic Center near Ground Zero."[44] For the vigil, participants were instructed not to bring signs, in order to make the evening one of unity and remembrance. Because it was the second day of Rosh Hashanah, and soon to be Eid al-Fitr, the end of Ramadan, some were unable to participate. A few hundred gathered; many wore white or carried American flags; some also wore clerical collars, kufis, kippahs, or saffron robes. One young woman wore a hijab with an American-flag design. Just around the corner from the vigil, as the candles burned in the darkness, two blue lights reached toward the sky to mark the place where the towers once stood.

The speakers that night included diverse faith leaders, elected representatives from New York, and Rep. Keith Ellison from Minnesota, the

---

[43] Mediagrrl9, "'I Fear for My Country,' Muslim Leader Daisy Khan 1," Democracy Now! Archive, YouTube, August 12, 2010.

[44] New York Neighbors for American Values, "Announcing New Coalition in Support of Cordoba House/Park51," https://web.archive.org/web/20100828022902/http://nyneighbors.org/.

first Muslim to be elected to Congress. Ellison greeted the crowd warmly: "When you stand up together, and you hold each other close, and you demand that our essential dignity is more important than anything that divides us, you lead the way for the whole country. You let us know that we all count, and we all matter."

Ellison emphasized that the focus—that night and on September 11—should be on those who lost their lives to terror. He continued by offering a story from the Gospel, the feeding of the multitudes, in which Jesus fed thousands with just a few fish. Ellison explained that there is often the perception that someone has to be left out. "Jesus perceived there to be enough, and where they thought there was scarcity, there was abundance." He continued, "And I'm telling you today, that there is enough for me; there is enough for you. There is enough for the Muslims, the Christians, and the Jews. There is enough for Buddhists and Bahá'í.... There's enough for all of us."

Ellison offered thanks to Mayor Bloomberg and other elected officials who stood up for the center rather than being guided by the polls. "They stood up and said, 'I will bear the disapproval for a worthy cause.' And they did. And I want you to remember that, because character is not what you would do in times of ease; it's what you do when times get tough." He concluded,

> Look: don't return hate for hate. Don't return rejection for rejection. Overcome evil with courage and love. Put out fire with water, not more fire. Don't respond to provocation; don't reward provocation with a negative response. Reward good deeds, and when people provoke you, you come together, and show them solidarity.[45]

September 11, 2010

The next day, the "9/11 Rally of Remembrance" drew thousands to Ground Zero, including a number of 9/11 families and many concerned citizens. SIOA estimated the crowd at forty thousand. The rally began with a memorial service, with prayers offered by a minister and a rabbi. Hosts Pamela Geller and Robert Spencer introduced the speakers,

---

[45] All quotes from support rally: Alex Kane, "On Night before 9/11, New Yorkers Voice Strong Support for Muslim Community Center," Mondoweiss, September 11, 2010, https://mondoweiss.net/.

including 9/11 family members, a former US ambassador to the United Nations, a US Senate candidate, journalists, and activists. The featured speaker, Dutch politician Geert Wilders, took the stage amid chants of "USA, USA" from the crowd.[46] Wilders, a charismatic speaker who was characterized by the BBC as "a deeply divisive figure"[47] for his views on Islam, received a warm embrace from Geller before addressing the enthusiastic crowd. "Ladies and gentlemen, let me start by saying: 'No mosque here!'"

After speaking of the tragic loss of life at the site, Wilders spoke of the plan to "build a mosque, a house of Shariah, here on this hallowed ground." He went on to quote Lincoln: "Those who deny freedom to others deserve it not for themselves." The crowd cheered. Wilders continued, "The tolerance that is crucial to our freedom requires a line of defense." Referencing Mayor Bloomberg's defense of the project in the name of "tolerance," he countered,

> A tolerant city, like your city New York, must defend itself against the powers of darkness. The forces of hatred. The blight of ignorance. It cannot tolerate the intolerant and survive. And that means that we can never give a free hand to those who want to subjugate us.

Wilders's speech continued for fifteen minutes, with occasional chants from the crowd of "No mosque here, no mosque here." He emphasized that the majority of Americans opposed the mosque and explained, "They understand that it is not only a provocation, but a humiliation." Wilders completed his speech: "In the name of freedom, no mosque here."

A few blocks away, the group that held a candlelight vigil the night before held a rally. Some chanted, "Hey hey, ho ho, Islamophobia has got to go!" Others carried signs saying, "No to Hate, Yes to Freedom of Religion!" and "Jobs Not Hate: Say No to the Tea Party Bigots" and "Jobs Schools Healthcare, Not Racism and War." They gathered at city hall and continued to the corner of Church and Park. The group numbered in the hundreds, rather than the thousands who rallied nearby.

Khan wasn't able to attend any of the rallies. By that time, security threats had intensified, and she and her husband were instructed to avoid

---

[46] All quotes from protest rally: Robert Spencer, "Video: The 911 FDI/SIOA Rally of Remembrance: Geert Wilders," Jihad Watch, September 13, 2010.

[47] "Netherlands Islam Freedom: Profile of Geert Wilders," BBC News, June 23, 2011, https://www.bbc.com/.

large public events. Also, they had a visitor in town: "We were under complete duress because Pastor Terry [Jones] showed up." Khan recalled, "He came to barter." Khan and Rauf weren't interested in having such a conversation; "We said we'd meet in the future to do a dialogue." The weekend of September 11, they were in constant communication with Evangelical Christian leaders and Christian clergy who provided "blocking and tackling." Khan noted that they shared a common concern: left unchecked, they were afraid that extremists would dominate the conversation.

Support, and a Surprising Turn

On September 20, national Muslim leaders convened in New York to discuss, and later express support for, Park51. They met with Rauf and Khan, as well as Sharif el-Gamal, their partner and real estate developer. Afterward, a spokesperson stated,

> From the discussion we had with the developer, they are committing to expedite the process, of making sure this project is coherent, has an advisory board from the Muslim community, from the Interfaith community, so this project will reflect America in terms of its spirit and its look at the future.[48]

In the months that followed, the controversy over a proposed Muslim community center faded from the headlines. While some believed that the shift coincided with the end of the election season, Khan thought the turning point came in early October, when ABC News televised a town hall debate: "Holy War: Should Americans Fear Islam?"[49] Khan felt the mainstream media was finally tackling the issue. The program provided a forum for Khan and two others who supported the project to face off with three opponents, including Robert Spencer of Jihad Watch and SIOA and Rev. Franklin Graham. Each group included a 9/11 family member. Khan later explained that the program was valuable for what it revealed about the opposition: "It was like Jerry Springer. . . . It was so telling. Whoever

---

[48] Ron Scherer, "US Muslim Groups Unite, See Mosque near Ground Zero as Test of Rights," *Christian Science Monitor*, September 20, 2010, 5.

[49] ABC News, "Town Hall Debate: Should Americans Fear Islam?" October 3, 2010.

saw it realized what it was all about. 'Oh, it is bigotry.'" Shortly after, she recalled, the intensity of the crisis and its coverage died down. "The phone stopped ringing. It was a big moment."

While the controversy continued to swirl online, as 2010 came to a close Khan and Rauf returned to the quieter work of bridge-building. In December 2010 Rauf announced the launch of the Cordoba Movement, "a multi-national, multi-faith organization dedicated to breaking the cycle of mistrust, misunderstanding, and fear of Islam."[50] Rauf also announced plans for a speaking tour.

Yet on January 14, 2011, the day before Imam Rauf embarked on his nationwide tour, Park51 issued a press release: "New Imam Joins Park51." The press release congratulated Rauf on his tour and stated that Imam Abdallah Adhami was coming on as a senior adviser. The statement continued, "Imam Feisal and Daisy Khan will not be speaking on behalf of Park51, nor will they be raising funds for the project. Imam Feisal will remain on the Board of Directors of Park51. The Cordoba Movement and the Cordoba Initiative are separate nonprofit entities from Park51 with different missions and leadership."[51]

Khan, once again, was shocked. Looking back, without bitterness but with sadness, she said, "Incomprehensible." They were no longer part of the Park51 project. She later explained, "We were the visionaries. To have this happen, it was like being told the child you conceived and gave birth to wasn't yours." She added, "The opposition puts so much pressure.... It is hard to stay together under so much pressure." Ultimately, Khan felt it was the last in a series of "terrible missteps." She noted, "The developer thought that changing the name would make the opposition go away. Then he thought changing the leadership would make the opposition go away. Guess what? [The opposition] pressed on."

Park51 would move forward without Khan and Rauf. It would also continue without Imam Adhami: after less than one month under intense scrutiny, Adhami resigned. At the same time, Khan and Rauf considered their next steps. Sitting in her Upper West Side office, Khan reflected, "Should we really build this in the shadow of this controversy? Or should we do something that is so completely unexpected?"

[50] Cordoba Movement, "Imam Feisal Launches Movement to End Spiral of Violence: Retaking Discourse among Cultures from the Hands of Extremists," press release, December 7, 2010, https://www.prnewswire.com/.

[51] Park51, "New Imam Joins Park 51," press release, January 14, 2011.

As Khan looked to the future and a new vision for the center, her voice rose with excitement, and she brimmed over with ideas: it could be a center for conflict resolution, a place for reconciliation and healing, for interfaith understanding. She noted, "Whatever the next step is, it has to be something that takes into consideration all the stakeholders' aspirations, and what was it that everybody was fighting for."

September 11, 2011

In early September 2011, Pamela Geller released her new book, *Stop the Islamization of America: A Practical Guide to the Resistance*. A few days later, on the tenth anniversary of 9/11, SIOA hosted its second Freedom Rally. Their film on the dispute, *The Ground Zero Mosque: The Second Wave of the 9/11 Attacks*, has been screened at the Conservative Political Action Conference, Tea Party gatherings, universities, and meetings of grassroots organizations.[52]

On September 21, 2011, Park51 held a "symbolic opening"[53] of the center with a photographic exhibit of New York City's children. No protesters were reported to be in attendance. Although the leadership of Park51 has changed, key elements of the original vision remain, with space for recreational and educational activities. While Park51 is "inspired by Islamic values and Muslim heritage,"[54] the dedicated place for Muslim prayers—later renamed as "PrayerSpace"—is an independent not-for-profit organization affiliated with Sharif el-Gamal.

In autumn 2011 Khan and Rauf began to detail their ambitious new vision for Cordoba House: "a series of multi-faith, multi-cultural institutions.... Our dream is to have a Cordoba House in every nation where religious tensions exist."[55] Khan reflected, "We started out thinking it would be a home for Muslims. Then we thought it would be a home for Muslims and outreach." After being at the center of a crisis for almost a

---

[52] Pamela Geller, "911 Freedom Rally at Ground Zero: America, Stand for Freedom," Geller Report, August 16, 2011.

[53] "Editorial: Making the Right Decisions," *Downtown Express* (New York City, NY), September 28, 2011, 10.

[54] Park51 Community Center, "Vision," accessed February 28, 2023, https://park51.org/.

[55] Cordoba Initiative, "Cordoba House," 2010 Cordoba Initiative Website.

year, Khan reflected, "There are people of all religions—good, compassionate people who believe in the oneness of humanity.... We need to create a home for that."

Postscript

The aspirational Muslim community center in lower Manhattan—known as Cordoba House, Park51, and more widely as the "Ground Zero Mosque"—was never built. Khan's imagined community center was never realized; she describes her dreams for the center as "shattered."[56] Looking back, she reflects, "All of these things happened with such intensity that it was a moment of spiritual growth." She continues, "There is a verse in the Qur'an that says, 'With every hardship comes ease.'" Khan added, "Other doors were going to open."

Since that time, Khan completed a doctorate in ministry, wrote her memoir, and published a book on fighting extremism in the Muslim community—with another guide on fighting white Christian supremacy in the works. She continues to lead the Women's Islamic Initiative in Spirituality & Equality (WISE), helped to develop the Global Women's Shura Council, and is completing a new book on women's rights in Islam. Khan's partner on the Community Center—now her ex-husband—directs a streamlined form of the Cordoba House organization that is no longer focused on brick-and-mortar projects.

Khan reflects that, although the "Ground Zero Mosque" controversy dominated the headlines and the public consciousness for months, "Often people think of it as this moment in history that happened, but they don't understand its consequences." She cites the work of journalist Spencer Ackerman, who connects the "Ground Zero Mosque" opposition with the rise of extremist voices and the era of Donald Trump. Ackerman writes, "The transformation of a proposed Lower Manhattan cultural center into an anti-American edifice—framing pushed by the right and reinforced by the mainstream media—was a crucial victory for the nativist coalition that would later rally behind the 45th president."[57] Khan continues, "So

---

[56] All quotes from Daisy Khan in postscript from Zoom interview with the author, July 15, 2022.
[57] Spencer Ackerman, "'The Scariest Thing I've Ever Seen in My Life': How

for me, that is the greatest regret: by not creating a center that would have amplified the voices of the moderates and rejected extremism, with faith communities coming together, we allowed this to happen—or, this movement has come to fruition."

In the years since the controversy, she reflects, "It's definitely gotten worse, because the extremists have an upper hand right now." She remembers the angry faces of the people at the protests and hearings. It was an America she had never seen before: "The hate-filled rhetoric, the anger, the vengeance, all that—I had never really experienced it because I was living in my own silo. . . . I was more involved in harmony-building and dialogue." Before the dispute, Khan was aware of extremism in her own community and saw the center—and her writings—as a way to amplify peaceful voices and reject extremism. During the dispute, she began to observe the rise of a different form of extremism linked to white supremacy. She adds, "So when the January sixth insurrection happened and people were so shocked—'Oh my God, I did not know these guys existed!'—And I said, 'Come on!'"

After the deluge of media attention, the "Ground Zero Mosque" disappeared from the headlines until 2021. On the twentieth anniversary of 9/11, Jonathan Greenblatt, the executive director of the Anti-Defamation League, wrote a letter of apology for Yom Kippur. The opinion piece, first published by CNN on September 4, 2021, began,

> Around the world Jews are celebrating the High Holy Days. During this time, Jews focus on the need for Teshuvah, or self-examination and repentance. But self-examination need not be limited to individuals.
>
> Institutions, especially century-old institutions like ADL, also can commit to the practice of self-examination and Teshuvah. And it is in this spirit that I have been reflecting on a stance ADL took 11 years ago when we opposed the location of the then-proposed Park51 Islamic Community Center & Mosque near Ground Zero in Lower Manhattan. . . . I believe the stance we took is one for which we owe the Muslim community an apology.[58]

the 'Ground Zero Mosque' Set the Table for Trump," *Vanity Fair*, August 9, 2021, https://www.vanityfair.com/.

[58] Jonathan A. Greenblatt, "ADL Head: On NY Islamic Center, We Were Wrong, Plain and Simple," *CNN Opinion*, September 5, 2021, https://www.cnn.com/.

Although Greenblatt was not at ADL at the time of the controversy, his letter thoughtfully outlined the mistake.

> Daisy [Khan] once explained how the goal of Cordoba House was to "repair the breach and be at the front and center to start the healing." Perhaps ADL should have helped facilitate such a discussion. And yet, we chose to weigh in differently. And through deep reflection and conversation with many friends within the Muslim community, the real lesson is a simple one: we were wrong, plain and simple.[59]

It was an apology "without caveat" that also expressed a commitment to "fight anti-Muslim bias as allies."

Khan learned about the ADL apology from a friend, and when she saw it on Twitter, she had a "visceral" response: she would have hoped that the ADL would contact her directly. The Council on American Islamic Relations tweeted back, "It took you and the ADL 10 years to realize this?"[60] Later, Jonathan Greenblatt and Khan had a "heart to heart" conversation about the impact of the decision and ways they might work together in the future. For Khan, the hurt from the prior statement would take some time to heal. She accepted the apology, but noted,

> Their statement allowed the extremists to get emboldened. Because them saying that it's insensitive meant that we were doing something wrong. For me, this is a much bigger issue about acceptance of new groups into America, and how the American Muslim community was the latest group just trying to fight for its acceptance. And there will be other groups behind us.

Khan explains that this is the same message she received from many Jewish organizations and individuals who stood by her during the crisis. "This is the American challenge. And we are the ones that are being tested right now." Only recently has Khan returned to the site of the proposed community center. "I find it very painful to go back there. The pain of 9/11, the pain of everything." While "the trauma is still there," she

---

[59] Ibid.

[60] @CAIRNational September 7, 2021, replying to @JGreenblattADL Tweet, September 5, 2021.

explains, "sometimes these traumas propel you to do other things." Khan's research about women in the early Muslim community have led her to a new idea, which she hopes to express in brick and mortar. She explains,

> At the time of the Prophet, women were so engaged in his community, right by his side. It was a vibrant community, a vibrant mosque. The mosque was one room where men and women and children were floating around everywhere, there were no dividers, no nothing.

She continues, "I've been sharing this information with a lot of women, and everybody's telling me that it's time for us to establish a new mosque in New York City designed around the Prophet's mosque." Khan would call it "The First Mosque." She adds, "I'm envisioning something very transformative, very freeing for women, and freeing for men. We need to go back to the seventh century to restore the wholeness of our community."

Khan hopes to build the project upon the lessons of the past:

> The Cordoba House was a vision of a grand scale. It could have come to fruition had it not become public and had we not received so much opposition. We would put everything in place first: the supporters, the sponsors, the helpers, the volunteers, everybody that needs to make it happen.

She notes, "It's not going to be the same thing that we had envisioned before, but something maybe even better."

When Khan reflects back on her experience with the community center, she emphasizes that there are "two Americas." During the controversy, she collected the correspondence she received into binders, dividing it into "hate mail" and "great mail." In Khan's estimation, these letters tell more than the story of the "Ground Zero Mosque": "It's also the rise of extremism. These letters that I received are the extremists of today that we are seeing out on the streets." As Khan flips through the binder of hate mail, she pulls out a few examples:

> This is a Christian nation! our people have fought and died to preserve our Christian Nation.... One day some noble leader will expel all you Muslims vermin from our country. Get out now!!!

... The Muslim plan is NOT to co-exist but to Convert + take over—stop all Muslim immigration.... Daisy (the new face of terror) Khan "another whore of Mohammed," Americans! Don't fall for the lies of this bitch and other Muslim leaders! Islam is not a religion of peace.[61]

Yet Khan observes that while extremists get attention, "you never really hear about the people that are rejecting that. That's what gave me consolation during our—the onslaught on us—because every nasty letter that we were getting there were other good letters coming." Khan pulls out another binder, and finds a few examples:

My wife and I completely support your project and urge you to stand tall against bigots and hatred.... I would like you to know that some 9/11 victims' families support what you are trying to accomplish. My wife died on American Airlines flight 77 when it hit the Pentagon on 9/11. You honor her and the other victims by being a courageous voice for moderation, freedom and tolerance.... Just throwing some good thoughts your way from Oregon. Sorry about all the mosque uproar you all are having to deal with. I'm beginning not to recognize our country. Please don't back down—our freedom is at stake. I'm sorry you all are having to fight for America's religious freedom, while so many in our country are too blinded by hate to realize it.... I just wanted to add my voice to what I hope is a growing wave of support for the community center. The backlash against your organization is crazy—and it shows just how much we need centers like yours. The protestors make me embarrassed to be human being, but you make me proud to be one, so I guess it all evens out.

She emphasizes, "We must never forget that the loving America has a huge potential to heal the divide." About half of the email expressed messages of genuine care and support; the other half was hate. Khan notes, "That's why I call it two Americas." She asks, "And so, which one is going to dominate? Which one is going to win?"

---

[61] All hate and support correspondence cited, email from Daisy Khan to author, August 11, 2022.

Part 5

Interfaith and Multifaith Challenges

A Question of Membership

While studies of interfaith or multireligious encounters regularly focus on communities, many families—and increasingly, individuals—identify with more than one religious tradition. For Sherry Chayat, born into a Jewish family and now a leader of a Buddhist community, this sense of "being both" was never an issue. Within the Zen Buddhist community, she is known as Shinge Roko Sherry Chayat Roshi. When it was time for Chayat's son to have his bar mitzvah, she and her husband scheduled a meeting with the rabbi of the local Reform synagogue to ask if their family could become members. How might the rabbi respond? Does it matter that she is a religious leader in another tradition? What criteria might he use to decide? What does it mean to "be both"?

(A) Case

Looking back, Rabbi Sheldon Ezring remembered few details about his meeting with Sherry Chayat to discuss her family becoming members at Temple Concord. While today Chayat often wears the robes and shaven head of a Buddhist monk, at the time, there were few outward signs that she practiced Buddhism or that she was a Zen priest. Ezring recalled, "She was a very nice, normal Jewish lady."[1] As Chayat sat in Ezring's office at Temple Concord, a historic Reform synagogue in Syracuse, New York, she approached the issue directly: she was a member at the local Conservative synagogue but wanted to join Temple Concord to enroll her son in the religious school and begin preparing for his bar mitzvah. Born Jewish, Chayat was also ordained in the Rinzai Zen Buddhist tradition; her husband, who converted to Judaism as a teenager, felt that his own Tibetan Buddhist practices enhanced his Judaism. Chayat recently

---

[1] All quotes from Rabbi Sheldon Ezring from phone interviews with Emily Sigalow, August 24, 2012, and September 12, 2013.

167

attended a bar mitzvah at Temple Concord and felt that this community would be a more compatible place for her family. Rabbi Ezring listened intently as Chayat spoke but knew that this was a question he could not answer right away.

Rabbi Sheldon Ezring and Temple Concord

Rabbi Ezring, like the temple he served, had a rich Jewish history. As the grandson of a *ba'al tefillah* (a leader of prayers), and with two brothers who are rabbis, he explained simply, "I was brought up to be a rabbi." Ezring was the sixth rabbi to serve the congregation in its long history. Founded as the Society of Concord in 1839, it is the ninth-oldest Jewish congregation in America. He brought more than a decade of experience to his role as senior rabbi: as a native of New York City, he found Syracuse to be more culturally midwestern and conservative than he expected, but the medium-sized Jewish community was thriving. The temple grew under Ezring's leadership to some seven hundred families. By the time Chayat requested a meeting, he had been at Temple Concord for less than a year.

A Decision

As a rabbi, Ezring often had to make difficult decisions—and sometimes he had to say no. Ezring reflected, "One of the problems with being a rabbi, and especially a Reform rabbi, is people think you can say yes to everything—so you can't say yes to everything." He explained, "I've had people come to me to convert, and I ask, 'You're Christian, so do you believe in Jesus as the Messiah?' And they say yes, and they say, 'I still want to convert.'" Ezring added, "And I have to say, 'Well, I'm sorry, I can't help you, because belief in Jesus as the Messiah is what makes you a Christian.'"

In many congregations, Ezring recognized, rabbis had faced major challenges when the lines of faith were not clear. This was particularly true if people promoted another religion: "Many, many rabbis over the past decades have had this happen when Messianics have secretly joined our synagogues, and then we've had to react to it." Chayat and her husband, however, were not being secretive: they brought up their meditation practice as well as Chayat's leadership role at the local Zen Center. They made it clear that they would not proselytize. The couple explained that they saw their Buddhist practice as complementary to their Judaism: at the

Conservative synagogue, their engagement with Buddhism was known, but not discussed.

In their conversation at Temple Shalom, Ezring recalled that Chayat and her husband described Buddhism as a philosophy rather than a religion, yet he remained unsure. As they detailed their practice, he wondered how meditation was any different from what would be described as a ritual. He considered, "Rituals are a major part of religion. They're a major part of Asian religions. They are Buddhists." Further, he continued, "I mean, no matter how you get around it, from a Jewish perspective, if you got a Buddha in your practice, you've got an idol in your practice." He added: "She was a Jew practicing Buddhism, and she wasn't only practicing Buddhism, she considered herself a Buddhist priestess. If you are a priestess, you're not practicing a philosophy; you're practicing a religion." And if Ezring said no to Chayat, he would have to say no to her husband and son as well: at the time, children could not join Temple Concord without both parents as members.

A Letter to the Central Conference of American Rabbis

Shortly after his meeting with Chayat, Ezring decided to pose the question to the Central Conference of American Rabbis (CCAR), seeking their perspective and advice. In return, the CCAR, the governing organization for Reform Judaism, would issue their opinion on the case. Codified in the form of "Responsa," they provide guidance on particular issues while leaving the ultimate decision to the rabbi.

Ezring had written to the CCAR once before regarding the removal of a feeding tube from a man who had no hope for recovery: the CCAR responded that it "was not permissible in light of Jewish Tradition."[2] In that instance, he chose to support the family's decision to remove the tube, rather than follow the guidance of the CCAR. While the question of the Chayat family's membership was not a life-and-death situation, it was still complex and charged with emotion. Ezring explained, "Sometimes if you have an opportunity to pose a question, it might provide insight to others and give you more complete knowledge of the decision that you are making."

---

[2] Central Conference of American Rabbis, "Hospital Patient beyond Recovery, 5750.5," Responsa, accessed February 28, 2023, https://www.ccarnet.org/.

Ezring reflected: "Judaism is not a syncretic religion like Buddhism, like Eastern religions. So, I really didn't know what to do with it." Yet, Ezring emphasized,

> I have no problem personally with Buddhism. I have no problem with any religion, as long as they respect other religions. I have a problem with all religions that say mine is the only way to God, because I believe God is bigger than that. Mine is not the only way to God, because I really believe one God created. If one God created, and there's more than one religion, then for some reason, God wanted there to be more than one religion. I'm not wise enough to know why.

He mailed his question to the CCAR and awaited their response.

Questions for Reflection

- How should the rabbi respond to Sherry Chayat's request for her family to join the temple? What sources would you reference to make this decision?
- Do you think this would be an issue if Sherry Chayat was not a leader of another religious community, but merely a member? Are there different considerations for each of the family members?
- Does the performance of rituals signify a religion? Is Buddhism a philosophy or a religion? He also notes that "If you got a Buddha in your practice, you've got an idol in your practice." How would you respond?
- What are the risks of accepting Sherry Chayat's request for her family to join Temple Concord? What are the risks of rejecting them?

(B) Case

As Rabbi Sheldon Ezring read the Responsa from the Central Conference of American Rabbis (CCAR), he considered the points it outlined. It stated,

Without in any way denying the depth of Buddhist philosoph-
ical and ethical doctrines, there are fundamental differences
between them and the teachings of Jewish tradition. The latter
clearly affirm this world rather than, as the majority of Buddhist
traditions would, denigrate its importance. Reform Judaism especially has downplayed the salvational aspects of our religion and
has taught that we have an obligation to perfect this world.....
Judaism is a deed-oriented rather than a contemplative religion,
and while the merits of the latter are great, it reflects a basically
different approach to the needs of everyday life, and therefore
Rabbi Leo Baeck took the view that Judaism and Buddhism are
complete opposites, "two religious polarities."[3]

Yet the CCAR also noted that the husband's meditation practice was
not a particular concern:

To be sure, there is no conflict between Judaism and meditative
practices—after all, Jewish tradition itself is familiar with it. But
we see a conflict when it comes to the world-affirming view we
hold and that of a world-denying Buddhism. It is therefore inap-
propriate to consider a Buddhist priest as eligible for membership
in the congregation. The husband alone *might* qualify, but as a
family the couple do not, as long as the mother maintains her
status as a Buddhist priest.[4]

The Responsa continued,

There is also the matter of appearance (*mar'it ayin*). The Jewish
community would be confused by what it would conceive as
an experiment in religious syncretism and a watering down of
Jewish identity. The couple must be brought to realize that with
all the respect we have for their Buddhist practices and beliefs, the
enlargement which they think they have brought to their Judaism

---

[3] Central Conference of American Rabbis, "Practicing Judaism and Buddhism,
5752.3," Responsa, accessed October 23, 2008, https://www.ccarnet.org/.
[4] Ibid.

may fit their own personal needs but does not fit the needs of a congregation. Their request to join the congregation should therefore not be accommodated.[5]

In this case, Ezring agreed with the CCAR. Ultimately he felt "a religion has to have some point of demarcation. A religion has to have some red lines that cannot be crossed." Ezring considered Sherry Chayat to be "a leader who wanted to still practice her religion and her Judaism simultaneously." He would have to tell Chayat that she and her family would not be welcome as members of Temple Concord. Having served as a rabbi since 1974, Ezring knew the conversation would be difficult. He explained,

> When you say no to somebody, you generally make an enemy, especially when you're a liberal rabbi. Orthodox Jews expect it. They may not like the answer, but their life is much more guided by the rabbi. Liberal Jews always assume that the rabbi can come up with the answer that they want because we're liberal. And there are certain times you just can't.

Ezring recalled, "She was better about it, I think, than many other people would have been, but we were never friendly again. I think her Buddhist tradition didn't allow her to be [angry]. That would go against her Buddhist philosophy, at least outwardly. Inwardly, I don't know."

Looking Back

Chayat raised the question of membership at Temple Concord back in the early 1990s. Since then, Ezring explained, "The world has changed." He reflected, "When I began my rabbinate, I wouldn't have thought of consecrating the marriage of two men or two women. Today if it's legal, I'm happy to perform the ceremony for it. I didn't officiate in interfaith marriages until about five years ago. I had to compromise what I did when I'd say a blessing, but I didn't officiate. Today I'm happy to officiate, and as a matter of fact, I will co-officiate." He said, "You grow. You expand."

Ezring left Syracuse for Ohio in 2009 and is now the Rabbi Emeritus at Temple Beth Shalom in Boca Raton, Florida. Before he retired, he reflected, "In the world back then, the congregation I'm in would not

---

[5] Ibid.

have been 75 percent interfaith marriage like the one I'm in now. In the world back then, I would have been very unhappy if either of my children married a non-Jew. Now I've already married one woman who was non-Jewish when I began to date her, and I'm in a relationship with another woman who was a Jew by choice. Things change."

Yet one thing hasn't changed for Ezring: If Sherry Chayat posed the same question of membership today, he would have the same response: "No, because again, she's a minister in another faith who wants to be a Jew and a minister in another faith. I have to say no. In that Syracuse congregation, I had an American Baptist and an Episcopalian minister married to members of my congregation. . . . They were interfaith families. The non-Jews weren't trying to also be Jewish." Further, Ezring supports the Union for Reform Judaism's position against bringing up children in two religions. "I think it is confusing for children." Yet he also acknowledged, "My congregation today is 65 to 75 percent interfaith married, and I wouldn't be at all surprised if a number of the people were bringing their children to both. I just don't ask the question anymore." One of his current congregants wrote a book about meditation and recently led a Moon Rite, yet Ezring doesn't raise the issue. "I don't want to get involved in those issues at this point in my life, because I've passed the stage I want to fight every windmill. I'm just—I'm not Don Quixote these days."

He recalled that, centuries ago, if according to Jewish law a person was considered a doubtful *mamzer* (a person born from a tainted or forbidden relationship), they were not permitted to be married. Yet Jewish law made an allowance that if they went to another city and found someone to marry, they could do so freely. "The unwritten rule there was you don't ask too many questions. Sometimes it's wise not to ask too many questions."

(C) Case

Looking back years later, Shinge Roko Sherry Chayat Roshi remembers little about the meetings with Rabbi Sheldon Ezring to discuss her family's membership at Temple Concord. When Rabbi Ezring told her that they could not become members but were welcome at services, she was "shocked."[6] At some point in their conversations, she recalled, the

---

[6] All quotes from Shinge Roshi Sherry Chayat in (C) case from phone interview with Emily Sigalow, May 14, 2013.

word "apostate" was used. She added, "To tell you the truth, I was so upset, I don't remember what he said. All I know is we were rejected." Chayat explained, "I guess I didn't know enough about Judaism to think that there would be such resistance on the part of a Reform movement, because I knew a lot of mixed marriages at that temple. And I felt, well ... it would be the perfect place for us because we're bringing each of us in a way a mixed marriage, Buddhism and Judaism, and so they'll understand. But of course I was wrong."

"A Strong Spiritual Craving"

Chayat explained that even as a young child, she had "a strong spiritual craving." Her early years were spent living with her mother and grand-mother in a predominantly Jewish area of Brooklyn. Her grandmother was observant and kept kosher, but her mother "had no use for religion whatso-ever." At age four, she and her mother, together with a new stepfather, left Brooklyn; ultimately, they settled in a town in New Jersey where they were the only Jewish family. When she was in second grade, her best friend told her, "My mother said you can't be Jewish because you don't have horns."

She recalled, "We were the only Jewish family, and ... we weren't that Jewish." They did not celebrate the Jewish holidays; indeed, each year, her family put up a Christmas tree. When Chayat's grandmother visited, she insisted that the tree be put outside, out of view. Her grandmother, however, wasn't interested in questions about the nature of God; instead, she told Chayat, "This is what we do. We just light the candles on Friday night. I don't have to know about God. I just do it, keep a kosher home." "So, I guess," Chayat reflects, "that was kind of my exposure to Judaism."

Living with her stepfather's undiagnosed mental illness left Chayat anxious and unhappy as a child, and she found solace in silent reflection. "I would sit outside next to a tree and just let everything go, and kind of allow a river to flow through me. And I felt at one, at peace, and outside of the little bubble of misery that I had been in." She would later learn that she was meditating. In the eighth grade, she came upon Zen Buddhism in a world cultures textbook and thought, *There is a name for this? I couldn't believe it.* "And so, then I knew. I had to go and find a teacher and I had to go and train somewhere." In the late sixties, she joined the Zen Studies Society in New York, and was ordained as a Zen priest in 1984. By the early 1990s she was the leader of the Syracuse Zen Center.

A Turning Point

As an adult, Chayat regularly celebrated the Jewish holidays and hosted a Passover seder at her home. After her son was born, she became more immersed in Jewish life. "I wanted to have my son feel identified as a Jew and let him make up his own mind if he wanted to follow the faith or not.... At least he would have the opportunity to grow up and see what that was like and learn Hebrew and do all those things that actually I never had." They were members of a Conservative temple in Syracuse that many of her friends from Syracuse University attended; however, after attending a bar mitzvah at Temple Concord, Chayat thought, *Maybe this would be a better fit for us.* The Reform temple seemed like "a nice place, and not too demanding." Before they could become members, they would need to meet with the rabbi.

Chayat recalled that the meeting with Rabbi Ezring began on a friendly note. After her husband mentioned their Buddhist practice, Ezring followed up with a few questions. When she described her meditation practice and her role at the Zen Center of Syracuse, she remembers, "I could just see that he was feeling very uncomfortable, just [his] body language and moving away and tightening up." She added, "His expression was a kind of mixture of fear and sympathy." Ezring told her that he would get back to her.

A Decision

Chayat was shocked and hurt when she learned that they would not be permitted to join Temple Concord. She explained, "I never felt this was something that God disapproved of. I really felt that what I was doing was what I should be doing and in no way was being a Zen Buddhist priest making it impossible for me to be Jewish. I was a Jew who was doing this. It was my spiritual path." This spiritual path would lead her, in the years that passed, to become a major figure in American Buddhism. Today, known as Shinge Roko Sherry Chayat Roshi, she is the abbot of the Zen Center of Syracuse and the abbot of Dai Bosatsu Zendo Monastery in the Catskills.

She noted, "I would say there's more of a private being Jewish than public interaction as a Jew, but my public persona is as a Zen priest. But I quote Jewish text all the time, so I never hide it when I'm doing a talk, a Zen talk. I often will bring in a reference to something I've been exploring or something in the High Holy Days text or something like that." She continues to celebrate the Jewish holidays; she and her husband still celebrate Hanukkah together. Her son had his religious training and bar mitzvah at Beth Sholom. As a young adult, Jesse "doesn't particularly follow any religious path.... He identifies as a Jew but spiritually and philosophically perhaps more Buddhist."

Chayat emphasized that she doesn't blame Rabbi Ezring. She explained, "I don't think he knew very much about Buddhism, and he didn't really want to go there.... I don't fault him for it. That was what he had to deal with." She added,

> Well, I think if you know anything about Buddhism, you'll know that there is no real such thing as Buddhism. "Buddha" means awakened one and to be a Buddhist means you're on the path of waking up from delusion and embracing all life in its interconnect- edness. That does not go against Judaism. And to be a Zen priest means that I have given my life to this practice of Zen, of medita- tion, of waking up and of helping others to do the same. It doesn't go against Judaism. And some people say, "Well, do you believe in God?" Well, I believe in what we might call the ground of being or the ultimate or the supreme wisdom. I don't have to call it God, but I can call it God. It doesn't bother me to call it God.

Through her work with a local interfaith organization, Chayat met the rabbi who succeeded Ezring after his retirement. Some twenty years after asking to join, Chayat became a member at Temple Concord. However, between writing, teaching, and shuttling between the Zen Center of Syra- cuse and the monastery in the Catskills, she isn't able to attend services as often as she'd like.

Postscript

Shinge Roko Sherry Chayat Roshi never confronted the rabbi about his decision to deny her family membership, nor did she contest the characterizations of Buddhism by the Central Conference of American Rabbis (CCAR). Chayat, who would be called Shinge Roshi in formal settings, notes,

I don't get into these conflict-related things, as much as possible. I'm here to teach how we all can understand each other and know what's important in life. What's our role in life? Why are we here? This is a big question in Zen Buddhism.... What is your precious life going to be about? Is it just self-absorption? Or is it true opening to all beings, and understanding their pain and how to respond? So, for me as a Jew who practices Buddhism, or as a Buddhist who practices Judaism—and I don't really care how it's put—they are interrelated.[7]

Chayat explains that the CCAR's description of Buddhism as "world-denying" in their response was "a very typical Western misunderstanding." She explains that in Mahayana Buddhism, of which Zen is a part, practitioners may follow a Bodhisattva path. "The Bodhisattva is one who, out of deep compassion, holds all beings' suffering, and responds to that suffering as the number-one reason for practice. So, it's no different really from Tikkun Olam." She continues, "The Buddha did not teach that we are not concerned about others. He taught that when he awakened, all beings awakened. In that sense, there is no way you can separate yourself from others."

Chayat later became a member at Congregation Beth Sholom-Chevra Shas, the Conservative congregation where her child Jesse became a bar mitzvah. During the pandemic, Chayat missed going to the synagogue for services. Given her age, she would only attend in person for death remembrances; otherwise, she participated via Zoom. She notes, "I would say I'm a fairly observant Jew. I don't keep kosher, but the older I've gotten, the more involved with Judaism I've gotten. I think that, in fact, my Zen practice has led me to cherish the teachings of what I would say would be the more mystical Jewish Rebbes throughout time." She notes that the synagogue is inclusive, recognizing that "people are Jews in many different ways, and we embrace them all.'"[8] Overall, she emphasizes, Beth Sholom-Chevra Shas has been "very welcoming"; they even invited her to give a talk to the congregation about her personal spiritual journey.

Her child Jesse, the catalyst for requesting membership at Temple Concord, now identifies as Jewish and Buddhist. Chayat notes that the

---

[7] All quotes from Shinge Roshi Sherry Chayat in postscript from Zoom interview with the author, September 2021.

[8] Congregation Beth Sholom-Chevra Shas, "About Us," accessed February 28, 2023, https://www.cbscs.org.

majority of her community, in both the Catskills and Syracuse, identifies with more than one faith. She continues, "And that's true of Zen in America. Almost everyone was raised in one religion or another, most in Christianity." While statistics on dual religious identity are slim, the Pew Religious Landscape Study indicated that one in five American adults were raised by parents with "different religious identities"; however, only half of these identify as "having been raised in more than one religion," and only six percent of those surveyed identified as "belonging to more than one religion."[9] Yet Chayat and other observers suggest that, in lived experience, dual religious identity might be higher than these statistics suggest—especially with the increasingly fluid identity categories of the next generation.

In Syracuse, Chayat explains, many members of the Zen Center were born into Catholic families and also identify as Buddhist. Over time, they become "more friendly" to the religion in which they were raised. "And they may go home to their families and say, 'Okay, I'm going to go to church with you or a synagogue with you.'" Whether they've returned to the fold, she adds, "They've stopped seeing things in dualistic—this and that—factions. So that's the teaching of Buddhism, we are all here interconnected, and there are many paths." For Chayat, "It's not about naming." She explains, "In Orthodox Judaism you don't say 'God,' right? You don't write 'God.' You write 'G-d.' This is throughout the Jewish texts: You cannot name. This is bigger than anything you can conceive of conceptually." It is the same, she notes, with Buddhism. "Temporarily, we use words. We say, 'Buddha.' What do we mean by 'Buddha'? It means awake. We want this to be our way of living in the world, to be awake to everything, even though it's painful, so that we can respond appropriately."

Chayat is unsure if the CCAR would issue the same ruling today: "I would hope they would look deeper, to really examine, 'What is it to be a meditative Jew? How does that differ from being a meditative Buddhist?'" For those who understand Buddhism as world-denying, she suggests, "Really investigate in a personal way. Do the reading, talk to a Buddhist practitioner, and find out that there are such similarities of concern about what to do about all of the suffering in this world." As a Buddhist teacher, she stays grounded in Jewish practice and spirituality in two ways: "feeling

---

[9] Michael Lipka, "Few Americans Identify with More Than One Religion," Pew Research Center, October 26, 2016, https://www.pewresearch.org/.

the emanation of that which cannot be named—and the spark in everything that Judaism teaches." She continues,

> We are all here to realize our ability as a human in helping others. So *tikkun olam* is really the essence, I think, of being a Jew in the world. But it has to be based on, again—and here Judaism and Buddhism are the same—it has to be based on insight. The mystical teachers are constantly harping on this: "Don't get stuck in your own limited views. This is far beyond what you can conceive of." There is that expression *Ein Sof*—nothingness. It's the same in Buddhism, to realize that everything comes from this nameless, wondrous place.

Looking back at the denial of membership, Chayat hopes that other religious leaders would approach interfaith families, and people, with respect. Yet, she adds, "I don't think that it was anyone's fault. I think that that particular rabbi was going along with his understanding, and that, of course, the CCAR didn't really do much work in terms of understanding Buddhism." She reflects,

> It's easy to come up with these views, but it's much harder to let the views go. Let the opinions go and open to the spiritual realm. What is the point of a religion unless it's going to encourage that?

Showing Up for Shabbat

After the massacre at the Tree of Life synagogue in Pittsburgh, Jewish communities across America sought additional safety, whether in the form of increased security, religious gatherings, or support from fellow citizens and interfaith organizations. It was the deadliest antisemitic attack in American history, with eleven people brutally murdered as they prayed. When Rabbi Joel Sisenwine learned that the American Jewish Congress was planning "Show Up for Shabbat" events the next week, he bristled. Was now the right time to open the doors to the synagogue? The safety of the community, both physical and spiritual, was in danger: Would an interfaith event be appropriate, or welcome? If so, who should participate? Should it be a traditional Jewish Shabbat service, at a time when the community most needed it, or an interfaith event? As he comforted his community and contemplated his sermon, he knew there were only a few days before people would be showing up for Shabbat.

(A) Case

As Rabbi Joel Sisenwine drove along Fifth Avenue into Midtown Manhattan for a brief birthday getaway with his wife, Heidi, his cell phone rang. The road trip from the Boston suburbs went by quickly, the trees still ablaze with autumn colors in late October. Sisenwine remembered, "At about Sixty-Ninth Street, I get the call."[1] He continued to drive as he listened to one of the temple educators describe the horrible details of gunfire erupting during Shabbat services at the Tree of Life synagogue in Pittsburgh. Many were feared to be dead. By the time

---

[1] Unless otherwise noted, quotes from Rabbi Joel Sisenwine in (A) and (B) cases are from interview with the author, Wellesley, MA, November 18, 2018.

Sisenwine reached Sixty-Fifth Street, just a few blocks south, New York's landmark synagogue Temple Emanu-El came into view. The large, historic temple was surrounded by the National Guard and officers carrying machine guns.

The rabbi's thoughts turned to his own synagogue: Temple Beth Elohim (TBE) back in Wellesley, Massachusetts. The next day, hundreds of people would be coming in and out for Hebrew school. *So, what's the procedure going to be?* Sisenwine wondered, as he considered whether to turn his car around and drive back to Massachusetts immediately. With a capable clergy team of five and plans already coming together for a vigil at TBE that evening, Sisenwine decided to return the following day: he would handle the calls about safety and security arrangements over the phone.

Safety, Sisenwine reflected, wasn't just a matter of a police presence or guards at the door. It was about community members feeling comfortable returning to the synagogue for regular Shabbat services the following week. With eleven confirmed dead, the Tree of Life shootings were the worst antisemitic attack in US history. Yet when Sisenwine heard the news, he realized that he wasn't surprised. He sighed, "I was not shocked. Just deeply sad." He reflected, "Right now it's just a matter of comforting people that they're going to be secure."

Back in Wellesley the next day, Sisenwine received an email from the American Jewish Congress: "Today we are launching #ShowupforShabbat, a new nationwide initiative aimed at filling synagogues across the country. Join us. . . ." As Sisenwine read the message announcing the initiative just one week after the shootings, he thought, *This is terrible. They just invited outsiders to come, when my synagogue is fearful, to open the doors?* He worried, *Now do we have to have metal detectors? Do we ask people not to bring bags? Do we ask them to RSVP?*

In addition to grappling with security issues, Sisenwine also needed to shape the service and write a sermon. As a leader, he reflected, "Ultimately, my job is to give the answer. But I have to figure out the question. If people come with one question and I'm answering a different question, it doesn't matter how good my answer is—the service didn't meet their needs." Friday's Shabbat services were in just five days, and the doors would be open whether he—and his community—were ready or not.

Temple Beth Elohim

The large, vibrant Reform Jewish community of Temple Beth Elohim (TBE) in Wellesley, Massachusetts, was first established in the 1940s. At the time, Jewish families were regularly prevented from purchasing homes in the wealthy, predominantly Protestant town; real estate agents routinely refused to show Wellesley properties to Jewish homebuyers even after the passage of the state's Fair Housing Act in 1946. Sisenwine acknowledges Wellesley's history of exclusion but notes that the town is more diverse today than its reputation might suggest: it is now home to growing racial and religious diversity and a vital clergy council. On the large, sloping lawn in front of Wellesley's stone Romanesque town hall building, the holiday display now includes a menorah alongside a Christmas tree—and, more recently, a crescent moon.

Today, of the more than thirteen hundred TBE families, some live in Wellesley, while others are drawn from thirty-five other cities and towns in the greater Boston area. TBE bustles with activity throughout the day, from the preschool in the early morning to the evening classes and activities, from the *b'nei mitzvah* and book clubs to "Tot Time" and Torah study. While many other religious communities are shrinking, new members join TBE each week. The stunning modern building, which opened in 2010, was designed to accommodate this growing community. The sanctuary at the heart of synagogue seats 450, with sliding walls to accommodate 700; another set of walls extends the capacity to over 1,000 for the High Holidays.

Within the building, inscribed upon the temple's wall, a quotation from the Mishna expresses the three pillars of the TBE community:

> The world stands on three things: on *Torah* (learning), on *Avodah* (worship), on *Gemulit Hasidim* (acts of loving kindness). (*Pirke Avot* 1:2)

The decoration and design of the purpose-built structure reflect the values of the community, such as ramps and accessible passageways to promote inclusion of people with physical disabilities. The design also elegantly incorporates another concern: security. Although the front of the building includes soaring glass walls and exudes a warm sense of welcome, visitors may only enter through one, central, alarmed door. After the Pittsburgh shootings in late October 2018, the doors of the synagogue are not left open or unattended: visitors buzz in at the front door, and a security guard stands outside. Rabbi Sisenwine notes that he receives many questions about the level of security provided. "We do not say publicly whether our guard is armed, but part of me thinks we should."

Rabbi Joel Sisenwine

Growing up in Philadelphia, Sisenwine experienced some anitsemitism. "But," he reflected, "minimal in terms of its potential danger: name calling, pennies thrown, things like that." His worries about anitsemitism in America began to grow after the white supremacist Charlottesville rally in 2017. "One can't separate [the Pittsburgh attacks] from that." For Sisenwine, it was also difficult to separate the synagogue attacks from the highly polarized political climate of 2018. The shooter in Pittsburgh targeted Tree of Life partly because of their affiliation with HIAS, a refugee aid group. Sisenwine noted, "We're a congregation that welcomes Syrian refugees. We're deeply involved in HIAS's work." The midterm elections would be held in less than a week, and issues like gun control and immigration could be divisive at TBE, as in any community. Sisenwine added, "When community is your agenda at a time of polarization, it's really challenging."

On the basketball court and on the *bimah*, Sisenwine sees himself as a community-builder. While a torn rotator cuff keeps him off the basketball court, his love of sports continues. He jokes, "I think there have been many Jewish boys who slowly started to shift their long-term dream from NBA player to something else, and that's what happened to me." When still in his teens, Sisenwine had to choose between playing on the high school basketball team or becoming more involved in the life of the synagogue. His choice reflected a "serious calling"; later, Sisenwine would go directly from undergrad to rabbinical school. And, for nearly twenty years, he has served the TBE community. During that time, he helped the community through other national tragedies, including 9/11 and the 2013 Boston Marathon bombings. Each of those had local impact: one of the planes that hit the World Trade Center originated in Boston; the synagogue is just a few blocks from the marathon route. Yet it was clear that the attacks at the Tree of Life synagogue struck even closer to home.

A Busy Monday at Temple Beth Elohim

On Monday, two days after the Tree of Life shootings, Sisenwine believed that the community's main question was: Will I be safe to come to synagogue? That morning, Sisenwine rose early. He wanted to be sure that he was standing at the entrance of TBE, next to the security guard, to greet the preschoolers as they arrived for the first time after the shootings. "It's not every day I'm there at eight o'clock," he laughed. "I felt like it was important to be there. To take the temperature ... and to convey a welcoming message." Afterward, in a discussion with a preschool parent, Sisenwine asked about how they felt regarding his presence and the additional security. The mother explained that the presence was welcome, adding, "My older son is in the elementary school, and they have lockdown drills all the time now." He added, "So the world has changed."

Later that day, Sisenwine and the clergy team gathered for a meeting to discuss the approach to the service. He stated to his team, frankly, "I have no idea what's going on right now. Let's put our ears to the ground until Wednesday." He wanted to be sure that the service responded to the community's needs. Meanwhile, logistical decisions had to be made related to opening the front doors of the temple. As a security measure, they would distribute name tags to the local churches if members of other communities decided to come to the services. Yet other questions remained: How many officers and security guards should be present, and what should they wear: A sweater? A jacket and tie? A yellow reflective jacket? Sisenwine wondered, "How do you protect yourself and maintain a culture of openness and welcome?"

In addition to opening the doors at the temple, there was also the question of opening the walls of the sanctuary. For weekly Shabbat services, the standard setup of 450 seats was more than adequate, but the space could be expanded to 700 or up to 1,000. Yet Sisenwine worried, what if they opened up the walls and no one showed up? He thought, "It would make people feel vulnerable ... alone. And the whole point of that service was to not feel alone."

As the busy Monday of meetings drew to an end, Sisenwine was struck by "a moment of deep, deep sadness." With all of the preparations, he had little time to think about what happened in Pittsburgh and how he felt about it. "It was just a tremendous sadness that this happened in a synagogue, that I have a security guard in an American synagogue right now." Sisenwine sighed. "He's there all the time. That's crazy, that I live in a country like that. In Poland, they don't have a security guard. That's the grounds of the concentration camps, of the death camps.... Something's wrong." Yet Sisenwine couldn't dwell in his sadness for long, as other matters needed his attention. In a few days, the synagogue doors would be open for Shabbat.

Planning the Service, Writing the Sermon

In the days that followed, Sisenwine received offers that might help him shape the service. A minister from a nearby church offered for his congregation to stand outside to welcome everyone and walk them into the building. A senator's office contacted TBE requesting to speak at the Solidarity Shabbat. As Sisenwine reflected on the message he wanted to offer his community and how to address the visitors who would be joining them, he considered the letter from George Washington to the Jewish congregation in Newport, Rhode Island. The 1790 letter affirmed the community's long-standing presence in America, which seemed far away from the polarized present-day political scene:

> For happily the Government of the United States, which gives to bigotry no sanction, to persecution no assistance requires only that they who live under its protection should demean themselves as good citizens, in giving it on all occasions their effectual support.... May the Children of the Stock of Abraham, who dwell in this land, continue to merit and enjoy the good will of the other Inhabitants; while every one shall sit in safety under his own vine and fig tree, and there shall be none to make him afraid. May the father of all mercies scatter light and not darkness in our paths and make us all in our several vocations useful here, and in his own due time and way everlastingly happy.[2]

As Sisenwine continued to write and revise, he received two emails from community members. One stated, "If you don't address politics in your sermon, you have failed moral leadership." Another warned, "If you

---

[2] "George Washington's Letter to the Hebrew Congregation of Newport," Touro Synagogue National Historic Site website, https://tourosynagogue.org/ history/george-washington-letter/washington-seixas-letters/.

address politics in your sermon, I'm leaving." Sisenwine thought, "I don't usually get emails in advance. I get them after the fact, so this is how vulnerable people are feeling, and how passionate."

The Solidarity Shabbat service was scheduled for the evening of November 2. The midterm election would come a few days later, on November 6; a few days after that, November 9, marked the eightieth anniversary of Kristallnacht. Sisenwine reflected, "And so all these things are brewing in people's minds. It was ripe." On Kristallnacht, "the night of broken glass" that took place in 1938, attacks on Jewish synagogues, homes, and businesses represented an inflection point in the hostility against German Jews, signaling the beginning of the Holocaust. Sisenwine knew that some people at TBE worried that the Tree of Life shootings might be a similar inflection point for American Jews. Yet he wanted his community to feel safe and not to "hunker down." And what did it mean to be having this conversation with the doors of the synagogue open to guests? Sisenwine wondered to himself: *Who would show up for Shabbat? And what would he say to them?*

Questions for Reflection

- What are some of the choices Rabbi Sisenwine must make in the immediate wake of the Tree of Life shootings? What does he identify as a primary concern?
- If you were a local clergy member or community member, how would you respond and support the rabbi and the community?
- At the end of the (A) case, Rabbi Sisenwine is asked by one community member to avoid politics; another says he must discuss it. What advice would you offer?
- What are the risks of opening the doors to those outside of the community? What are the risks of keeping them closed? How might these risks relate more broadly to interfaith activity?

(B) Case

In the week before the Solidarity Shabbat service at Temple Beth Elohim (TBE), Rabbi Joel Sisenwine wrote eight different sermons. On the evening of November 2, 2018, less than a week after the shootings at Tree of Life synagogue, Sisenwine was still unsure how exactly the service would unfold and who would show up. Security arrangements were in place, with plainclothes and uniformed police officers, nametags, and hospitable but watchful greeters. The service would be focused on the TBE community: although neighbors and supporters were invited in, it would still be a Shabbat service. Sisenwine reflected, "I wanted it to be a celebration of the Jewish community's place in America. The shooting made the Jewish community question whether they were welcome in America."

Sisenwine added a few new elements to the Shabbat service, including the song "America the Beautiful." He replaced the images that would be projected on the large screens, which usually depict Israel. "I didn't want it to be misunderstood that we're giving up on America as our home." Rather than iconic photos of Mount Rushmore and the Liberty Bell, they would feature familiar landscapes of New Hampshire or distinctive images of New Mexico. "I didn't want it to look kitschy." He also included a photograph of President Theodore Roosevelt at the Tree of Life synagogue, standing with the grandfather of a TBE member. "It was a picture to focus on. Because it messaged: We have been here. We are Americans, we are Jews, and the two belong together."

Wellesley police directed traffic along Cedar Street into Bethel Road, and the steady stream of community members and visitors quickly filled up the parking lots of TBE and neighboring Schofield Elementary School, with cars double-parked along nearby side streets. The doors of the temple stood open on the unseasonably warm evening, as greeters and security stood outside and hundreds flowed into the synagogue. Some guests arrived wearing name tags; others collected them from tables in the lobby before entering the warm, well-lit sanctuary. On either side of the *bimah*, large screens featured images of candles and the words "We are stronger together." Sisenwine was relieved that he decided to open the walls and bring in extra seating: by the time the service started, it was standing-room-only, with more than fourteen hundred people in attendance.

Sisenwine began the service with apologies for the late start and to the many people who were standing. After thanking his clergy team, sensing the mood of the crowd, he decided to tell a lighthearted story about how TBE estimates seating during the High Holidays through a "ticket-to-*tuchus* ratio."[3] This brought laughs across the crowded room and cut the tension of the evening. He followed that up by an admission: "In dark moments I thought, 'You know, we're gonna set up, we're gonna open

---

[3] All quotes from sermon by Rabbi Joel Sisenwine, November 2, 2018.

up the wall, make the guys work extra hard, it takes a long time to schlep those benches, and no one's gonna come.'" He continued,

> And I must say I want to thank our visitors. I know that in so many ways this service is foreign, and in an ancient tongue that you don't understand, but your presence here we understand very deeply, and it means a great deal to us. And so, I just want to thank you for being here once again. And I kind of want to apologize for the uniqueness of the service, and the fact that I want to share words for about fifteen minutes to our Jewish community. But I really—I'm so glad you're here to be with us.

He later reflected, "That is what interfaith relations should be: It's not compromising your authenticity. It's being authentic and supported along the journey."

In the final version of Sisenwine's sermon, he didn't draw from George Washington's letter to the Newport Jewish community, feeling it didn't work liturgically. Instead he focused on "the regulars," based on those who died at the Tree of Life, who might be a part of any synagogue community. Looking back at the service, which was interfaith in participation if not in content, he noted, "And while our expression is different, our deeply held values are the same. [The values of the regulars] were everything that was *not* the shooter, and that's what brought us all together in the first place. So while I say that this was a particularistic ritual, it was a deep embrace of the values that we share."

One of the moments that stood out most for Sisenwine was unplanned, when he asked those who were guests of the community to stand. Mixed into the crowd, hundreds of individuals rose from their seats and were met spontaneously with warm applause. Some TBE members were in tears, others offered hugs to the strangers and neighbors seated among them. Sisenwine also cried at the sight during the service. "I felt like I could have gone home, right then." He continued, "It had done what it needed to do. It said to us, 'We are Jews in America gathering for Shabbat, and here our neighbors came to say, 'We support you in being Jewish.'" He added, "And that's why I didn't have to address Kristallnacht." He didn't directly mention politics, nor did he avoid it entirely. Sisenwine encouraged the community to vote in the upcoming midterms, bemoaned the divisions of the current political scene, and reaffirmed TBE's work with refugees.

Unlike other local synagogues, TBE's service did not feature a special role for leaders of other faith communities or include elected officials. Although he invited clergy from the local interfaith group to attend, he did not invite them to participate in the service. Recognizing that this was a break with tradition, he explained to the clergy beforehand, "I'm not going to have you come forward. I'm not going to have you lead a prayer. But if you'd like to come it would mean a lot." As to the senator who offered to speak, Sisenwine responded, "This was not a time for electoral politics." While Sisenwine deeply appreciated the offer from a local church to stand outside the temple and welcome the Jewish community, he ultimately declined. "That didn't feel right. Come inside and be with us and worship instead. I want people to feel embraced in their norm, not to enter and say, 'This feels different,' but that we're doing what we always do, surrounded by immense love."

Afterward, Sisenwine described the community's response to the service as overwhelmingly positive, even from the two TBE members concerned about how he would reference the current political scene. One community member was upset that his references to immigration, about having "open hands," were too political. Sisenwine reflected, "The metaphor was intended to imply that we need to be open to the stranger.... I'm happy to stand by that notion, even though I understand its complexity." A few community members who expressed appreciation about the service questioned their rabbi's approach to the interfaith element. Sisenwine recalled, "They wanted a service that was completely accessible to the visitors, saying, 'That's what it means to be a good neighbor'—that there is no place of where it's group identity, and that there are no boundaries, in a sense." But Sisenwine explained, "In this case, I think it was clear, and that was I think what made it so beautiful: that this was a Jewish community gathering in prayer authentically, and we support that embrace. And that's what it means to be an American. That one need not compromise their expression of faith."

Postscript

Looking back to the Pittsburgh shootings and the impact on his community at Temple Beth Elohim, Rabbi Joel Sisenwine reflects, "That was a watershed moment in American Jewish life."[4] The murder of eleven

---

[4] Quotes from Rabbi Joel Sisenwine in postscript are from Zoom interview with the author, August 22, 2022.

members of a congregation gathered in prayer was a tragedy that, Sisen-wine explains, "punctured our sense of security in America." He notes, "I think Pittsburgh was the moment when we realized how vulnerable we were. It has not stood apart; now there's kind of a continuum."

*   *   *

On January 15, 2022, Rabbi Charlie Cytron-Walker and a volunteer were preparing for Shabbat services at Congregation Beth Israel in Colleyville, Texas. As they were getting the slide deck together and setting up streaming, they heard a knock: it was a cold morning, and the man at the door appeared to be unhoused. Cytron-Walker invited him in and asked if he wanted a warm drink. He asked the visitor if he had been to a Jewish service before and later noted that "he was polite and personable and there was no agitation. There were no red flags."[5] When the temple's vice president arrived, he greeted the visitor. "It wasn't for security purposes; it was more about hospitality." Cytron-Walker added, "Hospitality and security often can go together."

The visitor sat at the back of the small sanctuary and services began: only three congregants were in attendance; others were participating over Zoom and Facebook Live. Cytron-Walker was turned around, facing in the direction of Jerusalem, when—during the *Amidah* (standing prayer)— he thought he heard the click of a gun. "I hoped that I heard wrong." During the silent prayer portion, he went back to speak to the visitor: "You know, if you just wanted to warm up, you don't have to stay for the whole thing.... You're welcome to, but it's going to be over an hour." That was when the visitor pulled out the gun. They would be held hostage for some eleven hours.

Cytron-Walker would later credit security training he received— from the FBI, local police, the Anti-Defamation League, and the Secure Community Network—in helping them navigate the crisis. He would later explain that the active-shooter training "was most beneficial";[6] however, he also referenced his training in clinical pastoral education (CPE). Whether as a hospital chaplain, at a funeral, or speaking with

---

[5] Unless otherwise indicated, all quotes from Rabbi Charlie Cytron-Walker are from the Tri-Faith Initiative public Zoom event, "The Pros and Cons of Welcoming the Stranger," Wendy Goldberg with Rabbi Charlie Cytron-Walker, May 26, 2022.

[6] Rabbi Charlie Cytron-Walker, email with the author, December 21, 2022.

a member of the congregation in crisis, Cytron-Walker explained that CPE teaches to be present for the individual with a calm, non-anxious demeanor. "How do you be present for that individual in that moment because they're the person who needs care? And so how do you take the emotions that come up and not have them overwhelm you or get in the way?" When the gun came out, Cytron-Walker recalled, "I wanted to be non-anxious because I didn't want to set him off. I just tried to be present." He and his congregants stayed calm as the hours passed; only when the hostage-taker became agitated did they decide to act—identifying access to the exit, throwing a chair, and fleeing.

Reflecting back on the incident, which ended in the death of the hostage-taker, Cytron-Walker stated, "He didn't come in wanting to kill Jews ... but he could have." He described the hostage-taker's tirades, repeating antisemitic tropes: "that Jews control the banks, Jews control the media." Cytron-Walker noted that this sort of anitsemitism, often casually disseminated on social media, is rarely confronted. "And the fact of the matter is, it's not true. It's really damaging, and this guy believed the whole thing." He added, "It led to a really challenging, challenging day that could have gone a lot worse."

After the incident, Cytron-Walker and the Congregation Beth Israel community received an "incredible outpouring of love and support." They shared an interfaith healing service at a local United Methodist church; others issued statements or reached out with words of support. Cytron-Walker added, "I will tell you that words of support, after what we went through, mattered." Cytron-Walker recalls that many touching responses came from members of other faith communities. He noted, "One of the messages that I really stress is that all of our traditions would want us to live our values.... We want to have that sense of integrity and bring the values that we espouse into the world."

Cytron-Walker considers security trainings to be "vitally important." He noted, "Unfortunately we are not living in the world that we would hope to live in." He continued, "We don't want to live in a world where we have to have training, where we have to talk about hardening our facility. We don't want to live in a world where—at schools, houses of worship, grocery stores, and so many other places ... where this kind of violence can exist. And yet this is the world that we're in."

* * *

Sisenwine explained that the hostage-taking at Congregation Beth Israel "reminded us of our vulnerability." He asks, "Even after Pittsburgh and all the security decisions we made, were we going to close our hearts off to someone in the cold asking for a cup of tea?" He adds, "We could have as much bulletproof glass and locks as possible, but it wouldn't matter. When someone in need knocked at our doors, we want to continue to be who we were—to be a caring community." If a stranger knocked at Sisenwine's door, he emphasized, he would open it. Like all Jewish communities, he explains, they must take safety precautions, engage in training, and be wise about security—without closing off the outside world. Whether in terms of anitsemitism or COVID-19, Sisenwine notes, "There's a level of danger in the world, but one cannot isolate oneself forever."

Colleyville and other events continue to shake the community. However, Sisenwine reflects that without the strong show of support after Pittsburgh, "We would have felt very different with … other antisemitic moments." Sisenwine and the Temple Beth Elohim community are acutely aware of increasing anitsemitism at a national level, with a 61 percent increase in attacks against synagogues and JCCs and a staggering 167 percent increase in assaults in 2021.[7] In Greater Boston, it is difficult to ignore instances of vandalism and violence, including the stabbing of a rabbi in a nearby town. Sisenwine observed, "Anitsemitism's been on the rise, but we haven't had a thousand people fill the sanctuary like that. I think we needed that evening to survive what was to come."

In a polarized and divisive moment, and after years of contending with COVID-19, Sisenwine reflects that leadership in a diverse community is even more challenging. He explains, "Some religious communities are defined by social justice calls. They're easy to work with in this environment. It's harder to work in an environment like what I've created, which is dependent on a diverse community." He understands that political parties that are on the fringes are growing, but centrist political parties that span a spectrum are harder to sustain. While Temple Beth Elohim is a place where people challenge each other and engage around difference, he notes, those conditions are increasingly threatened. "We have a news

---

[7] Anti-Defamation League, "ADL Audit Finds Antisemitic Incidents in United States Reached All-Time High in 2021," press release, April 25, 2022, https://www.adl.org/

environment where people can only listen to what they want to hear and have the algorithm that feeds them only stories that they agree with."

To address this, the temple hosts regular trainings on civil discourse. Yet Sisenwine recognizes, "For some people, they are only looking for an echo chamber of affirmation, and so even though we have these programs, they basically say, 'You know what, we don't want civil discourse, we want a religious community that just agrees with us on our social issues and political issues.' And we're not that." He explains, "Some people come armed to speak, to convince, without a sense of openness and curiosity, but a desire to change people's opinions. And I think growth really requires heartfelt listening, and an openness to challenge one's belief system, and a sense of humility." Sisenwine adds, "The challenges are daunting."

The temple's interfaith work continues, primarily through the local Clergy Council; their work with refugees and food insecurity have expanded. Still, security and safety are ongoing concerns. "We're constantly thinking about these things, sadly enough.... You know, it's the state of our world, and so it is frequent and constant with every shooting in America these days." He elaborates, "Every time we read the paper we're reminded, because we are a school; we have young children in here all day, and so it's a constant question."

When thinking about his community's future, Sisenwine reflects,

> We did not have a Jewish state for two thousand years; we perished at the hands of our enemies without any sense of control. We now have a state for the last seventy-five that we can go to. I'm leading a community that lives outside of the Jewish state, where, if I feel that insecure, I actually owe it to my community to lead them to the Jewish state.... I believe in America wholeheartedly, and my patriotism is deep. I just want to continue that deep embrace of Jews' love for and appreciation for America, which in some ways is getting harder and harder as civil society fractures.

Yet Sisenwine maintains some sense of optimism: "The love for America is a continual embrace of American values and a protection of democracy where it's being whittled away, and I think our people are working hard on that." He emphasizes, "We have work to do. Democracy cannot be taken for granted. It's our obligation—and America's increasing obligation—to protect its minorities. I hope we continue to do so."

Part 6

Navigating Crisis and Change

A Quandary in Queens

Jamaica Bay is a vast, largely undeveloped wetland, roughly equal in acreage to Manhattan. In Queens, New York, it is adjacent to the beautiful Jamaica Bay Wildlife refuge as well as the busy John F. Kennedy (JFK) International Airport. The refuge, and the shores that face JFK, are part of the Gateway National Park. The National Park Service manages the beaches, cleaning up what visitors leave behind—and what washes up from the bay. Yet beginning in the early 2000s, they began finding something new amid the trash: coconuts, *murthis* (images of deities), saris, and other offerings. For the National Park Service, this was a clear violation of their "Leave No Trace" policy; for the growing Indo-Caribbean Hindu community, this was a sincere expression of faith and practice. Aminta Kilawan-Narine heard the range of opinions within her own community: some thought this was a religious freedom issue; others wanted to address the negative impact on the environment. Yet she also read the news stories, which referred to the offerings as "trash." Aminta understood respect for the environment as core to her Hindu faith. She also understood that, for many in the Indo-Caribbean community, the offerings to the sacred waters were a way to preserve an identity across two diasporas: first, from India to the Caribbean, and then, from the Caribbean to America. As the first American-born in her family, Aminta wanted to respond, but wondered, How? What options might Aminta, and others in the Indo-Caribbean community, have for addressing the issue? How might the National Park Service assist? Is there a way to address environmental concerns that also honors the deeply held religious beliefs and practices along Jamaica Bay?

197

(A) Case

Aminta Kilawan-Narine cherishes her earliest memories of coming to the sacred waters: she would often accompany her father after a family *puja*. They brought their offerings—a coconut, a flower, or a *murthi*—and her father released them into Ma Ganga (Mother Ganges), known locally as Jamaica Bay. Aminta's father explained that their ancestors made the same offerings to the rivers of India, and to the waterways of Guyana, before coming to America and settling in Queens, New York.

As a child, Aminta[1] gave little thought to the practice, simply enjoying the walk with her father along the vast shores of Jamaica Bay. Each year, when she joined the Hindu temple's beach clean-up for Earth Day, she was careful not to pick up the occasional religious offering in the midst of the litter. She understood that it would be inauspicious to remove these items left at the beach with intention and devotion—unlike the bottles, socks, and other discarded items carelessly littering the shoreline.

As a young adult, Aminta came to understand the offerings as a practice that connected her family and other members of the Indo-Caribbean community to a new sacred landscape; their traditions proved resilient across centuries of dislocation. Yet Aminta also began hearing some of the debate within her own community—and outside of it—about the offerings at the beach. Complaints were rising in nearby Gateway National Park about the increasing number of items left on the shore and in the water. Aminta recalled, "There were different opinions about it."[2] Some said, "Who does the government think they are to get in the way of our worship practices? We're going to continue to worship here, and we have a right to do that, based on the United States Constitution." Others thought the practices needed to change: "No, this is not good for the environment." Aminta added, "These are folks who are coming from generations that have really had to struggle to maintain their identity." Even at a young age, she understood that there wasn't a simple solution: it was just one of the many challenges that her uncles and aunties, and parents and grandparents, had to navigate in their new home of "Little Guyana."

---

[1] The protagonist is referred to throughout by her first name, Aminta, for clarity: her last name changes during the case.

[2] Unless otherwise indicated, all quotes from Aminta Kilawan-Narine are from Zoom interviews with the author, December 21 and December 27, 2021.

At Home in Little Guyana

The first in her family to be born in America, Aminta was also the only Hindu, Indo-Caribbean child in her Catholic school when she enrolled. She tried to hide her mass of curls in a braid and tried to ignore the dots her classmates drew on the faces of her textbook covers. Those textbooks described Hinduism as polytheistic; to her peers, it was foreign. But at home, she learned that her faith was monotheistic: "One God in many forms," her parents would explain. Aminta relished the warmth and support of her family, faith, and community.

In Little Guyana, colorful *jhandi* flags announced the Hindu presence, whether in front of a tidy home or outside one of the many storefront temples in Queens, New York. Here—unlike school, she recalled—the faces looked more like hers: Punjabi, Afro-Caribbean, and Indo-Caribbean. Roti shops were on every corner, with the smell of garam masala wafting through the air. Music inflected with Caribbean beats blasted from passing cars along the street; inside her home, the sound of *bhajans* rose from her grandmother's cassette player.

Aminta joined her grandmother every morning to sing, learning the forty-verse "Hanuman Chalisa" (a Hindu devotional hymn) by heart. She adds, "I owe a lot of my understanding of my faith to her." The *bhajans* were in languages neither she nor her grandmother understood; they were always sure to look up the meaning in English. Her own name, Aminta, means "defender," and even as a child she was not one to accept things passively. Her family still laughs at the memory of a young Aminta, confronted by a Guyanese cousin speaking negatively about America: Aminta, with her small frame, began loudly singing "The Star-Spangled Banner" in protest.

Aminta regularly sang *bhajans* at the temple, Shri Trimurti Bhavan, and embraced the leadership roles that the pandit sought to cultivate in this first generation. Although they were part of a large and vital community, with Guyanese Americans constituting the fourth-largest immigrant population in New York,[3] they were often marginalized or misunderstood by the broader Hindu American community—with a history and heritage unknown to most Americans. Aminta was proud of the strength and resilience of her community, and their ability to preserve their faith across a double diaspora: from India to Guyana, from Guyana to America.

---

[3] Mayor's Office of Immigrant Affairs, "2021 Report," accessed March 1, 2023, https://nyc.gov.

Under British colonial rule, Indians were sent to British Guyana as indentured laborers beginning in 1838. Part of a larger wave of forced migration from India to the Caribbean, they were separated from their homeland, culture, and language and forced to assimilate. They lost their mother tongues but preserved core aspects of their faiths. Hindus transmitted their faith through song and in the tattered copies of the *Bhagavad Gita* and *Ramayana*, brought over on the ships. In Guyana, political instability, racial divisions, and other ongoing echoes of colonialism would later send many Indo-Caribbeans in search of another home: long refused reentry to India, they looked to America. Beginning in the late 1980s Indo-Caribbeans began arriving in New York and establishing places of worship. While the community comprises diverse faiths, the largest of these is Hindu.[4]

A Screening, an Organization, a Project

In college, Aminta began feeling disconnected from her faith. Outside of her Indo-Caribbean "bubble," she noticed an emphasis on caste and Indian politics. At the same time, she was deepening her own commitment to social justice but was unsure how this resonated with her Hindu faith. *Was faith about preservation and protection*, she wondered, or *about progressive action?* Her boyfriend Rohan, who grew up in the same temple community and whose uncle is a pandit, shared these views. Aminta continued on her educational path toward public service, enrolling in law school after college. And soon Rohan would become her husband, but not before a moment of activism refocused their commitments.

In 2011 Rohan wanted to screen a film that was critically acclaimed but, for some, controversial: *Sita Sings the Blues*. Aminta laughed warmly remembering her then-boyfriend's "crazy" idea: why not show the short film at the temple? Adapted from the Ramayana by a non-Hindu, with an animated, buxom depiction of Sita and a blues soundtrack, they understood that the film pushed boundaries. Aminta and Rohan both appreciated aspects of the film; he thought, if it was deemed problematic, why not watch it together as a community and discuss it? They were not surprised when his uncle said no, feeling it disrespected the tradition; yet Rohan pushed forward, booking the Starlight Pavilion, an event space in the neighborhood.

---

[4] Aminta Kilawan-Narine, in "Diverse Hindu Leaders Share 'Lived Religion,'" Interfaith Center of New York, YouTube, July 18, 2019.

Rohan considered the film to be art—and worthy of discussion: many of those condemning the film had never seen it. And thanks to more than one thousand angry letters to the Starlight Pavilion, the public screening would never take place; it would be moved to his parents' living room. Rohan and Aminta were shocked by the tenor of the dispute and the hate mail he received. She reflected, "Look, I'm not into call-out culture. I would rather call people in.... Maybe we don't agree, but at least we don't agree respectfully." She understood that there were those who think Hinduism is "under threat." Aminta reflected, "I actually think that lends itself to a weaker Hinduism. To me it's counterproductive. I like to come from a place of strength."

Through media coverage of the film controversy, Rohan and Aminta connected with a well-established South Asian Hindu activist, Sunita Viswanath. Together they recognized the need for a stronger progressive voice in the Hindu community. Soon after, they launched Sadhana, meaning "faith in action." Aminta embraced Sadhana's organizational mission to "empower Hindu American communities to live out the values of their faith through service, community transformation, and targeted advocacy work."[5] They would address a range of issues, well beyond a film screening. And one of those would be the offerings at the beach.

The National Park Service: Leave No Trace

The Gateway National Recreation Area on Jamaica Bay is managed by the National Park Service (NPS). Beginning in 2007 the NPS regularly engaged in outreach to the local Hindu community, concerned about the offerings left in the water and on the shores. For the NPS, standard warning signs and punitive fines were not effective, nor were they desirable. Instead, NPS staff educated themselves about Hindu practices, visited local temples, and encouraged pandits (priests) to share the policy of "leave no trace" with their communities. The NPS launched an internship program for members of the Indo-Caribbean community, participated in dialogues, and attended a Ganga *puja*.[6] They also regularly acknowledged that the ceremonial offerings were not solely Hindu; some were related to smaller subsets within the Hindu community, others to Afro-Caribbean

[5] Sadhana, "Mission, Vision, and Values," accessed March 1, 2023, https://www.sadhana.org/.

[6] National Park Service, "2012 Dialogue with Hindu Community," February 26, 2015, https://www.nps.gov/.

practices. Early outreach from NPS included the two main streams of the Indo-Caribbean Hindu community—*Sanatana* and *Shakta*—and a range of religious organizations: the Hindu Learning Federation, the Federation of Hindu Mandirs, and the USA Pandits Council.

Yet conversations among beachgoers and news reports described an increasing number of offerings left behind on the beach: "discarded coconut shells, candles, rotten fruit and flowers, pieces of paper and plastic, soiled rags and garments, religious statues, flags, broken glass, rats, and sometimes body parts of slaughtered animals."[7] The NPS outlined the environmental impact:

> Offerings of cloth can damage boat propellers and smother new shoots of marsh grass in the spring. Marsh grasses are the basis of the salt marsh ecosystem, which acts as a nursery for many recreationally and commercially important fish, crabs and other marine life. The statues offered during the rituals can be a hindrance to barefoot beachgoers. Although food and flowers are biodegradable, they attract rodents and contribute to the overloading of nitrogen in the bay. Nitrogen acts as a fertilizer and causes overgrowths of algae in a process known as eutrophication. When the algal blooms decompose, oxygen is removed from the water, which can cause fish and other marine life to die. The policy of the NPS is to "Leave No Trace." No items can be left on our shores, period.[8]

Within the Indo-Caribbean Hindu community, some leaders advocated for change; others advocated for rights; some advocated for both. Even if there was mutual agreement between the NPS and the diverse Hindu community about the need to protect the environment, the question of how to do so—without restricting religious practices—remained unclear.

Project Prithvi and the Practice of Puja

Through Sadhana, Aminta found her faith and social justice efforts coming together in new ways. At the heart of the work were core Hindu values: *ekatva* (oneness of all), *ahimsa* (nonviolence), and *seva*

---

[7] Lee Landor, "Gateway Volunteers Forced to Clean Litter Left on Shores after Rituals," *Queens Chronicle*, November 20, 2008.

[8] National Park Service, "2012 Dialogue with Hindu Community."

(service).[9] Aminta was aware of the efforts of NPS to work with the Hindu community and its occasional cleanups, like the ones she participated in as a child. But she also recognized that these efforts were not gaining enough traction. Sadhana formed Project Prithvi (meaning "earth") to explore new approaches—and to coordinate regular cleanup efforts. For Aminta, it seemed like a perfect project for a Hindu social-justice organization: "What does it mean to be a champion of change but still maintain your faith?"

Aminta explained that offerings were made for numerous reasons, whether to achieve something positive or to remove negative energy. "Somebody has passed away in their family, and they have to release an offering; or they're getting married; or they're struggling with infertility or terminal illness; or they've just had their annual family *puja*. And their priests told them, 'Don't put these items in the garbage, go to the bay and put this in the water, put this in Mother Ganga." She added, "There's a certain pride in doing that, and there's a deep devotion in doing that as well. It's so beautiful, and ... unwavering."

Aminta noted, "The people that you'll find going to the bay are those that are really firmly planted in their faith and that have a strong belief in the power of the water to provide blessing in somebody's life." Yet she also struggled with the fact that some of the practices meant to honor the earth also harmed it.

Within the Indo-Caribbean Hindu community, there were diverse practices: although the majority of this community practiced vegetarianism and emphasized *ahimsa*, some groups practiced a form of worship that involved animal sacrifice. Aminta was among those who identified as Sanatan Hindu, who do not engage in animal sacrifice; yet as a public voice for the community, she also represented those who identified as Shakti worshipers, or Madrassi Hindus, whose religious practices had some variance with her own.

From the beginning, when listening to the elders discussing the offerings at the beach, there were a range of opinions, but few actionable steps. "It's just a really hard conversation to have." Aminta regularly reminded those who saw the issue as intractably polarized about the nature of change: she believed that they needed to educate the broader community about the practices, and work within the Hindu community to reduce

[9] Sadhana, "Mission, Vision, and Values."

the negative environmental impact of offerings in the bay. She would regularly offer the reminder that when these ritual practices originated in India, Styrofoam didn't exist. When Aminta went to the beach with her father as a child, she didn't leave the offerings herself. Most times, when she goes to the bay, she leaves nothing more than the words of a prayer or a *bhajan*. "That would be my form of offering, usually; not an actual tangible thing."

After years of dialogues between the Hindu community and NPS about the issue, she observed, "Conversations were good ... but there's still a real big issue at Jamaica Bay." Aminta thought, "It's better we approach the issue than we expect Park Rangers to come to our temples to be environmental advocates, right?" Together with her husband, Rohan, she wondered, "What can we do as a group to address these issues in a culturally responsive way, in a respectful way, but in a way that is culture-shifting?"

Questions for Reflection

- What advice or ideas would you offer to Aminta Kilawan-Narine as she seeks to be both culturally responsive and culture-shifting?
- Should the National Park Service adjust its "Leave no trace" policy? How might the NPS help to resolve this issue?
- What additional information do you need to know about Hindu religious practices to understand this case?

(B) Case

The first step for Aminta Kilawan-Narine was to formalize a relationship between Sadhana and the National Park Service. They soon developed a memorandum of understanding, agreeing to do cleanups together on a monthly basis from April to November. "They were really, really excited and happy—and thankful that a group like ours was emerging." For the cleanups, co-organized with her husband, Rohan, NPS provided the gloves, the pickers, the garbage bags, and staff; Sadhana brought the volunteers and the food. They have built a close relationship with the Park Rangers: "The folks that we've worked with, they are really good listeners. So they may not have understood a lot of things, and are still learning for sure. But I love that they don't approach things with any presumptions."

Aminta's next step was to reach out to her own community: "Let's look at what we can do to change this. Let's mobilize people from all different Hindu communities. And let's think outside of the box about solutions."

A Guide to Eco-Friendly Practices

"A leaf, a flower, a fruit, or water; if any of these are offered with love and devotion, I will accept them."[10] These words of Lord Krishna from the *Bhagavad Gita* are at the top of Sadhana's one-page guide, "Performing Eco-Friendly *Pujas*." The guide was developed collaboratively with the community: it grew out of consultations with local pandits (priests) and careful considerations of how to mitigate the environmental impact of devotional practices within the Indo-Caribbean Hindu community, with input from the National Park Service. For one of the most familiar offerings at the bay, *murthis*, the guide outlined the following:

- Take the *murthi* back home after immersing it.
- See if your temple can install a tank or large tub for devotees to immerse their *murthis* and perform *puja*.
- Use *murthis* made entirely of soft clay, with no paint. These will dissolve almost immediately in the water, causing no harm.
- Use a coconut as your *murthi*, and when the *puja* is over, cook or eat the coconut as prasad [sanctified food].
- Do not place *murthis* or any objects which are not completely biodegradable into the bay.

Taking a practical and adaptive approach, it offered guidance by each type of offering, in addition to *murthis*: bamboo; fruits and flowers; saris and fabrics; *diyas* (lamps); and other religious items, including specific types of food, oil, and incense. The guide outlined eco-friendly options: instead of immersing a sari in the waters of Jamaica Bay, donate it to a needy person. If you wish to float a small *diya* upon the bay, make it of dried

---

[10] All references in "A Guide to Eco-Friendly Practices" section from "Performing Eco-Friendly Pujas," https://www.sadhana.org/.

leaves rather than clay. Bamboo sticks can be used as fencing, or supports for garden plants, rather than being left behind. It also warned that fruits and flowers, while "technically biodegradable," can cause environmental damage due to pesticides.

The guide, designed to be distributed at local temples and mandirs, concluded with an invitation to join Sadhana's Project Prithvi for monthly beach cleanups, a form of *seva* (service). The final words, in bright orange at the bottom of the guide, stated, "Please show your devotion to Prithvi Maa (Mother Earth) by ALWAYS taking your *puja* materials home with you!" The National Park Service would also distribute a shorter version of the guide, designed as a rack card for easy distribution at the park. It included a photograph Rohan took during a clean-up, depicting a *murthi* of the Goddess Lakshmi amid seaweed and debris on a local beach.

Sacred Waters Exhibit

In addition to the eco-friendly *puja* guide and the rack card, Aminta, Rohan, and others at Sadhana considered more ways to respond. "We started to also try to bring more visibility to the issue, whether it be through newspaper articles [or] public awareness campaigns." An exhibit and panel discussion at the Queens Museum proved one of the most visible efforts. *Sacred Waters: A Collection of Hindu Offerings from Jamaica Bay*, aligned with Aminta's two primary goals: to work with her own community to embrace eco-friendly worship practices, and to educate the broader community about the significance and meaning of the offerings at the bay. The advertisement for the exhibit featured the same striking photograph of the Goddess Lakshmi on a Queens beach. In the exhibit, *murthis* were displayed in the context in which they were found; one was next to a broken bottle.

An article about the exhibit, written by a journalist who was also a member of the Indo-Caribbean community, explained, "The act of worship at the water's edge, called a *puja*, is a set of rites that involves the offering of food and items, such as saris and *murthis* (idols) to patron deities. The intention of this practice is to return these items to the Earth."[11] The article quoted Aminta: "'We saw the vast amount of Hindu

---

[11] Prem Calvin Prashad, "Hindu Relics from Jamaica Bay Featured in Exhibit," *Flushing Times*, October 10–16, 2014, 14.

offerings left at Jamaica Bay.... It was very jarring,' she said. Aminta described their dismay at the sight of broken *murthis* and other materials, such as saris and aluminum pans. 'Part of Hinduism is to protect the environment, a lot of our *pujas* are meant to respect the environment,' she said."[12]

The same article quoted Charles Markis, Park Ranger at Gateway National Recreation Area: "We want people to come and enjoy the bay," he said. "However, leave no trace—take nothing, leave nothing." Markis explained, "We could be going out and ticketing people ... but that isn't really the relationship we want with the community." The article noted that prior to the partnerships and cleanup efforts, the beach was a "veritable junkyard" and resembled an "underground parking lot"; the efforts were beginning to improve the beach, but the work of cleanups and education was ongoing.

Sadhana hosted an opening reception for *Sacred Waters* with a panel discussion on the themes of the exhibit. But the response was not what Aminta expected. Many in her community said, "Oh my gosh, what are you doing? First of all, you can't be taking these items out of the bay; the second thing is, why are you displaying broken items that are extremely religious?" She and Rohan heard, "They don't belong on display: they belong where they were left, and you're incurring negative karma by picking them up."

Since the cleanups began, the issue of what to do with the sacred items continued to be "a struggle." It wasn't merely a matter of how to honor the earth or how to balance religious freedom and expression with "leave no trace"; it was a question of what to do with the sacred items on the beach. Those items without religious symbols—bamboo, containers used for ritual items, ripped saris, coconuts—could more readily be disposed. But the *murthis*, the flags with images of deities, the items brought with honor and supplication to a sacred place? Aminta noted, "This is the challenge."

Managing the Murthis

Aminta, who often served as a bridge to other communities, is regularly called upon to explain the offerings left on the beach, particularly the *murthis*. She notes, "I don't call them litter because I don't think they are

---

[12] All quotes in this and the next paragraph also from ibid.

litter. I would call them items left at the bay. I also try not to call *murthis* 'statues' either. Because they're not statues to me." Aminta explains, "They come in various iterations, and what I always try to explain is that in Hinduism we believe in one God, but in many forms. So, we're not a 'polytheistic' faith, but these are all the different visuals of different gods and goddesses that represent different things for our various populations." She notes, "There's no shortage of *murthis* to show the Park Rangers, and they know, trust me, they know what these are. They are certainly collecting them as well, whenever they walk up and down the bay."

During Sadhana's beach cleanups, which include Hindus and non-Hindus, she explains, "Some of the items that you may see at the beach you may not want to pick up. They manifest the gods and the goddesses, and we recognize that you may not want to pick up those items up because you don't want to mess with what those items may carry." The impact of the beach cleanup extends beyond the thirty people or so who come each month; social media has aided their cause. Aminta explains, "We're able to reach that many more people with pictures. And some of pictures are really—I would even venture to say that they are graphic.... We're not afraid of posting photos that are literally what we're seeing at the beach. This could include *murthis* with their heads chopped off or their arms chopped off, and these things which are hard to watch, but important to see."

Aminta adds, "I don't like to perpetuate a perception that the things that are left at the bay are only Hindu offerings because they're not... We collect a lot of beer bottles and a lot of liquor bottles, and we collect condoms, and we collect all these different things that are not Hindu offerings." She notes, "We need to think about the impact to the items that we're leaving and the impact on the environment as well. This is Mother Earth, this is Ma Ganga, and we're doing this, and this is not okay."

From the first clean-ups, Aminta notes, "We had this issue where we didn't want to throw the *murthis* in the garbage, but we just didn't know what to do with them." For the first couple of years, Rohan housed the *murthis* in his parents' garage and a small shed of Aminta's parents, but soon, they were running out of space. For a period of time, leaders of Sadhana would drive the *murthis* to Pennsylvania, where a cow sanctuary provided refuge on their acres of land. Yet the distance proved challenging. As the cleanups and advocacy continued, she knew they would have to find a solution to reenvision or recycle the *murthis* left as offerings. She notes, "I don't think of it as 'disposal,' I think it is finding a new home."

Postscript

Walking along the beach in winter, not far from JFK airport, traces of Hindu religious practice are visible along the Jamaica Bay shoreline. The coconuts are a confounding sight, far from a climate that would be hospitable to coconut trees. On this day in 2022, along a small beach by the Cross Bay Boulevard Bridge, an orange sari is tangled in the rocks below a graffiti-covered bridge. Bright colors from broken *murthis* and *diyas* can be seen amid the grays and browns of the sand and stones along this sacred landscape. A collection of mostly intact *murthis* have been gathered together, placed on the sand near the busy public parking lot. The gods and goddesses look toward the beach and bay, and beyond.

It is more difficult, perhaps, to measure the impact of the exhaust from cars along the bridge or the airplanes departing and arriving. There are traces left behind from other visitors to the beach: a broken beer bottle, a sock, the arm of a doll, a dead turtle, and an empty plastic bottle. A family of three arrives with a plastic bag, and performs a brief *puja*, huddled up in their winter jackets along the shoreline. Airport and traffic noise compete with the sounds of the birds overhead. They place their store-bought flowers reverently in the bay and return to their minivan, carrying their empty plastic bag.

Aminta Reflects

From the beginning, Aminta emphasized that the goal was much greater than cleaning up the beaches: "The goal is to shift cultures and honor the earth." Aminta wanted to shift her community's practices to be more eco-friendly, but also to expand the broader community's understanding of Indo-Caribbean practices. When it comes to the offerings at the beach, Aminta emphasizes, "It isn't about shaming but understanding why it happens." Whether attending heated civic association meetings or hearing pushback from her own community, this can be challenging work.

For more than ten years, Aminta—joined by Rohan and other Sadhana members, National Park Service staff, and a diverse and dedicated set of volunteers—rises early on the first Saturday of each month to clean the beaches of Jamaica Bay. Aminta reflected, "We, including NPS, have seen the landscape change for the better." Today, she and Rohan consider the Park Rangers to be friends. Awareness of eco-friendly worship, reinforced by small placards displayed on NPS signage, is increasing. But, she notes, ritual items continue to be left at the bay. Other local organizations continue their own clean-up efforts as well: the United Madrassi Association (UMA), an organization of Shakti worshipers, holds cleanups and advertises a "Murti Rescue Mission" on their website. UMA's site states plainly, "Our Murtis Are Not Garbage." They provide a phone number to call for free, and confidential pickup of offerings and other items that would otherwise be left on the beach.[13] UMA also launched a project in collaboration with the Interfaith Center of New York for "Eco-Worship dialogue" between spiritual leaders from diverse traditions within the Hindu community.[14]

While Aminta still participates in Sadhana's monthly cleanups, often leading the opening prayer, her husband, Rohan, has taken over coordination of volunteers. In 2021 Aminta formed another local effort, the South Queens Women's March (SQWM). Her Queens neighborhood is home to the vital Indo-Caribbean community, Aminta explains, but also large Afro-Caribbean, Punjabi, and Latinx communities: they are of diverse faiths but share common concerns well beyond Jamaica Bay. Aminta explains, "We're struggling with some of these issues around social justice, economic empowerment, gender justice, all of that, and I really wanted to mobilize across faiths and tackle that from an intersectional perspective." Once again, Aminta is a bridge. Her goal is "to stop organizing in silos, just among our own, or who looks like us—because we share so many of the same struggles, we live in the same neighborhoods."

After years of beach cleanups, she reflects, these events are easy to organize; the intersectional, interracial conversations of SQWM are "happening for the very first time in the community, which would warrant more time for me." She adds, "I feel like I'm dealing with issues literally related to human lives, right now, if somebody is experiencing violence in their life right now." Aminta explains, "Sadhana is still important to me, for a number of reasons, including filling the Hindu progressive space." Even beyond cleanups, she and Rohan still think together about new approaches to the offerings at the beach.

---

[13] United Madrassi Association, "Ongoing Missions," accessed March 1, 2023, https://www.madrassi.org/.

[14] Interfaith Center of New York, "ICLA Senior Fellows' Community Projects," accessed March 1, 2023, https://interfaithcenter.org/.

Aminta reflects, "I think there's a couple things that haven't been explored but that require permissions and governmental approval and things like that." She elaborates, "We're not there yet.... What it could look like to have a designated space that is maintained and maybe adopted by a different temple every month, for example, that is attached to a local body of water?" She notes, "There are options, but again, we run into the regulatory schemes that prevent some of that from happening." They wonder together about ways to repurpose found sacred items: could they be made into stepping-stones, or could they create large murals to be displayed at the bay?

Most recently, Aminta and Rohan have been experimenting with a 3-D printer to create a mold for an eco-friendly *murthi*. The molds, she explains, would be used to gather up the natural materials in the image of a deity. "Whatever is offered, we're hoping it can be native to Jamaica Bay, for example—or whatever the local body of water is that is accepting the offering. So, one thought was literally to just have a street cart and have different shapes of molds for different gods and goddesses." The sand from the beach, she explained, could then be molded into a deity and offered into the body of water. "Then it just dissolves on its own." She smiles as she describes their experiments: "We're trying to figure this out, and we're certainly not scientists or anything." They hope to involve students at local universities and have begun exploring this idea with NPS.

Looking back at her organizing efforts and her role as a bridge builder, Aminta comments, "My faith has really carried me through all of my struggles in life." She adds, "I think that helps me to approach things from a compassionate perspective and not judge quickly. Because it's so easy to judge.... It's so easy to start to point fingers and to not understand why people are the way they are and how their life experience might have informed that—even from people that I strongly disagree with." Between her full-time job, advocacy work, writing for the local Indo-Caribbean newspaper, and other commitments, Aminta has the kind of schedule that often requires her to work through lunch. Sometimes, when working from home, her father or husband will stop at a roti shop and bring her lunch. Each morning, Aminta still sings the "Hanuman Chalisa," the *bhajan* she learned from her grandmother to bring her strength and focus.

With competing demands of work and activism, rising stress, and health concerns, Aminta recently went to Jamaica Bay to offer a prayer. Usually she leaves nothing more than a drop of water or the words of a prayer along the shoreline, but on that brisk afternoon, standing before the expansive Jamaica Bay, she placed a small yellow flower in the waters and watched it drift away. Aminta later noted, "I do believe—like, in my heart of hearts believe—that Mother Ganga exists in local bodies of water." She added, "And I firmly believe in her power to heal."

Forty-Nine Days

The COVID-19 epidemic brought with it unprecedented levels of hate crimes against Asians and Asian Americans. For Chenxing Han, trained as a Buddhist chaplain, these were painful to watch and deeply personal. Han, together with her colleagues and friends Funie Hsu and Duncan Williams, wanted to craft a Buddhist response, but wondered if a written statement was sufficient to the magnitude of the unfolding crisis. They considered, What purposes do such formal statements serve? What might their statement convey? How would they address the larger historical context of anti-Asian violence in America? And can a statement truly help to heal?

(A) Case

In early 2020, even before the lockdowns and soaring cases of COVID-19 in America, attacks against Asians and Asian Americans were rising. In February 2020, Los Angeles County officials hosted a news conference cautioning against "anti-Asian stereotypes, panic, and misinformation"[1] with increased reports of hate and hostility.

Asian American communities responded in various ways—including efforts to support those who were targeted by teaching self-defense, facilitating reporting, and tracking incidents. In March 2020 Stop AAPI Hate launched to document hate incidents against Asian American Pacific Islanders: in its first week, the group received six hundred reports; in one month, almost fifteen hundred reports streamed in.[2] Other attacks were recorded by security cameras, the brutal incidents often going viral;

---

[1] City News Service, "L.A. Officials Fear Anti-Asian Racism amid Coronavirus Worries," *Los Angeles Daily News*, February 13, 2020, https://www.dailynews.com/.

[2] Stop AAPI Hate, "National Report: Two Years and Thousands of Voices: What Community-Generated Data Tells Us About anti-AAPI Hate," 2020, 2, https://stopaapihate.org/.

however, many went unrecorded or unreported, or took the form of a more subtle hostility. By the end of 2020, incidents of hate and violence against Asians and Asian Americans in Los Angeles increased 76 percent,[3] close to the FBI's estimate of 73 percent nationally.[4]

Chenxing Han, author of *Be the Refuge: Raising the Voices of Asian American Buddhists*, found it emotionally taxing to read the news reports, let alone watch the viral videos of elderly people being attacked. These hate incidents weren't abstract for her: Han witnessed the verbal abuse of an elderly Vietnamese man in the parking lot of an Asian grocery store; two of her Asian American women friends had also been the target of verbal attacks in California. She felt keenly the suffering of these incidents. Han drew on her training in Buddhist chaplaincy when considering how to relate to this suffering: "Not to flinch away; to be a witness. To accompany in their suffering."[5] Yet as the hate and hostility continued, Han felt a growing sense of "helplessness and despair." She was at a loss for how to intervene in the face of ongoing violence: "It's a terribly disempowering feeling."

Han was grateful to be in close touch with her friend and colleague Funie Hsu during this time: "We always know that if we have something we want to talk about, especially regarding the Asian American Buddhist community, we can just pick up the phone or text." As scholar-practitioners who work on Asian American Buddhists, each brought an acute awareness that anti-Asian violence and erasure were not new. Increasingly, their conversations turned to how to respond to the rise in hate. In November 2020, at Huong Tich Temple in Santa Ana, California, fifteen Buddha and Bodhisattva statues were spray-painted: it was the sixth incident of vandalism against Buddhist temples in L.A.'s Little Saigon that month. The police called the vandalism a hate crime: one of the statues had "Jesus" spray-painted across its back.[6] Across the United States, seventeen Asian American Buddhist temples reported hate incidents in 2020.[7]

---

[3] Los Angeles County Commission on Human Relations, "2020 Anti-Asian Hate Crimes Los Angeles County," 1, https://hrc.lacounty.gov/.

[4] Sakshi Venkatraman, "Anti-Asian Hate Crimes Rose 73% Last Year, Updated FBI Data Says," NBC News, October 25, 2021, https://www.nbcnews.com/.

[5] All quotes by Chenxing Han unless otherwise indicated are from Zoom interviews with the author, October 5 and October 21, 2022.

[6] Caitlin Yoshiko Kandil, "Buddhist Temple Attacks Rise as COVID-19 Amplifies Anti-Asian American Bias," Religion News Service, December 10, 2020, https://religionnews.com/.

[7] Ibid.

Hsu contacted Han to ask, "Should we write a statement? How do we craft a Buddhist response?" They invited their friend Duncan Ryūken Williams, a professor of religious studies and Soto Zen priest, to join the conversation. Han considered the issue from a chaplaincy perspective: "How much does a statement heal?" She believed that a statement can have educational and moral value, but "The risk is when it feels more performative. When it's just a statement, and not followed up by any action.... A statement is not, ideally, an end step."

A Collective

While recognizing that the three members of their collective were all of East Asian heritage, Han observed, "We come from different Buddhist backgrounds, different ethnicities, different generations and life experiences." Han, the youngest of the group, considered Hsu and Williams to be friends, but also mentors and teachers: their work was defining and disruptive. Hsu had long challenged the American Buddhist community to confront its legacy of racism and erasure of Asian Americans. When her piece "We've Been Here All Along" was published in a Buddhist magazine in 2016,[8] some readers reacted with anger and defensiveness.[9] Over the years, Hsu has helped to reframe and recenter Asian American Buddhist practices, bringing a historical perspective to structural bias and exclusion. Han's own work, which included a new book on young Asian American voices, resonated closely. Williams, the most senior of the group, wrote the award-winning book *American Sutra: A Story of Faith and Freedom in the Second World War*. His scholarship has a special focus on the Japanese American experience and—as a priest—emphasizes ritual and ceremony.

Han, Hsu, and Williams brought diverse perspectives and came from different fields, yet shared a common approach: the importance of perseverance. Han and her colleagues often described it as "trying to capture something of the Asian American spirit." She recalled, "There's a beautiful expression in Japanese that Duncan [Williams] cites often: 'Fall down seven times, get up eight.'"

---

[8] Funie Hsu, "We've Been Here All Along," *Lion's Roar*, Winter 2016, https://www.lionsroar.com/.

[9] Tynette Deveaux and Ajahn Amaro, "A Response to Critics of 'We've Been Here All Along," from the Winter 2016 Buddhadharma, December 1, 2016, https://www.lionsroar.com/.

A Buddhist Chaplain

Growing up in an atheist family, Han wanted to be a writer; she didn't know what a chaplain was. "I was a sensitive child attuned to the suffering of others, especially those who felt marginalized." Han came to Pittsburgh at four years old; only sense memories remain from her early years in China. Han reflects, "I can't actually remember a time when race was not a part of my consciousness." At her inner-city school, Han was "a little anthropologist trying to learn the language, trying to learn what was going on." Racial hierarchies quickly became clear, and as one of five Chinese girls at the school, Han was sometimes mocked and taunted. Racism didn't end when she left the schoolyard. As she grew up, she had to contend with another form of bias: the hypersexualization of Asian women. When asked about her experiences with bias, she sighs. "There were countless moments—so it's deeply and completely personal."

Han began exploring Buddhism as she graduated from college and was later drawn to chaplaincy, completing three rotations at a hospital in Oakland. She explains, "Buddhism supports the chaplain's impulse to identify and alleviate suffering." She was encouraged by her chaplaincy supervisor to pursue writing as an act of spiritual care: Han recently completed her second book, *one long listening: a memoir of grief, chaplaincy, and spiritual care*. While she doesn't intend to become a full-time hospital chaplain, she draws upon her clinical pastoral education in writing, co-teaching, and everyday life. She would also be challenged to apply those skills to the crisis of rising hate in America.

February 22: A Meeting

Han, Hsu, and Williams first met to discuss writing a statement in February 2021. Though busy schedules and geographic distance made it difficult to find time, they decided to meet every Monday over Zoom. Having known each other for many years, the COVID distancing and geographic divide—Han and Hsu were in the Bay Area, Williams in Los Angeles—were easily overcome. Together they considered how to craft a Buddhist response and what they might include in a statement. When reflecting on the value of a statement, Han noted, "It's a matter of how statements are created, and how are they used. If the creation of the statement really made an organization dig deep and work collectively, that could lead to powerful ripple effects. If a statement was used in a more public setting—in a sermon, for example—it might also have more of an impact."

Yet, from the first meeting, Han recalled, "We were questioning the efficacy of the statement, whether that was appropriate to the magnitude of what was happening." They wondered, "Maybe a video is more impactful?" They didn't have experience creating videos, but felt it was important to connect to real people, and—as much as possible—to the people directly affected. But they wondered, "How do we talk to people, especially victims' families, in a respectful way?"

As Han reflected on the options, she thought, *What will people remember in five or ten years? Will they remember a statement about George Floyd, or will they remember having marched? Probably the latter.* Not only does a march engage the body and the senses, she explained, it is "with other people, in community." After their first meeting, it was clear that they needed to craft something more than a statement. "Something else—something more visually and sensorially engaging." But the question remained: What?

February 25: Another L.A. Temple Attacked

Then, on February 25, 2021, Higashi Honganji Buddhist Temple in Los Angeles was vandalized. The community has a rich history in Los Angeles, dating back to 1904. In the 1940s, many members interned at Manzanar maintained their Buddhist practices, and some even managed to send donations to preserve the temple in their absence. Later, Higashi Honganji would serve as a hostel for families returning from internment and host a growing Young Buddhist Association. The community celebrated America's bicentennial in 1976 with the construction of a new temple in the heart of Little Tokyo: built in a traditional Japanese style, it serves a thriving community that includes multigenerational Japanese Americans.[10]

The temple enjoyed relationships with civic, religious, and cultural groups in L.A. Under the leadership of Nikkei Progressives (NP), many of these organizations came together to launch an online fundraiser on GoFundMe: "Beloved Little Tokyo community institution ... was

---

[10] Higashi Honganji Buddhist Temple, "Centennial History," accessed March 1, 2022, https://hhbt-la.org/.

recently vandalized with a smashed window, lanterns broken, and lantern stands burnt, an event that has shocked and saddened us all."[11] Their goal was to raise thirty thousand dollars for repairs and enhancement of the temple's security measures. It was not the first incident at the temple in recent weeks.

Higashi Honganji issued a statement and posted on the temple's Facebook page, stating, in part,

> We will work to repair the damage and to restore the temple. But we need to repair the damage to ourselves as well. Like many others in our AAPI community and beyond, we feel hurt and saddened and even angered by the recent attacks on those of Asian and Pacific Islander descent. For many of us, the temple is a second home, and this feels like an attack on our culture, our history, our community, our family. Together, we will grieve, and we will heal.[12]

A Visit to a San Francisco Temple

Two days later, Han's husband, Trent Walker, showed her a story in the *New York Times* with the headline "He Came from Thailand to Care for Family. Then Came a Brutal Attack."[13] It told the story of Vicha Ratanapakdee, an elderly grandfather who was slammed to the ground in San Francisco while out on his morning walk. The article, published a few weeks after his death, included a photo of a woman grieving at Wat Nagara Dhamma: she was holding her father's photo. Eighty-four-year-old Ratanapakdee, with gray hair, black glasses, and a distinguished bearing, had a hint of a smile in the framed portrait.

Han recalled, "It was a shock to see the picture in the *Times*." This was a temple that, pre-COVID, she and her husband visited on several occasions. Despite their concerns about COVID, they decided to visit the temple. Han considered asking the monks about connecting with the family for a video. "But I had a lot of reservations around it." She wanted

---

[11] "Support for Higashi Honganji Buddhist Temple!" GoFundMe Website.

[12] Rinban Noriaki Ito, "Our Temple in the News," Higashi Honganji Buddhist Temple, February 28, 2021, https://hi-in.facebook.com/.

[13] Thomas Fuller, "He Came from Thailand to Care for Family. Then Came a Brutal Attack," *New York Times*, February 27, 2021, https://www.nytimes.com/.

to respect the family's privacy, and she also wondered if a video was feasible, since the vaccines were not fully rolled out. Producing a video posed unique ethical and logistical challenges.

On March 3 she and her husband visited Wat Nagara Dhamma to pay their respects. There on the altar was a framed photo of Vicha Ratanapakdee. Han fought to hold back tears. She recalled, "I hadn't been in a temple for so long. To smell the incense, to bow at the altar, just to be there ... it was really moving." After a brief conversation with the monks, she returned home with even greater resolve to honor those who were lost to violence.

A Strong Response

In the weeks after the vandalism at Higashi Honganji Buddhist Temple, support was strong and swift: the fundraising goal of thirty thousand dollars was surpassed in less than twenty-four hours.[14] The effort brought together a dozen community partners, most based in Little Tokyo, with donations streaming in from across the United States. Many of the donations were anonymous: they came in smaller increments of twenty dollars and larger donations by families. On March 12 Rev. Peter Hata wrote a column in the *Rafu Shimpo*, a Japanese American newspaper. Hata acknowledged that some may see this as a "wake-up call." He wrote, "In this case, it has made us aware of the threat of anti-Asian hate. But in our Buddhist tradition, we often speak of a different kind of 'call,' one that is 'calling us to listen' to the Buddha's teachings."[15] He continued,

> The essence of these teachings is the reality that all our lives are not only unpredictable and in constant flux—something certainly in evidence on the evening of Feb. 25—but all our lives are also interconnected. And that especially in times of difficulty, in the shock and dismay we all felt upon seeing the damage to the temple, we are most able to sense this interconnectedness of our lives.
>
> This interconnectedness has many layers of meaning. On the one hand, the vandalism has brought us closer to our fellow

---

[14] GoFundMe, Updates to "Support for Higashi Honganji Buddhist Temple!," https://www.gofundme.com/.

[15] Peter Hata, "The Vandalism at Higashi Honganji: Waking Up to Our Interconnection," *The Rafu Shimpo*, March 12, 2021, https://rafu.com/.

temple members, but on the other, the public outpouring of support has also underscored our ties to the community, locally, nationally, and internationally.[16]

Within three weeks, and after more than fourteen hundred donations, the fundraiser was closed with $90,165 raised for the temple—more than three times beyond the original request.[17] These were the moments that helped carry Han and her colleagues forward—moments of resilience and hope. But that feeling would not last for long.

March 16: Atlanta-Area Murders

On March 16 a gunman killed eight people at three spas across Atlanta and Cherokee County, Georgia. His first stop was Young's Asian Massage, where four people were killed; he continued to Gold Spa and Aroma Therapy Massage, killing four more. Seven of those killed were women, six of them of Asian heritage.[18] For Han, Hsu, and Williams, this was an inflection point. "Things just became very clear, right after that."

For weeks, they had been meeting and thinking together. "When the Atlanta shootings happened, it felt like the magnitude of the emotions that people were experiencing—ourselves included—needed to be met." Han explained, "We felt like, 'Okay, the statement is not going to work. A video is not going to work.' We need something bigger, something where people could actually participate in real time." She added, "It felt very personal, maybe especially for me and Funie [Hsu] as Asian American women. Very visceral and personal."

Williams thought there needed to be a ritual, or some way to mourn, to grieve—and that it needed to be on a national level. Han agreed. "Ceremony and ritual bring people together. They are healing; they are spiritual acts of care." Yet gathering in person seemed risky and complicated during COVID. Any event would need to draw from the diverse umbrella of Buddhist Asian America with its myriad lineages and languages. Han suggested that the memorial service, following in the practice of many Buddhist traditions, be held seven weeks after the shootings. The team wondered, what could they create in less than forty-nine days?

---

[16] Ibid.

[17] GoFundMe, Updates to "Support for Higashi Honganji Buddhist Temple!"

[18] Richard Fausset and Neil Vigdor, "8 People Killed in Atlanta-Area Massage Parlor Shootings," *New York Times*, March 19, 2021, https://www.nytimes.com/.

Questions for Reflection

- How effective are formal statements in a crisis? If writing a formal statement from your own location, what would it include?
- How might a chaplaincy lens inform Chenxing Han's perspective?
- What is important for the reader to know about historical anti-Asian violence and erasure to understand this case?

(B) Case

After a soft ringing of bells that echoed through the warm, wooden-walled Higashi Honganji Buddhist Temple, chanting began in Japanese:

Bu jou mi da nyo rai niu dou jou
San ge ra ku

We respectfully call upon Tathagata Amida to enter this Dojo
As we joyfully scatter flowers of welcome ...[19]

A traditional opening for Jodo Shinshu services, on this day the *Sanbujo* (Three Respectful Callings) was plaintive. As Bishop Marvin Harada of the Buddhist Churches of America continued to chant, a solemn procession began from the back of the temple. Monastics with shaven heads and robes of yellow and orange entered, joined by other Buddhist leaders in black and gray: the diversity of the American Buddhist community was evident in the colorful yet somber display. All were wearing surgical and N-95 masks; many also chose to don the white paper masks Rev. Shumyo Kojima of Zenshuji Soto Mission handmade for the event, painted with "Homage to the Three Jewels" in Japanese calligraphy. One by one, they processed in slowly and reverently bowed at the altar before taking their seats in the wooden pews.

---

[19] Buddhist Study Center, "Sanbujo," accessed March 1, 2023, https://sites. google.com/site/buddhiststudycenter. Transliteration of chants and ceremonial program: "Ritual Manual for May 4," Chenxing Han, October 11, 2022, in author's possession. Manual compiled and written by Chenxing Han, Funie Hsu, and Duncan Ryūken Williams. Additional quotes from May We Gather, "May We Gather: A National Buddhist Memorial Ceremony," YouTube, May 6, 2021.

With the ringing of bells, the procession continued. A second chant began, led by Bishop Noriaki Ito from Higashi Honganji Buddhist Temple. Since the vandalism a few months prior, the host temple for the ceremony had been repaired and restored. As Noriaki and Harada chanted *Juseige* (Three Sacred Vows) in Japanese, a single white *paritta* thread stretched in front of the altar. Although not part of this temple's tradition or practice, the protective thread—common to Theravada practice—was woven into the ceremony. The seven-minute procession included some forty-nine monastics and leaders from each of the Buddhist lineages.[20] After the procession and chanting, Chenxing Han, dressed in black with a vivid blue scarf, came to the front. She began, "Venerable members of the *sangha*, distinguished guests, beloved community participating in the livestream—We welcome you to May We Gather: A National Buddhist Memorial for Asian American Ancestors."

With those opening words, Han felt a palpable shift in the energy of the room, a coming together. She also felt a strong sense of connection to those participating online, despite not being able to see them and not knowing how many people were tuning in. "I was surprised to feel so connected despite this barrier of digital media space. I just felt a profound sense of not being alone." She would later learn that some seventeen hundred people across the United States gathered for the livestream service. It was held on May 4, 2021—forty-nine days after the Atlanta-area shootings.

Han later reflected that May We Gather was only possible with Duncan Ryūken Williams's optimism, Funie Hsu's determination, and the contributions of so many others. There had been obstacles to overcome, many of them practical, logistical, and technological. Han's husband, Trent, assisted with translation, including invitations in multiple Asian languages; other volunteers stepped in to help with everything from calligraphy to outreach, from ceramics to web design. The challenges related to intra-Buddhist differences were overcome in the context of a memorial service, with a sense of "generosity." Somehow, through collective effort—and more than a few sleepless nights—it all came into place in less than forty-nine days.

With the compressed time period, they had to move quickly through many decisions. The easiest decision was related to place: Higashi

---

[20] For more information, see Lion's Roar, "Prominent Schools of Buddhism," accessed March 1, 2023, https://www.lionsroar.com/.

Honganji was a natural option, and they would follow the temple's COVID protocols. The most difficult issues were about selection: who should be invited, who should speak, and most importantly, who should be memorialized in the ceremony. Planned as a national ceremony, Han, Hsu, and Williams reached out via email and phone to the diffuse and diverse networks of Buddhist organizations, and even in-person visits to temples; they also leveraged social media, posting a colorful graphic with the hashtag #MayWeGather.

May We Gather honored ancestors across multiple eras and of diverse backgrounds. They remembered some of those lost in the past year: Korean American mother Yong Ae Yue, killed in the Atlanta shootings, and Thai American grandfather Vicha Ratanapakdee, who died after being knocked to the sidewalk in San Francisco. They memorialized two Vietnamese American young men: Tommy Le, shot by police in 2016, and Thien Minh Ly, stabbed to death by a white supremacist in 1996. They honored Kanesaburo Oshima, a Japanese man murdered at an internment camp in 1942, and Sia Bun Ning, a Chinese miner killed in the Rock Springs, Wyoming, massacre in 1885. For each, a ceremonial tile was placed upon the altar, while the central ceremonial tile was dedicated to all who lost their lives through racial and religious animus.

At the ceremony, Funie Hsu acknowledged the American Buddhist leaders gathered together from Chinese, Japanese, Khmer, Korean, Taiwanese, Thai, Tibetan, Sri Lankan, and Vietnamese Buddhist traditions. Hsu noted,

> We gather as Asian American Buddhists and allies in an expression of our fundamental interconnectedness. We do not suffer alone, nor do we heal alone. Only when we join together as a *sangha* can we truly support each other's freedom.

After describing exclusion and violence faced by earlier Asian Buddhist immigrants, she added,

> In the face of nearly two centuries of xenophobia and systemic violence, Asian American Buddhists have long joined together to rebuild our communities. Piece by broken piece, we sutured the jagged edges of altars, statues, incense burners, and our very bodies and minds back together. This mending is part of our Buddhist practice in America. Each act of rejoining reveals

how compassion can arise out of racial suffering, how fragments are inseparable from wholeness. We mend them as a declaration of our interconnectedness, as an expression of gratitude to our ancestors, and as a way to cultivate the karmic conditions for American Buddhism's continued flourishing. As we confront yet another wave of violence, vandalism, and exclusion targeting Asian Americans and Asian American Buddhists, let us honor our ancestors by continuing their legacy of gathering and mending.

Next, they shared a video clip from the *Atlanta Journal-Constitution*'s website about Yong Ae Yue, one of those murdered in the Atlanta-area shootings who was honored in a memorial tablet on the altar. In the video, Yue's sons Elliott and Robert remembered their late mother with love and respect, noting that she spoke out against discrimination and encouraged them to embrace their identities as African American and Korean. The video was followed by chanting in Pali by a group of six Theravada monastics from three different L.A. temples: the Three Refuges chant affirmed the centrality of the Buddha, the *dharma* (teachings), and the *sangha* (community).

Co-planner Duncan Ryūken Williams delivered the *Hyobyakumon*, a pronouncement of intention. Once again he recited the names Yong Ae Yue, Vicha Ratanapakdee, Tommy Le, Thien Minh Ly, Kanesaburo Oshima, and Sia Bun Ning. He also recited other names: George Floyd, Daunte Wright, and Amarjit Sekhon. Williams concluded,

Together we join today to repair the racial karma of this nation because our destinies and freedoms are intertwined. And though the mountain of suffering is high and the tears of pain fill the deepest oceans, our path compels us to rise up like a lotus flower above muddy waters. Medicine also comes from a saying attributed to Bodhidharma: *nana korobi ya oki*; fall down seven times, get up eight times. This means we've come back to our breath when our mind wanders or sit up straight when we slump off the meditation cushion. Other times we return to our precepts and vows when we fall off the noble path, but sometimes it requires us to gather.

And today, we the Sangha of the United States of America have gathered to recall our interconnectedness, feel the presence of those who have gone before us, and to get back up. And though we may fall a million times we rise again a million and one times in honor of our ancestors and our loved ones who have passed. May we gather.

The ceremony was punctuated by *dharma* talks on each of the six *pāramitās*, or perfections of awakening beings. Dr. Larry Ward, a prominent black Buddhist leader from Ohio, spoke of *dāna* (generosity); Sister Kinh Nghiem from Deer Park Monastery in rural California offered comments on *śīla* (appropriate conduct); Bhante Sanathavihari, a Mexican American monk from L.A. delivered his *dharma* talk in Spanish about *kṣānti* (patience); Rev. Cristina Moon from the International Zen Dojo in Hawaii spoke of *vīrya* (effort); Bishop Myokei Caine-Barrett offered a prerecorded teaching about *dhyāna* (meditation) from her temple in Texas; Bishop Noriaki Ito of the host temple delivered a *dharma* talk on *prajñā* (wisdom).

While each *dharma* talk was powerful and distinct, one was particularly emotional. Rev. Moon asked, "After an exhausting year, many are probably wondering, where can we find such spiritual strength?" Moon suggested that the answer can be found in temples and dojos and in the methods, teachings, and archetypes of the Buddhist tradition. She added, "But more importantly, we need only look around, finding examples of spiritual strength in our families and ancestors who risked everything to build a brighter future." Her voice broke as she recited the names of the women killed in the Atlanta-area shootings. After a pause, she continued, "The strength they had to make America their home, working multiple jobs and navigating a new world for the sake of their families, was tremendous. Let us commit to matching their spiritual strength, their *vīrya*, today and every day to come as we remember and honor them."

In addition to chanting, the recitation of names, and dedication of merit to the deceased ancestors, offerings of light and incense were made in front of the memorial tablets. At this solemn moment, livestream viewers were invited to make their own offerings, to show respect in silence, or by reciting the names of those who died.

Central to May We Gather—ritually and symbolically—was the gilding of a white ceramic Kintsugi Lotus. As Funie Hsu explained during the ceremony,

> *Kintsugi* is the Japanese art of repairing broken ceramics by mending the fractures with golden lacquer. The lotus flower,

rising clean from muddy roots, symbolizes the purity and potential of the Buddha's awakening. The cracks in this *kintsugi* lotus will now be gilded by several of our monastics in attendance, transforming brokenness into beauty.

Han added,

> The work of repairing our communities requires remembering, rather than hiding, the ways in which we've been hurt.
>
> The careful rejoining process of *kintsugi* embodies our collective efforts to heal the wounds of racism and religious bigotry.

The large ceramic lotus, displayed near the altar, had fractures on every petal. As a small group of monastics gathered to paint the cracks in the lotus carefully with golden paint, the chanting continued in Korean and later in Tibetan.

The ceremony concluded with the protective *paritta* ritual. Led by the abbot of Wat Phrathatphanom of America in Yucca Valley, California, a group of monastics recited the *Ratana Sutta* (Jewel Discourse) in Pali. As they did so, Hsu explained,

> The two long white threads emanating from the altar will be empowered with the blessings of these chants. These cords weave together the Buddha as represented on the altar; the Dharma as manifest in the *paritta* chants; and the collective protection and interconnectedness of everyone participating in this event, in person and online.
>
> These threads will guide us as we leave this space to share our aspirations for peace and healing with the world.

Tied to an Amida Buddha statue on the altar, the protective thread would now be connected to the stone lanterns outside of the temple—the same stone lanterns vandalized months earlier. As chanting continued in Pali, those gathered for the ceremony processed out of the temple in pairs: two by two, connected by a common thread.

The final chant connected an ancient story with the contemporary context: in a place where people had been living with death and despair, the chant brought healing and protection.[21]

---

[21] Dhamma USA, "Ratana Sutta—The Jewel Discourse," March 2020, https://www.dhammausa.com/.

Yānīdha bhūtāni samāgatāni, bhummāni vā yāni va antalikkhe,
tathāgataṃ devamanussapūjitaṃ, Saṅghaṃ namassāma suvatthi hotu.

Whatever beings are assembled here, terrestrial or celestial, come let us salute the perfect Sangha, honored by gods and men. May there be happiness.[22]

As the procession concluded, with the chants fading, the final frames of the video focused upon the flickering flames of candles in front of the memorial tablets, followed by, "We the Sangha." The *sangha* included a list of hundreds of Asian American Buddhist partner temples and organizations, allied *sanghas* and organizations, and individuals.[23] May We Gather received extensive media coverage, including features in the *New York Times* and the *Los Angeles Times*, and was also highlighted by a range of Buddhist publications. In the weeks and months that followed, thousands more would watch the virtual ceremony.

Feelings and Reflections

Chenxing Han later observed, "In a way, we did write a statement." Posted on the website, and offered as part of the invitation to participate, it was composed with a ritual and poetic sensibility. She explained that, like the *mettā* chant, "May all beings be happy; may all beings be well," it was expressive of "an ongoing aspiration." The statement began, "May We Gather. When someone is hurting, we come together as community. We gather because our lives are inexorably interlinked. We do not suffer alone, nor do we heal alone. Only when we gather as a *sangha* (community) can we truly support each other's freedom." The statement unfolded, "May we gather to remember.... May we gather the pieces.... May we gather to repair.... May we gather to liberate together."[24]

Reflecting back on her experience, Han explained that her feelings of "grief and rage, helplessness and despair" began to shift as they prepared and convened the memorial ceremony. For Han, it was empowering to come together with friends and mentors, volunteers, and communities across the

---

[22] Ibid.; see also May We Gather, "May We Gather."
[23] May We Gather, "One Year Dharma Reflections: To Honor the One-Year Memorial of the March 16, 2021, Atlanta-Area Shootings," accessed March 1, 2023, https://www.maywegather.org/.
[24] Ibid., "49 Days Ceremony."

United States to co-create May We Gather. More so, Han explains, "The very process was profoundly healing." She adds, "And that makes a lot of sense. Like a forty-nine-day memorial, you're grieving along the way."

Postscript

One hundred days after the Atlanta-area shootings, the team released a short video with highlights from May We Gather: A National Buddhist Memorial Ceremony for Asian American Ancestors.[25] Designed for use in temples, *sanghas*, and classrooms, the organizers hoped that the short version would continue to promote dialogue and foster healing. One year after the Atlanta-area shootings, on March 16, 2022, they marked the anniversary with reflections from the broader community.

These short reflections powerfully expressed the ongoing impact of the May We Gather ceremony, which—less than one year later—had been viewed over nine thousand times. Posted online, it included a message from Han, Hsu, and Williams: "Our collective voices are a powerful reminder that we are not alone, in suffering and in healing." Others wrote,

> When we remain aware of the Atlanta shootings + the ongoing conditions in which anti-Asian violence has increased by 339% this year, it compels us into discerning actions to alleviate our collective delusional hatred of each other, as opposed to a passivity or hopelessness. May we find the strength + resources together to live our historic resilience over + over again, as shown by our capacities to more than survive the concentration camps, the exclusion acts, even the killings. The least we can do for those lost lives is to honor them by more than surviving oppressive forces, but to transform those forces + thrive in creating the beauty of our cultures. (L. Yang)
>
> . . .
>
> At this anniversary time of two years into a global pandemic and 1 year anniversary of this targeted violence against our Asian kin especially sisters, daughters, mothers, aunties . . . we honor our interconnected[ness] through great vehicle of compassion at the suffering that reverberates through all of our hearts. We see

---

[25] Ibid.

and feel deeply the harm that was caused by seeds of hate and othering, and we vow to heal these fractures by coming together in unison to sing, chant in love. We gather to heal and remember this wounding. May all beings be protected and safe from harm, may all beings be remembered, honored and celebrated while living and passing. May the seeds of violence be dissolved by the collective forces of wisdom, compassion and love. (S. Parikh)

. . .

May we continue to gather, to heal, and to seek liberation for all beings. (E. Yoshikami)[26]

The planners now face a new dilemma: "How do you continue?" Han reflects, "We were able, in that short amount of time, to pull it all together with the help of a lot of people. This happened once, and it's powerful, it's symbolic, and time passes." The question then becomes, "How do you keep the momentum going?" She noted: "People shared how moved they were, and then wanted to know, 'Can we have more of this? What are you going to do?'"

Han and her co-creators recognize that the gathering emerged out of a very particular set of circumstances, with a unique sense of urgency. Looking to the future, it is perhaps more difficult to imagine what would be needed: Han explains, "We don't know what the world is going to look like geopolitically. . . . There could be another pandemic." Although there is much uncertainty, the team is continuing to meet and shape the next gathering, which they hope will be in person. She adds, "When people are able to gather, this can touch and resonate on a different level than doing things online."

Chenxing regularly emphasizes that May We Gather is not the only multilineage, multiethnic gathering, nor was it the first. "Multilineage events are regularly happening at smaller scales, by local community members or local temples—and by people who go to more than one temple." Some events may not be publicized or may not receive extensive media coverage. Well before May We Gather, she notes, Buddhists for Black Lives Matter held a "Great Awakening Walk" in June 2020.[27] The

---

[26] Ibid.

[27] Do LA, "Great Awakening Walk / Buddhists for Black Lives Matter," June 13, 2020, https://dola.com/.

"slow, silent marching meditation led by Buddhist monastics" traversed the courtyard of the Japanese American National Museum to Los Angeles City Hall. Planners of the event wrote,

> There was a time when a movement reverberated worldwide, calling upon people of all faiths to come together in solidarity for the envisioning of a grand, new nation. We believe we again stand at that precipice today—and, as it was then, we stand beside you now. We unequivocally support the demands set forth by #BLACKLIVESMATTER that their just pursuit of freedom be truly realized, and that those elected as servants of the people honor their sworn vows. For as it is written, "[They] that violate [their] oaths, profane the divinity of faith itself." We stand in awe of this precious opportunity that the black community has granted us, that the nation may awaken to the true nature of its suffering, that we may move forward towards a right vision of a more compassionate humanity, one that honors and recti- fies the egregious disproportion of suffering currently existing in our country. Only when black lives matter, can all lives matter. For the great awakening happens when the wave realizes it is the ocean. We see you, we love you, hold fast!

The Great Awakening Walk was organized by Han's friend David Woo, founder of Burning Pride Meditation. Han notes, "It was a powerful moment of multilineage, and of solidarity, in response to anti-Black racism, anti-Black violence."

Other religious responses to anti-Asian hate have included interfaith efforts, many of them on the local level. In Chicago, the Uptown Rally Against AAPI Racism was also held in early May 2021. With the parking lot of the Buddhist Temple of Chicago as the venue, the rally brought together Asian American Christians and Buddhists with a diverse group of other local congregations.[28]

Stop AAPI Hate continues to track anti-Asian hate, with 11,467 inci- dents reported in the two years between March 2020 and March 2022.[29]

---

[28] Maggie Phillips, "Buddhist Temples Seek a New Path to Combat Anti-Asian Violence," *Tablet*, August 12, 2021, https://www.tabletmag.com/.

[29] Aggie J. Yellow Horse, Russell Jeung, and Ronae Matriano, contributors,

Their two-year national report noted that this "is just the tip of the iceberg," with a survey indicating that one in five Asian Americans experienced a hate crime in that two-year period.[30] California remains the state with the largest number of reported incidents. It has also been a center for response: in San Francisco, a street was renamed Vicha Ratanapakdee Way.[31] In the years following his murder, the advocacy group Justice for Vicha works to ensure that "his death was not in vain, but rather serves as our inspiration to continue the fight for Asian justice."[32]

In diverse ways, the community continues to heal, to remember, and to advocate. As Han explains, there is also a powerful urge to create, from a Thai American artist's *Unseen* exhibit in Omaha, Nebraska,[33] to New York's MOCA (Museum of Chinese in America) interactive exhibition, *Responses.*[34] The Japanese American National Museum hosted an online art exhibit, *An American Vocabulary: Words to Action*, with flash cards in multiple languages to illustrate four themes: ancestor, voice, persistence, and care.[35] The same museum is the host for Williams's newest project: an interactive, monumental light exhibit honoring those incarcerated during World War II. It includes a recitation of names, integrating ritual and remembrance.

With plans for another gathering underway, Han notes, "Ongoing ritual and ceremony are so important." Reflecting back on May We Gather, she says, "We were lucky. A lot of karmic circumstances came together to make this event more visible. Hopefully, it serves as a seed."

"Stop AAPI Hate National Report, 3/19/20–12/31/21," Stop AAPI Hate, 2, accessed March 3, 2023, https://stopaapihate.org/.

[30] Ibid., 3.

[31] Danielle Echeverria, "S.F. Street Renamed for Beloved 'Grandpa Vicha,' Whose Death Sparked a Movement, *San Francisco Chronicle*, October 1, 2022, https://www.sfchronicle.com/.

[32] Justice for Vicha, Past events page, accessed March 1, 2023, https://www.justice4vicha.org/.

[33] Charles Kay Jr., *Unseen*, The Kaneko, October 13, 2022–April 27, 2023, https://thekaneko.org/.

[34] MOCA (Museum of Chinese in America), "Responses: Asian American Voices Resisting the Tides of Racism," July 15, 2021–May 21, 2023, https://www.mocanyc.org/.

[35] JANM (Japanese American National Museum), "An American Vocabulary: Words to Action," October 8, 2022, https://www.janm.org/.

Afterword

A Pedagogy of Pluralism

Diana L. Eck

I was lucky to start my teaching career at Harvard during the presidency of Derek Bok, who thought a lot about the nature of the university, its moral and social responsibilities, and its teaching mission. He was especially interested in the growing educational research that supported case-study teaching and what we now call "active learning."

My first encounter with case studies was as a first-year teacher. I was a graduate student with my first discussion section as a teaching fellow in a large religion course. Business School professor C. Roland Christensen had become well-known for his work on teaching by the case method, and President Derek Bok was determined to improve the quality of teaching throughout the university. He tapped Christensen to lead a workshop for graduate students and young teachers on "Developing Discussion Leadership Skills" and I signed up for that workshop. I loved it and learned from it and I'm sure it improved my work and confidence as a teaching fellow. However, I couldn't quite imagine how case-based teaching and learning could translate to the substance of a class on religion or on India's literary and artistic cultures. We did not have an arts and humanities faculty that was busy writing cases to use in teaching. There was certainly no library of relevant cases such as that being collected at the Business School.

As an assistant professor, I began teaching with the usual mix of lecturing and section discussions. I loved preparing lectures, coordinating my lecture with the slide carousels—and later PowerPoints—that brought a "visual text" to life. I was enthusiastic, and that generated a positive classroom ambiance and the disposition to learn. But eventually I realized that in preparing elegant lectures, I was the person who learned the most.

That was the very point that Bok's research and writing on higher education was making. Students enjoyed the class, took notes, and thought about it all for their midterms, final exams, and papers, but on the whole they were not active in their own learning. They read books, they listened to me, and the research claimed they wouldn't remember much a few months later.

At the same time, the world of higher education was in a state of rapid and profound change. The key drivers were immigration and technology. On the technology front, it was in the 1980s that many of us got our first computers; in the mid-1990s we accessed the internet. As for immigration, one generation after the immigration reforms of 1965, the religious and cultural "other" was right here, in our neighborhoods, schools, and classrooms. I had Hindu and Muslim students in my religion classes and in my classes on India. They asked their own questions and challenged some of mine. The fact that we were all "other" to one another made for vibrant discussions in and out of class. I loved it, but it was clear I needed to switch gears.

I had spent years doing fieldwork in India, primarily on Hindu pilgrimage and temples. Now I would do a bit of fieldwork right here at home in Boston. This began with a seminar on "World Religions in Boston." Who was here, now? Week after week, our seminar discussions would be focused on the experience, the interpretations, and the questions produced from the "field." For most students, and for the communities they visited, these encounters were a new experience. Something was happening that could not be studied in the library. It required our curiosity and our presence, our attention.

This was the genesis of the Pluralism Project. Students did summer research and our fall-term seminars were bursting with reports. Focusing on the local, getting to know the religious centers nearby became the guiding methodology of this early phase of our work. Why begin with a textbook rather than by meeting Muslims and following the set of questions that emerge from that encounter? Might we think of Chicago, with its dozens of mosques, as part of the "Islamic world"? What would that mean for the way we approach education? The same questions might accompany the study of Christianity, Judaism, or any other religious tradition.

As the work of the Pluralism Project grew, however, it became clear to us that the challenges of a more diverse religious America were ubiquitous. Students like Ellie Pierce were documenting the new Hindu temple openings, but also learning about opposition, even hostility. The micro-histories of an Islamic center or Jain temple often included moments of resistance and neighbors downright opposed to having such a new religious center. How did the Muslims or Jains respond? What happened next, and how are they doing now? Maybe these would be the sites of a set of case studies.

These encounters were not just about religious people engaging with those of another faith, although the theological encounter was one very important aspect of our interest. There were many civic and legal issues. Indeed, virtually every public institution in America had new dilemmas in navigating the more complex reality of American life. They came up in business and management, in educational institutions, in hospitals and courts, in city councils and zoning boards. Our orientation for research included visiting religious communities, of course, but also visiting zoning boards and public schools and local newspapers. Among the actors on the local scene were emergent interfaith initiatives: often they were the first to speak up or weigh in when a new community was threatened or harassed.

The first step Ellie Pierce and I made as we began to think about case studies was to consult with Willis Emmons at the Christensen Center at the Harvard Business School (HBS). We attended some Business School classes and watched how the professor leads a class. Our experience was eye-opening. Both of us had attended classes at Harvard Divinity School and in the Faculty of Arts and Sciences, and there was no comparison in terms of the energy and intellectual discussion we encountered in these classes across the river at HBS. Their classes made clear the way in which the case study redefines the educational experience for professors and students by foregrounding specific problems and decisions to make. This places issues of leadership, decision-making, and policy on the ground in specific companies, with real issues and dilemmas.

As senior researcher and case writer, Ellie Pierce had just the right sense of how a case might be constructed to allow us into the kinds of dilemmas and decision-making that people encounter as they grapple with questions of diversity in a multicultural and multireligious society. At first, I introduced two cases of Ellie's cases in a seminar on religious pluralism in America: "A Mosque in Palos Heights" and "Fliers at the Sikh Parade." Eventually I was able to develop an entire course around case studies in the Ethics and Civics section of Harvard's General Education program: "Pluralism: Case Studies in American Religious Diversity."

In this course we ask, "What challenges do people of different religious or cultural communities face as they encounter one another in neighborhoods and public institutions, schools and businesses?" We are asked to take the perspective of mayors and concerned citizens, teachers and executives, religious and civic leaders—all confronting the choices and changes of a dynamic society. The cases are specific and local, but they all have implications for other communities and for the wider world. The dilemmas will likely engage and enable us to clarify our own perspective as well. Being able to articulate the mayor's position is important, but equally important is the ability to articulate and defend one's own perspective. This is surely what education is about.

I often describe the course as bringing together perspectives from religious studies, American studies, immigration studies, civics, and constitutional law. The cases are not opinion pieces nor are they research papers, but they are designed to provoke reflection and debate. This a pedagogy for pluralism. A well-constructed case puts us in the shoes of someone, a protagonist, who is confronting a new challenge without precedents and with choices that are not clear and might be risky. In the changing religious landscape of America today, there are a lot of such dilemmas as we try to navigate new terrain of our religious and cultural diversity. This book presents some of these cases. In my experience, all of them have elicited thoughtful and spirited discussion. They are not constructed to teach truths about this religion or that. Rather they require the protagonist—and we ourselves—to think in the context of a new and often complex situation. They ask us to draw upon our religious values or our civic commitments as citizens and to bring these to bear on a new situation.

Of course, reading the case carefully and more than once is a prerequisite for class participation. And digging into some background reading will be necessary for students unfamiliar with the religious tradition at hand. Our cases do ask students to find out what they need to know about Sikhism, Islam, or Buddhism in order to get a handle on the case. This sense of not knowing enough is not unique to students in the class; it is at the core of the dilemmas faced by our protagonists as well. We never really know enough, but nevertheless we have to listen attentively, to think and to act in new situations.

Coming to class, students should be prepared to discuss the case and should not be alarmed to be called up to respond. The "cold call" is difficult or even traumatizing for some students, so I try to think carefully about whom to call upon, at least at the beginning of the class. Everyone eventually becomes more comfortable with this format. I have to become comfortable with it as well, since I don't have my lecture notes and PowerPoints. I can anticipate what might happen, but I can't completely control it. Frankly, it makes me nervous, and I spend my preparation time embedded in the case and imagining where the discussion might move.

What kinds of questions might launch the class? Informed by the guidelines of the Christensen Center at HBS, I begin with a question of assessment rather than ask for a descriptive summary of the situation.[1]

> What is at stake here?
> What keeps our protagonist up at night?
> What are the options our protagonist faces?

Listening carefully to the first responder enables me to stick with that student and follow up with some probing questions:

> Why is that?
> Could you say more about that?
> What do you think the protagonist is feeling at this point?

Opening the conversation to a broader class discussion, I might ask,

> Who are the other stake-holders here?
> Are there allies? Antagonists?
> What interests do they have in the outcome?
> What other perspectives do we need to consider?
> Are there people missing from this discussion?

Broadening the discussion will also include questions such as,

> What are the issues here?
> Are there religious issues at stake? Civic issues? Legal issues?
> What assumptions are being made—or questioned?
> What are people feeling? Are there emotional issues that underlie
>   this dilemma? Fear? Nostalgia?

---

[1] This section draws from "Questions for Class Discussions," C. Roland Christensen Center for Teaching and Learning, Harvard Business School, https://www. hbs.edu/teaching/.

Looking at the implications of a case for wider issues, I might ask,

What can we learn from this case?
Does this case have implications for other dilemmas in our
    society?
Who else might learn something from this situation? A teacher?
    A mayor? A pastor?
How do those engaged in this dilemma understand religion?
In the various cases we have discussed, what understandings of
    religion have been at work?

Breaking into small groups might enable students to discuss some of
the secondary readings:

How does Bellah's articulation of American "civil religion" apply
    here?
Does Martin Marty's understanding of the dynamics of "belon-
    gers" and "strangers" help in understanding this case?
What does Martha Nussbaum mean by the "inner eyes," and how
    might that apply to this case?

In small groups, students are also able to generate proposals.

What would be a successful way to make religion tangible on the
    National Mall?
What would you propose for holiday decorations in the Sea-Tac
    Airport, or in the Harvard House where you live?
What would you propose as a member of a local citizens' group?

In the civic studies context, the question shifts from "What should
he, she, or they do?" to "What should *we* do?" Whether as a committee,
a working group, or imagining the issue in the context of our own college
or community—discussion participants offer a collaborative and constructive solution. When working on an individual basis, students might be
asked to prepare a speech for an embattled leader, write a letter to the
editor, or even draft their own decision-based case study.

For the individual reader, teacher, or discussion participant, here are a few suggestions:

- For the first reading of the case, resist the impulse to look beyond the page, and consider—whether in reflection or in discussion—the range of options and risks based solely on the case narrative. The lack of complete information gives a case greater fidelity to decision-making in real life: rarely do we know all of the dimensions of a problem when we are initially called to solve it. After reading the (A) case, reflect and develop a response; then explore other sources to deepen, expand, and explore new dimensions, beginning with the (B) case.
- Each case includes within it a range of themes for exploration, many of which can be unpacked by asking the questions: What do I need to know? Are there legal dimensions referenced? What do I need to know about Free Exercise or the Establishment Clause? Do I have sufficient religious literacy to understand the terminology—or the meaning for those within the tradition? How does internal diversity, gender, or race inform the dispute? How does the media respond to—or intensify—the problem?
- Cases also—by their very structure—invite reflection with the pause between (A) and (B). After reading the (B) case, common questions include: What surprised you about the outcome? When considering the problem, What did I miss? What assumptions did I make? What was missing from the case, and why? How has this issue played out in my own local area? What do I want to learn more about? Look for what is missing: perhaps it reflects the protagonist's blind spots, or might be predictive of the outcome. The case is a starting point for discussion and reflection.

Over the years, educators in diverse contexts have utilized these cases—in interfaith and religious studies, civic studies, negotiation, leadership development, and seminaries and rabbinical schools. Case studies have also been embraced by faith communities and interfaith organizations seeking new forms of engagement.

While we speak of case studies as a pedagogy for pluralism, it is a pedagogy not at all restricted to the classroom. It is at the heart of inter-faith work and, in an ideal context, is at the very heart of the workings of legislative democracy.

Index